THE BIBLIOGRAPHIC CONTROL

OF AMERICAN LITERATURE

1920—1975

by

Vito Joseph Brenni

The Scarecrow Press, Inc.
Metuchen, N.J., & London
1979

Library of Congress Cataloging in Publication Data

Brenni, Vito Joseph, 1923-
   The bibliographic control of American literature,
1920-1975.

   Bibliography: p.
   Includes index.
   1. American literature--20th century--Bibliography
--Theory, methods, etc. 2. American literature--20th
century--History and criticism--Bibliography. I. Title.
Z1224.5.B73 [PS221]   016.810'8'0052   79-12542
ISBN 0-8108-1221-5

PREFACE

This book is concerned with that aspect of bibliography which is called bibliographic control. This term as applied to literature would mean all the various studies that list publications by and about authors. For the purpose of this book, only works dealing with publications by American writers are considered, "publications" being defined as novels, short stories, plays, and poems. Juvenile literature, dime novels, travel and captivity narratives, anecdotes, folklore, essays, biographies, and manuscript and archival material are omitted. Ethnic and immigrant literature are also excluded. The main aim of the book is to trace the growth and development of the bibliographic control of American belles lettres between 1920 and 1975. A secondary aim is to examine carefully some of these titles in order to point out their merits, faults, and deficiencies. The book concludes with an assessment of the achievement and failure of the efforts over a period of more than a half century to bring under control the large body of creative literature Americans have produced since the early colonial period.

The main tools of bibliographic control are the bibliography, the bibliographic essay, and the anthology. The anthology is included because it brings together a group of writings for a particular purpose. Because it provides title and author, two essentials in bibliographic description, it can be used as a substitute for a bibliography or as a supplementary aid to existing bibliographies. Some anthologies are better than others in that they give complete bibliographic information about the selections or they contain biographical sketches for the authors included. The anthologies listed in the Appendices were chosen with the idea that they do contribute, individually and collectively, to bibliographic control.

Bibliographic control does not have for its aim a full description of the writings in a subject field. It is concerned primarily with a brief identification of each publication. This identification consists of author, title, imprint, and pagination for a book, and author, title, serial location, volume, pages, and date for all publications which are serials or which are located in serials. Most of the bibliographies cited in this study, therefore, are enumerative. Some descriptive bibliographies are included because they list publications not found in other bibliographies. This is particularly true of many author bibliographies which are as nearly complete as the compilers can make them.

Belles lettres differ from publications in other areas of the humanities in that they are more difficult to classify by brief subject headings. To think of a great novel or poem, for example, is not to reduce it to a few words. An essay is needed. The huge number of writings about individual works in American literature do not fall within the scope of this study. Many of these writings are critical in nature and belong to literary criticism and the subject bibliography of American literature. The MLA International Bibliography, for example, is a subject bibliography in the sense that it lists writings about literature. It is not a bibliography of belles lettres in modern literature.

While this study does intentionally omit critical writings about authors and their works, it does not exclude all such studies. A critical study of the American political novel, for example, would be included if it has a separate bibliography of novels at the end of the essay and/or if the essay gives the intellectual content of a fair number of novels. The idea is that, while bibliographic control is concerned primarily with bibliographic description, it does not entirely neglect the content of writings. Librarians and scholars have been, and always will be, interested in the subject analysis of literature. One need only be reminded of the subject headings in library card catalogs and the content annotations in some bibliographies to understand the extent to which readers require a subject approach to the world of print. The critical works included in this study are not those which examine the writings of one author but rather those which discuss a whole group of titles by many authors. The critical works discussed and/or listed in this study represent some of the most useful studies for bibliographic purposes.

The titles discussed in the text and the additional titles given in the Appendices were selected from a great many sources, some of which are listed in the bibliography at the end of this book. The sources that supplied the greatest number of entries are the Cumulative Book Index (1920-

75), Tanselle's Guide to the Study of U.S. Imprints (1971), the bibliography volumes of the Literary History of the United States (1948, 1959, 1972), Gohdes's Literature and Theatre of the States and Regions of the U.S.A. (1967), Nilon's Bibliographies in American Literature (1970), Havlice's Index to American Author Bibliographies (1971), and McNamee's Dissertations in English and American Literature (1968, 1969, 1974). All titles have been verified in library card catalogs and in the printed catalogs of the Library of Congress. Most of them were examined in the libraries of Michigan State University and the University of Michigan and in the Newberry Library in Chicago. A fair number were borrowed from other libraries on interlibrary loan.

The titles in the Appendices may be said to contain the history of the bibliographic control of American belles lettres for the years 1920 to 1975. The words of the titles speak for the efforts of many individuals and groups to record the products of the American mind and spirit. By themselves the titles are a shorthand account of these efforts. The essay, on the other hand, may be considered a verification of selected attempts at bibliographic control and an expansion of the short account provided by the words of the titles. The book, therefore, consists of two major parts: the bibliographic essay in four chapters plus notes, and the titles in the Appendices.

For convenience both parts of the book are divided into three periods: 1920-1939, 1940-59, 1960-75. Within each period the discussion will begin with the comprehensive bibliographies, continue with the national genre lists, regional, state, and local bibliographies, historical sources, humor, and author bibliographies. Humor is included as a separate category because it has been a tangible quality and a constant element in American writing.

Some bibliographic terms need to be defined because some publishers and compilers of bibliographies have used them rather loosely. In this study a checklist is a list of publications with only a minimum of bibliographic description. A descriptive bibliography is one which gives a fuller description of the physical appearance of the books, such as binding, paper, exact transcription of the title page, and collation. The collation of a book gives the assembly of the pages in a book in the order in which they appear: frontispiece, dedication, table of contents, text, blank pages, appendices, bibliography, index, ads, etc. A biobibliography is a list of books by many authors giving brief biographical data about them.

Many thanks are due Michigan State University professors Arthur Sherbo, Joseph Waldmeir, Roger Meiners, and especially Russel Nye, who directed the work here shown and encouraged the author with much patience and understanding. Except for his gentle and friendly persuasion this book might never have been begun; and, had he not allowed the author so much freedom to follow "his natural bibliographic bent, " the work might never have been completed.

As a librarian the author can hardly fail to appreciate the generosity of the university library in securing many books on interlibrary loan. The reference librarians and the interlibrary loan staff conveyed their support and interest in the study by welcoming all requests for publications not found in the Michigan State University Library. If some publications were not easily located--and I think a few must have been--the librarians did not give up the search without having tried many times. I should be remiss if I did not acknowledge their many efforts on behalf of this book.

TABLE OF CONTENTS

Preface iii

1 The Cambridge History of American Literature
and Its Aftermath 1

2 The Literary History of the United States, the
Bibliography of American Literature, and other
Bibliographic Studies 27

3 The Golden Years, 1960-1975 53

4 A Backward Glance and Some Recommendations 83

Chapter Notes 91

Appendices: Bibliographic Control of American
Literature
A 1920-1939 129
B 1940-1959 145
C 1960-1975 167

Bibliography 192

Index 197

Chapter 1

THE CAMBRIDGE HISTORY OF AMERICAN LITERATURE AND ITS AFTERMATH

The history of the bibliography of American literature may be said to begin near the end of the eighteenth century with the publication of the first anthologies of poetry. Many more anthologies were published in the nineteenth century, including Samuel Kettell's three-volume Specimens of American Poetry (1829), John Keese's two-volume Poets of America (1840-42), and Rufus W. Griswold's anthologies.[1]* These anthologies enabled many people both here and abroad to read and enjoy American poetry. Without the anthologies many poems would have gone unread because they were scattered in many books and periodicals. They took the place of poetry indexes and bibliographies; indeed, one might say that the American literature anthology was the chief bibliographic aid in American literature before the twentieth century.

Before the end of the nineteenth century two significant events occurred: the first bibliography of first editions of American authors was published and the first single-author bibliography was compiled.[2] Francis G. Leon, a Polish nobleman and bookseller living in America, made a list of first editions for a sales catalog in 1885, and Beverly Chew, a New York bibliophile, did a Longfellow bibliography in the same year. Although both are very modest publications by modern standards, intended mainly for the book collector, they did call attention to American literature, and they served as a stimulus to similar bibliographic activity.

In the closing years of the nineteenth century and in the first two decades of the twentieth century, a number of bibliographies were published on American poetry, drama, and fiction, and on American writers. One bibliographer

---

*For all references see Chapter Notes, beginning on page 91.

and one publisher deserve special mention for the quality and
quantity of their work. Oscar Wegelin compiled long lists of
early American fiction (1902; second edition, 1913), poetry
(1903, 1907) and plays (1900; second edition, 1905). [3] They
are all carefully done, giving full description for all titles
and notes for some of them. The Houghton Mifflin Company
published between 1906 and 1908 bibliographies of six authors:
Hawthorne (1905), Lowell (1906), Henry James (1906), Oliver
Wendell Holmes (1907), Henry David Thoreau (1908), and
Ralph Waldo Emerson (1908). [4] All but the Henry James
volume have more than 200 pages and attempt to be complete.
Francis H. Allen's A Bibliography of Henry David Thoreau
is an especially admirable volume for the many notes revealing the interrelations between Thoreau's Journal and his published writings. The full index, pages 175-201, gives titles
of all his books, poems, and lectures.

The second important period in American literary bib-
liography--and the years with which this book is concerned--
begins with the completion of the Cambridge History of American Literature (1921) and extends through 1939. [5] The CHAL
was a notable event because for the first time students and
teachers could turn to a long authoritative account of American literature written by several scholars. For the first
time also there was a long comprehensive bibliography on
the subject, for each of the chapters in the history has a
bibliography. In all there are more than 500 pages listing
titles by and about authors and on many topics in American
literary history. Many titles on the social, political, and
cultural history are also listed. Unfortunately for many
titles bibliographic information is lacking for pagination and
publisher. This is a very serious defect of the work, especially for periodical articles. To have only the month and
date for a periodical article means that the reader must
check the periodical's table of contents, or turn pages until
the article is found. The compilers of the bibliographies,
most of whom remain unnamed, were obviously more interested in listing many titles than in giving complete or even
adequate bibliographic data. That the compilers made a
great effort to provide a wide range of titles on American
life and thought there is no denying, for one has only to look
at the bibliography at the end of one of the volumes to note
that hardly a subject has been omitted. The greatness of
the bibliography, therefore, lies in the quantity and broad
selection of its titles rather than in its bibliographic description.

The CHAL was for many years an invaluable aid for many students and scholars who did not have access to major research libraries having large dictionary catalogs and specialized bibliographies.   Although less useful now for many reasons, the scholar will still want to refer to the bibliographies if only because the titles were selected and arranged for the chapters in the history.   If his study falls within one of the chapters, he may want to begin his research by looking at the bibliography for that chapter.

A little more than a decade later a bibliography by Bradford Fullerton appeared under the title, Selective Bibliography of American Literature 1775-1900. 6 In the words of the Preface: "The book is designed to serve as a guide to noteworthy achievements in American letters between the years 1775 and 1900..." (page viii).   For most titles only place and date of publication are given; for other titles such additional information as line readings, errata slips, misnumbered pages, and color of binding is given.   Biographical information varies from 50 to 350 words.   This is a more lengthy work than a similar title by Merle Johnson, which appeared a few years earlier. 7   Johnson's American First Editions (1929) contains checklists for 105 authors and has some notes about issues, editions, title pages, and bindings. The bibliography lists books and pamphlets only.

A much more selective bibliography appeared in 1924 in the form of a sales catalog for the Stephen H. Wakeman collection of nine American authors of the nineteenth century. 8 It lists first editions, inscribed presentation and personal copies, original manuscripts, and letters.   Reproductions of some title pages are given.

The first attempt to cover the bibliography of contemporary literature in one volume was published in 1922. 9 The authors, John Manly and Edith Rickert, exclude all authors who died before 1914 and living authors who have produced no work since then (page v).   Contemporary American Literature gives titles of books for each author, some critical studies, and brief biographical information.   The book is mainly for the student and quick reference purposes.   Because the work contains only very brief bibliographic description, it had at the time only very limited value for the scholar.   The revision by Fred B. Millett published seven years later is a much more useful volume because it has many more authors and contains essays on the novel, drama, poetry, biography, and literary criticism. 10   Both volumes

have more value for the student who wants literary criticism
and biography than for the scholar who wants bibliographic
information. They deserve a brief mention, however, for
with all their limitations, they did serve a purpose at a time
when many twentieth-century authors were not covered by
separate bibliographies.

In 1938 the Oxford University Press in New York
came out with an anthology which has become, among other
Oxford anthologies, fairly well known and highly regarded. [11]
The Oxford Anthology of American Literature was compiled
by William Rose Benét, poet and critic, and Norman Holmes
Pearson. The volume contains 152 authors, many selections,
and a biographical commentary for each author. The commentary includes titles of books with place and date of publication. A short bibliography with more of an author's works
plus biographical and critical writings completes each commentary. As a very select bibliography these commentaries
served very well for ten or more years, especially for the
beginning student in American literature. For short stories
and poems the selections in the anthology provide titles for
a short, eclectic bibliography. The table of contents is especially good for compiling such a bibliography because the
selections are listed under the authors' names. For Walt
Whitman, for example, 46 poems are listed with page references under his name.

One yearbook of the period contains information about
American literature. The American Yearbook was first published in 1910 and continued to appear annually through 1950.[12]
Each volume has a bibliographic essay on American fiction
and one on poetry. The 1930 volume divides the essay on
fiction as follows: "Outstanding Novels, " "Realism in Current
Fiction, " "Problem Novel, " "Historical Novels, " "Detective
Stories, " "The Short Story, " and "Conclusion and Tabulation. "
The latter lists about 50 works of fiction. This fiction section runs from pages 772 to 775. The poetry section follows,
pages 776-780, and is divided as follows: "Narrative Fiction
in Poetry, " "Satire, " "Lyrics, " and "Books About Poetry. "
The work has considerable value as a yearly record of American fiction and poetry.

American historical novels are included in Jonathan
Nield's fifth edition of A Guide to the Best Historical Novels
and Tales (1929). [13] The book, which is based on a careful
examination of novels, contains critical and descriptive annotations of 1-10 lines. A new feature in this edition is a

detailed subject index enabling the reader to locate novels on specific periods, states, battles, etc. The index gives 35 page references for the American Civil War, 12 for the War of Independence, one each for North Carolina and Massachusetts, two for Williamsburg, Va., and seven for the Battle of Gettysburg. This work plus the shorter lists by N. J. Thiessen and Rebecca W. Smith were among the few keys to information about American historical fiction.[14]   Thiessen's An Annotated Bibliography of American Historical Fiction (1938) lists the novels in ten historical periods and provides annotations of 25 to 150 words. It has separate indexes for authors and titles. Smith's list, which appeared in the Bulletin of Bibliography between 1939 and 1941, has only fiction about the Civil War and its aftermath. Many of the titles came from her 1932 University of Chicago dissertation on the subject.

Several other theses contain notable bibliographies on fiction. Lisle A. Rose has a rather lengthy bibliography on economic and political fiction in his dissertation: Appendix A, pages 270-294, contains fiction published between 1865 and 1901, and Appendix B, pages 295-299, covers 1909 through 1917.[15]   Robert L. Shurter did a nine-page critical bibliography of American utopias between 1865 and 1900 for a dissertation on the subject.[16]   Claude R. Flory made a four-page list of twentieth-century utopian fiction for his dissertation.[17]   Flory provides brief critical annotations. Dorothy E. Wolfe's thesis is an annotated bibliography of the short story, listing many local-color stories by such Americans as Bret Harte, Mary W. Freeman, O. Henry, Sherwood Anderson, Hamlin Garland, Sarah O. Jewett, Jack London, Thomas N. Page, and Ruth Suckow.[18]   The annotations are very brief, rarely exceeding 50 words.

Two annual anthologies of short stories may be said to constitute a current bibliography of some of the best short fiction in America.[19]   The O. Henry Memorial Award Prize Stories was first issued in 1920 for the short stories written in 1919. The series was begun by the Society of Arts and Sciences in New York City and published by Doubleday, Page in Garden City, New York. From the beginning the Society's aim as given in the first volume was to include in a yearly volume the very best short stories by Americans writing for American magazines. Blanche Colton Williams, professor of English at Hunter College, was on the Committee of Award in 1919. An Honorary Committee advised the judges and nominated short stories. The Committee in its early years

included such distinguished names in literature and criticism
as Gertrude Atherton, Fannie Hurst, Hamlin Garland, James
B. Cabell, William A. White, John Macy, Max Eastman, and
Robert Morss Lovett. Each volume contains between 15 and
19 short stories, many of them by names well known to fiction readers, including F. Scott Fitzgerald, Edna Ferber,
Booth Tarkington, and Sherwood Anderson.

The other annual anthology is called Best Short Stories
of [year] and the Yearbook of the American Short Story. Edward J. O'Brien, poet, critic, and translator, began the anthology in 1915 and served as editor until 1940. Each volume
contains between 20 and 30 short stories which are, in the
opinion of the editor, among the best written in the previous
year. They are stories which have "the distinction of uniting
genuine substance and artistic form in a closely woven pattern
with a spiritual sincerity so earnest and a creative belief so
strong that each of these stories may fairly claim ... a posi-
tion of some permanence in our literature. "20

The part of each volume called the "Yearbook of the
American Short Story" contains an index to short stories in
magazines, such as the Atlantic Monthly, Century Magazine,
Saturday Evening Post, Scribner's, Woman's Home Companion, Lippincott's Magazine, and many other titles. Foreign
authors with stories in these magazines are included. Beginning with the 1921 volume the yearbook lists the American
authors separately. For many stories the editor uses aster-
isks for quality: one for a story meritorious for either form
or substance, two for a story outstanding for both, and three
for a story such as those selected for inclusion in each vol-
ume.21 The yearbook gives the name of the periodical containing the story and the date. A special list in each volume
called "the roll of honor" gives the names of the very best
short stories for the previous year and biographical information for the authors. The 1918 volume has a critical summary of the 60 best American stories published between January and October 1918 (pages 374-383). A short critique is
given for each story in the form of an annotation from 40 to
150 words in length. The 1918 volume also does the same for
books of short stories published in that year (pages 354-367).
This volume also begins a section listing stories in books
(pages 397-411). The number for the first page of a story is
given but not the imprint for the book.

Two outstanding bibliographies of American poetry were
published in 1930: Oscar Wegelin's second edition of Early

American Poetry and Ola E. Winslow's American Broadside Verse from Imprints of the 17th and 18th Centuries.[22] Wegelin corrected many errors in the 1903 edition and added many new titles. Full title, imprint, pages, size, and many notes about editions, original publication, location of copies, and content are given. For a 1771 London broadside, probably printed in London, of Phillis Wheatley's ode on the death of the Rev. George Whitefield, Wegelin writes in a note that "this issue differs from the usual version, for after the line 'Till life Divine reanimates the dust,' there follow eight lines in double column, and 'The Conclusion,' six lines" (page 85). In the same note he gives the exact title of the 1770 Boston Broadside and the page references to the poem in the 1771 London edition of Ebenezer Pemberton's Sermon on the Death of Whitefield. He does not hesitate to give a probable location for a poem when he cannot give the first appearance in print, even if only to state that "the original of [Freneau's "The Expedition of Timothy Taurus"] was probably printed in a newspaper about 1775" (page 35). He does locate the poem in Freneau's Poems (1909). For Michael Wigglesworth's Day of Doom he gives in a note to the 1701 Boston edition the dates and place of publication of the various editions printed before 1800 (page 90). At the end of the note he refers the reader to a bibliographical account of the poem in the American Antiquarian Society Proceedings, April 1929. In the note to John Trumbull's An Elegy on the Death of Mr. Buckingham St. John he writes that this 1771 broadside was his first separate publication. He locates a copy in the New York Historical Society (page 79).

The user of this bibliography will not fail to note the care and scholarship of the author. The foregoing description of the work gives only a small indication of the amount of reading and research Wegelin did over a period of thirty years or more. Wegelin's own collection of American verse numbered 1600 pieces when he sold it to C. Waller Barrett in 1953.[23]

Ola E. Winslow's American Broadside Verse from Imprints of the 17th and 18th Century (1930) represents the first sizable collection of broadside verse ever published. As the author states in the Preface (page ix), "no considerable body of this material has ever been assembled." The poetry is arranged in groups according to general subject matter: "funeral verses and memorials," "meditations on portentous events," "dying confessions and warnings against crimes," "wartime ballads and marching songs," "comments on local

incident, " "admonitions and timely preachments, " and "New
Year's greetings. " For each broadside the author provides
an introductory note giving information about authors and
events and, occasionally, extracts from contemporary annals,
e.g. the Boston Gazette and the Boston Weekly News-Letter.
The book has an index of titles and first lines and a separate
index for proper names. The author was a professor of
English at Goucher College.

Although not so well done as one would like, the Biographical Dictionary of Contemporary Poets (1938) does have
some bibliographic information.[24] Titles cited in the sketches
contain the year of publication, and each sketch is followed
by a list of anthologies, magazines, and newspapers in which
the work of the author has appeared. The text of one poem
for each poet is given.

For many years, 1913-1929, William S. Braithwaite
was the editor of an anthology of magazine verse.[25] Each
volume contains poems and a yearbook. The latter varies
somewhat, but in general includes an author index to poems
in magazines, an author list of new volumes of poetry, and
a select list of books about poets and poetry. Although the
work is not restricted to American poets, a good many of
them are in the anthology section and the index. The 1926
volume has "A Biographical Dictionary of Poets in the United
States, " part 4, pages 3-43. Many titles of books with dates
are given.

Some anthologies of verse came from individual magazines. The New Yorker published a volume in 1935 containing poems which first appeared in print in that magazine
in the years between 1925 and 1935.[26] The book has 300
poems by 100 contributors familiar to readers of poetry in
the 1930's. The well-known names are there, such as Eli-
nor Wylie, Ogden Nash, Dorothy Parker, E. B. White, Conrad Aiken, Phyllis McGinley, William R. Benêt, and many
others. Less well known are poets like Frances Frost,
Raymond Holden, Selma Robinson, and Patience Eden. Bibliographically the book has value because it is a fast way of
locating a number of poems written in that period and a
quick way of sampling a number of early poems of some
distinguished poets. The book would be even more useful
as a location tool if it had an index with title of poem and
page. Lacking this aid, the reader is not delayed too much
because it does have a separate author index with page references to the selections.

Another periodical poetry anthology published annually in this period was called Davis's Anthology of Newspaper Verse.[27] The 1940 volume contains about 400 poems by that many people. The poems come from big- and small-town newspapers from all parts of the country. The seven pages of acknowledgments following the title page list the newspapers with the names of the poets who have published in them. The newspapers include the Caspar (Wyoming) Tribune Herald, the Farina (Illinois) News, the Gladbrook (Iowa) Northern, the Boston Herald, the Los Angeles Times, the Kansas City Star, and many others. An alphabetical list of authors with poems and page references appears in the front of the book. The volumes in this series help to preserve many poems that would otherwise be buried in newspapers. In this period very few newspapers had published indexes.

Several other anthologies were published and are important bibliographically because as a group they contain many poems that would be lost or difficult to locate if they had not been collected in these volumes. Many of the selections are by minor writers who wrote only a very small quantity of verse. Even such a collection as Edith Warren's Important American Poets (1938) would contain many forgotten names among the 700 writers represented.[28] Lois E. Dann, Nell B. Knorr, Amy Hefner, and Philip Schipior are a few of the poets in the volume. The volume gives one to four poems by each poet and has biographical notes that give book titles and sometimes dates. The notes refer the reader to the Biographical Dictionary of Contemporary Poets discussed above.

Henry Harrison, the poetry publisher, came out with two volumes of contemporary poets in the 1930's.[29] Thomas Del Vecchio's Contemporary American Men Poets (1937) has poems by 459 living poets. The poems were selected from magazines, literary journals, and books. According to a note on the title page, the poems have not appeared in any previous anthology. Many of the authors would not be known to many students of literature, except perhaps to very avid poetry readers of the time. Byron A. Vazakas, Nixon Waterman, and Roger L. Waring are a few of these poets. The table of contents lists the poets alphabetically by author with titles of poems. One to four selections are given for each poet. A companion volume on contemporary women poets by Tooni Gordi was published in 1936.

In 1936 Burton Stevenson revised his 1908 edition of

Poems of American History.[30] It is a remarkable book because it has a good many poems on American history subjects. The editor used a wide range of sources: the works
of major and minor English and American writers, anthologies, newspapers, magazines, and collections of Americana
(Introduction, page xii). For many poems he gives a note
containing historical information about background, events,
and proper names. Additional notes are given at the end of
the volume plus indexes of authors, first lines, and titles.

There was considerable bibliographical activity in
drama in this period. The greatest contribution was made
by Arthur H. Quinn, professor of English at the University
of Pennsylvania.[31] The first volume of this history of
American drama, published in 1923, contains a list of plays
written between 1665 and 1860 (pages 419-462). The plays
are arranged alphabetically by title, and for each title he
gives place and date of publication and production. Four
years later he completed the second half of his history in
two volumes. The play list in the second volume, pages
263-335, is arranged by author rather than by title, with the
works of the author in chronological order. Biographical
and critical books and articles follow the works of each author. The text in both halves of the history has bibliographic
value for the subject analysis and synopses of individual
plays. In his 1936 revision of A History of American Drama
from the Civil War to the Present he updated the play list
and made some of the author lists complete. For other playwrights he gives a representative list only. Manuscripts are
included if they were actually identified. Only playwrights
whose works are discussed or cited in the text are included
(pages 314-315). For a more complete list of early American plays the reader needs to consult Frank P. Hill's American Plays Printed 1714-1830 (1934).[32] It contains 327 plays
by 151 authors and 78 plays by unknown writers. The plays
are in three lists: an alphabetic arrangement of authors and
anonymous titles, an alphabetic list by title, and a title list
in chronological order.

Two other works, one by Margaret G. Mayorga and
the other by Allen G. Halline, contain useful bibliographies.[33]
The Mayorga volume comments on American plays prior to
1920 and contains a lengthy bibliography, pages 358-458, giving
date of publication, and for some plays, place and publisher.
Halline's American Plays (1935) is a collection of plays with
critical introductions and bibliographies. The bibliography,
pages 751-767, gives names of plays with dates of production
and publication but no other information.

The volumes best known for information about plays produced in this country are called Best Plays of [year] and Yearbook of the American Drama. 34 Because for many years the series was edited by Burns Mantle, the volumes are known by many drama fans by his name.   Published annually since 1919, each volume contains excerpts of 10 of the best plays of the year.   Publication information is given in a separate section called "The Plays and Their Authors." Another part of the volume has a list of plays produced in New York City for the previous year.   Many of the foreign plays can be identified from the brief information about the author and title given for each play.   This is especially true for plays translated from foreign languages.   The student who is compiling a list of plays by American playwrights will have some difficulty, for the note following the title of some English-language plays gives no clue to the country of origin. Sometimes the cast of characters, or the setting, or the very short synopsis may suggest the nationality of the author or the play.   If the student knows the names of many modern American playwrights, he will find much useful information about American drama in this section.   Because bibliographic information is lacking, he will have to consult other reference works.

A special volume in the Burns Mantle series was published in 1933 giving information about the New York theater for the period 1909-1919, the years preceding the first annual volume. 35 It contains excerpts from 10 plays plus a very long list of plays (pages 395-658) produced in New York between 1909 and 1919.   Although no publication information is given, the list is useful for names of playwrights, titles of plays, and dates of production.

Three titles containing the text of one-act plays began in this period: the Yearbook of Short Plays (1931-1940), Best One-Act Plays (1937-1960), and One-Act Plays for Stage and Study (1925-1938). 36 While the individual volumes do not have many plays, together they would contain many titles and authors.   The six volumes of the Yearbook of Short Plays contain a total of 138 new nonroyalty plays with brief biographical sketches of the authors.   The sketches vary in bibliographic value: some give titles and some do not, and some give titles without dates.   The sketches vary also in length from eight lines to a half page.   The George Savage sketch is one of the longer ones and contains titles of eight plays with dates (first series, 1931, page 328).   A brief note preceding each play gives some idea of the content,

moral, and mood. The note for Louise Helliwell's "Light
Competition" in the sixth volume reads, "The beauty and
spirit of Xmas decoration--to say nothing of Xmas festivities
in general--are often marred by the growing rivalry and pre-
tentiousness brought about by civic competitions. How one
family handled the unpleasant situation is the basis of this
amusing play" (page 271).

Best One-Act Plays was an annual anthology from 1937
through 1960. Each volume has between 10 and 12 plays by
writers born in America and abroad. The brief biographical
sketches identify the authors and their published works but include little or no imprint information. One-Act Plays for
Stage and Study (1925-1938) contain in each volume between
20 and 25 plays by American, English, and Irish dramatists.
The American writers can be identified by the biographical
sketches preceding the plays. These sketches contain other
titles written by the authors.

By the 1920's the various regions of the country were
sufficiently developed economically and politically that many
people began to take a closer look at their cultural identity,
especially as it related to literature. New England and the
South had already written literary histories and compiled collections. One is not surprised, therefore, to note an awak-
ening on the part of the West to organize and collect its
writings in bibliographies and collections. Ralph L. Rusk,
a native of Illinois, was one of the first to list the early
literature of the Midwest. His 1925 Columbia dissertation,
"The Literature of the Middle Western Frontier," was published by the Columbia University Press in two volumes.
In volume two he lists works by citizens of the Middle
West and by travelers who described the country and the people. Lists for fiction, poetry, and drama are given on pages
351-363. For the Southwest a 600-title bibliography is included in Southwest Heritage (1938) by Mabel Major, Rebecca
W. Smith, and Thomas M. Pearce.[37] Belles-lettres titles
are identified among other titles, and imprint is given. The
text itself evaluates leading examples of all types of literature from the beginning through a portion of the 1930's. Book
titles are cited with dates, and individual poems mentioned in
the separate poetry chapter may be found in volumes cited in
a footnote on page 122.

Several authors turned their attention to regional fiction and poetry. Rowena Longmire did a dictionary catalog
of three Midwestern states' short stories for a 1932 dissertation

at the University of Chicago.[38] Carl B. Spotts wrote a
lengthy essay which ran through several issues of the Missouri Historical Review on the development of fiction on the
Missouri frontier.[39] The third, fourth, and fifth articles
are on the short story, and the sixth is on the novel. He
gives place and date of publication for many titles. The essay is based on his Ph.D. thesis at Penn State University.[40]
Another essay of bibliographic value was written by Levette
J. Davidson in 1933.[41] In it he provides content information
with dates of publication for 17 early works of fiction of the
Rocky Mountain region. Hilton R. Greer performed a valuable service when he edited two volumes of short stories
from the Southwest, one in 1928 and the other in 1931.[42]
Both Benjamin A. Botkin and B. S. Ivey edited anthologies
of southwestern poetry.[43]

Bibliographic aids were also done for the South. Janet
Agnew did A Southern Bibliography: Fiction 1929-1938 (1939)
and William Y. Elliott did a bibliography on local color in
southern literature (1929).[44] The Agnew bibliography is classified, with annotated titles for such subjects as farm life,
mountain people, poor whites, town life, and family life. The
work also has separate author, state, and title lists. The
Elliott thesis, which includes poetry and drama as well as
fiction, is also annotated and classified. It includes literature on other kinds of topics, such as coast and sea, river,
swamp, blue grass, and cane break. The brief annotations
give information about time and locality.

One of the best volumes published in the admirable
American Writers Series is on Southern poetry.[45] Edd W.
Parks edited Southern Poets in 1936 and covered 36 poets,
including such minor figures as Abram J. Ryan, Cale Y.
Rice, and Theodore O'Hara. The short biographical sketches
preceding the selections contain titles of books with dates.
Additional titles are given in the Selected Bibliography, pages
cxxxi-clviii. Many biographies and critical works have annotations which refer the reader to bibliographies and to texts
of poems. For George W. Ranck's The Bivouac of the Dead
and Its Author (Baltimore, 1875) the annotation reads as follows: "Although the author over-praises O'Hara, his 4-page
book contains valuable information, and the best texts of 'The
Bivouac of the Dead' and 'The Old Pioneer'" (page cxli). For
Irwin Russell's Poems (New York, 1888) Edd W. Parks writes
that this edition "contains a laudatory preface by Joel Chandler
Harris; the 1917 edition is more inclusive, and has an excellent biographical sketch of Russell by Maurice Garland Fulton"
(page cxlviii).

Much bibliographic work was done in this period on the literature of individual states. Bertha S. Hart's Introduction to Georgia Writers (1929) is one of the best because it contains a great many authors and titles in separate lists for humorists, fiction writers, poets, editors and journalists, historians, legal and political writers, scientists, and writers on religion.[46] Each chapter begins with an essay containing biographical and bibliographic information about some of the leading writers of Georgia. Next in order is the bibliography, and then a few selections. The chapter on poetry, pages 96-131, includes 93 authors in the bibliography and 10 poems, including Sydney Lanier's "Song of the Chattahoochee" (pages 118-119). The entry in the bibliography for Lanier lists 12 works of prose and poetry with imprint (page 113).

Another excellent example of a state literature bibliography is A Handbook of Oklahoma Writers (1939).[47] The book begins with separate essays on fiction writers, poets, dramatists, historians, and writers of general nonfiction. The essays are followed by a town list of Oklahoma writers, pages 220-225, a bibliography of Oklahoma writers, pages 226-305, and an index. The bibliography, which is set in small type, contains a great many titles, with imprints.

Edgar J. Hinkel's lengthy California bibliography is in three volumes, one each for fiction, poetry, and drama.[48] It contains works of native California writers and Californiana by other writers. More than 2800 authors are included with place and date of birth and death. The 6304 titles include imprint but not pages.

In 1937 the Wisconsin Library Association published a list of Wisconsin authors who lived between 1836 and 1937.[49] The authors are listed according to subject: economics, religion, philosophy, fine arts, political science, etc. Poets, novelists, and dramatists are located in three separate lists, pages 46-56, 59-77, and 78-84. Imprint and pages are given for the titles.

The Michigan list by Madge K. Goodrich is limited to authors of published books, with only a few exceptions.[50] For each author the years for birth and death are given and the titles are listed with date of publication. For many authors Goodrich refers the reader to the Readers' Guide to Periodical Literature and other bibliographies for titles of short stories, poems, and articles. Titles of reference works containing biographical information are listed. For

many minor writers of Michigan the book is a valuable tool
for research.

A rather lengthy bibliographic study of Missouri
writers was done by Alexander N. DeMenil for the Missouri
Historical Review in 1920. [51] The authors include historians,
clergymen, politicians, teachers, poets, novelists, and playwrights. The sketches vary in length from a short paragraph
to three pages and contain titles of books with dates, and
often with place of publication. For Mark Twain there are
13 titles; for Elizabeth Meriwether, six novels; and for William V. Byars, six poetry volumes. Eugene Field submitted
nine titles for inclusion. DeMenil writes briefly and criti-
cally about some titles. He evidently was fond of Kate
Chopin's Bayou Folk (1894), for he praises "the facility and
exactness with which Mrs. Chopin handles the Creole dialect,
and the fidelity of her descriptions of that strange remote
life in the Louisiana bayous..." (page 118). Unlike most of
the other sketches, which are highly factual, the one for Mrs.
Chopin is a eulogy, for he knew her as a child and later as
an author. He compares her with George W. Cable and finds
that "her touch is far more deft than Mr. Cable's; her insight
is femininely subtle (if I may use the word); pain, sorrow,
affliction, humbled pride, rude heroism--enter more completely into her sympathies. She feels and suffers with her
characters" (page 118).

North Carolina is one of the few states that listed current literature of the 1930's in an annual bibliography. [52]
Poetry and fiction by North Carolina writers or about North
Carolina are listed each year in the April issue of the North
Carolina Historical Review. The first listing, which is in
the 1934 volume, lists titles published between 1931 and 1933;
later volumes list books for the previous year and a few from
earlier years. The author's full name, title, imprint, and
pages are given for all titles. The compiler of this annual
bibliography in the 1930's was Mary Lindsay Thornton of the
North Carolina collection of the University of North Carolina
at Chapel Hill.

One volume called Arizona in Literature (1935) by
Mary G. Boyer is remarkable for including in its pages a
wide variety of writings about Arizona, including 11 short
stories, 112 poems, and selections from 16 novels. [53] The
brief biographical sketches preceding each selection contain
titles with dates and sometimes publisher. For short stories
in periodicals the name and date of the magazine are given.

The author of this anthology was a professor of English at Arizona Teachers College at Flagstaff.

Separate bibliographies for state fiction and poetry appeared in this period. Bernice M. Foster did a short bio-bibliography of Michigan novelists giving very brief information about the authors and listing titles with year.[54] She refers the reader to further biographical information in standard reference works such as Who's Who in America. Lizzie C. McVoy and Ruth B. Campbell did an annotated bibliography of Louisiana novelists, which is particularly good in listing titles on Louisiana subjects.[55] The subject index has entries like "Indians," "Mississippi," "plantations," "swamps," and "race problems."

More and better work was done on state poetry. Worthington C. Ford made a long list of broadsides printed in Massachusetts in the seventeenth and eighteenth century.[56] The chronological arrangement is of great value to scholars doing historical studies. The book was published by the Massachusetts Historical Society.

Two masters' theses, one on Texas poetry and the other on South Carolina poetry, contain many names and titles.[57] Venice Wallenberg's bibliography on Texas poetry contains vital statistics about the poets and titles of books with imprint and pages. The brief annotations characterize the content and value of the poetry. Gertrude Jacobi's essay discusses or mentions 111 South Carolina poets of the past 300 years. The essay is divided into six chapters, each one covering a chronological period. Besides the biographical and bibliographical information in the essay she includes a short anthology of poems in Appendix E.

Minnie Brashear wrote two long essays on Missouri verse in two issues of the Missouri Historical Review for 1924.[58] They contain names for many poets and poems and selected lines for poems. The second essay lists books of verse published before 1870 and for each of the decades between that year and 1900. She gives place and date of publication.

Many state poetry anthologies were published between 1920 and 1940. The volume of Virginia fugitive verse by Armistead C. Gordon is particularly outstanding.[59] The author defines fugitive verse as "that which may have been published in magazines or newspapers--or which may even never have been published.... Infrequently it appears in the course of a work of prose fiction, used per se, and probably written for the occasion" (page 11). The book contains an essay on Virginia fugitive verse, followed by an anthology of poems, pages 137-369, and brief biographical sketches of the poets in the anthology. This is an example of an anthology of considerable bibliographic value because most of the poems have never appeared in a published volume. The author was an assistant professor at the University of Virginia when he wrote it.

The state anthologies came from all parts of the country, and some states are represented by more than one volume. Walter J. Coates compiled four volumes of Vermont verse under the title of Favorite Vermont Poets. [60] Utah Sings, published between 1934 and 1942, is in three volumes.[61] Three volumes of Texas verse were published between 1936 and 1939. [62]

Henry Harrison of New York City was the chief publisher of state anthologies. The volumes of contemporary poets for Florida, Georgia, and Michigan are slim volumes of fewer than 150 pages. [63] The longest one, California Poets (1932), contains 244 poets and 500 poems.[64]

The poetry societies of America issued many collections of poetry in this period that must serve as documents for state literary historians. The Poetry Society of Georgia published a collection of prize poems by its members in 1925. [65] In 1949 the Society celebrated their twenty-fifth anniversary by publishing a commemorative volume. [66] Most of the annual publications from these societies were very modest volumes of 40 to 80 pages. Occasionally the societies put out a special volume such as the State Anthology (1936) of the Poetry Society of Oklahoma, which contains poems by 169 writers. [67]

City literary anthologies were published for Battle Creek, New London, Baltimore, Peoria, Cincinnati, New York City, and San Diego. [68] The local branches of the National League of American Pen Women compiled the collections for the last two cities. Rarely does an historical encyclopedia for a city contain poems, but one that does is Seattle and Its Environs (1924). [69] Volume one has a fair selection of poems by Seattle writers on pages 577-605.

Some bibliographies in subject fields other than

literature contain lists of belles lettres, but many of them are too short to make any contribution to bibliographic control. Lester J. Cappon's Bibliography of Virginia History Since 1865 (1930) is an exception. [70] It contains a lengthy list of poetry, drama, and fiction by Virginia men of letters. Some of the poetry can be identified by the word "poems" following the title, or in a note below the title. Novels are identified by the words "novel" and "romance." The Bibliography gives full imprint, pages, size, and such miscellaneous information as frontispiece, plates, portraits, dates for later editions, variant titles, and original publication for those books which were first published in magazines and newspapers. The index entry "poets" gives the poetry volume by entry number. There is no index entry for drama and fiction.

Some encyclopedic state histories contain information about authors and books. Stanley T. Williams, professor of English at Yale University, wrote the essay on Connecticut literature for volume two of History of Connecticut in Monographic Form (1925). [71] The essay cites many titles with dates. New Jersey: A History (1930) includes a chapter in volume four, pages 1285-1325, on writers of the nineteenth and twentieth century. [72] Information varying in length from four lines to a page and a half is given for a rather sizable number of authors. These multi-volume historical works would have greater value if they included, in addition to the essay, separate lists, of some length, of poems, plays, and fiction, written by natives of the state, giving full bibliographic information. The editors of future works may prefer, however, to list only belles lettres with scenes or setting in the state, or with information about the state.

The one-volume state histories sometimes have information about literature. In Early Days in Dakota Edwin C. Torrey has a section called "Early Poets in South Dakota" pages 65-74. [73] He gives brief biographical information about several poets and includes selections. If bibliographies of South Dakota poetry are few or nonexistent, one can rejoice that the author did not ignore the poets in an early history of the state.

Native American Humor (1800-1900) by Walter Blair is a classic on the subject. [74] The author states in the first line of the Preface, page vii, that his aim is "to trace the mutations of 19th century humorous treatments of American characters." In a long scholarly essay, pages 3-162, the author writes about aspects of the evolution of writing of this kind. Some pages in the essay, for example, 63 and 64, have a quantity of biographical and bibliographic information: 10 authors are listed with brief identification and principal works. One author is described this way: "Joseph M. Field (1810-1856), St. Louis actor, actor-manager and journalist, whose newspaper and periodical sketches make up The Drama in Pokerville (1847)" (page 63).

The bibliography of humorists in this book, pages 175-197, is, according to the author, "a somewhat more extensive one than any other which has appeared..." (Preface, page viii). It lists published books with place and date of publication. A few books and articles about the authors follow. The notes in the back of the book give additional information but only for those selections in the anthology which constitute the larger part of the volume. The note for Mark Twain's jumping frog story states that the author wanted it to appear in Artemus Ward's Travels, but that it arrived too late for inclusion. The Saturday Press printed it on November 18, 1865 (page 560).

The authors and titles of the writings in the volume would constitute a short bibliography of American humor of the nineteenth century. The familiar authors are there, with some of their famous stories. Some writers not so well known, such as Melville D. Landon, John S. Robb, and Madison Tensas, are represented by single selection. Anonymous selections are represented by some hilarious stories from the Farmer's Almanac and by examples of tall talk from the old Southwest. The author of Native American Humor was an assistant professor of English at the University of Chicago in 1937.

Another very useful bibliography, especially for book collectors and others interested in first editions, was compiled in 1937 by a New York bookseller by the name of Howard S. Mott, Jr.[75] Three Hundred Years of American Humor (1637-1936) has 186 entries, most of them first editions. The notes, some of which are rather lengthy, contain additional information and comment on the content and significance of the titles. The comments include quotes from standard reference works and from books about American humor, such as the study by Walter Blair described above.

Two other anthologies published in the 1930's supplement Walter Blair's Native American Humor. Franklin J.

Meine compiled Tall Tales of the Southwest (1930), and Arthur
P. Hudson edited Humor of the Old Deep South (1936).[76] The
first has 49 stories from southern and southwestern authors
of the period 1830-1860. The second contains more than 200
selections from a wide variety of sources, many of them
from travel books, histories, biographical writings, volumes
of poems, almanacs, and periodicals. Of these sources regional and state newspapers account for the largest number,
and include such titles as the Mississippi Free Trader,
Natchez Weekly Gazette, the Aberdeen Sunny South, the New
Orleans Delta, the New York Spirit of the Times, Field
Sports, and Literature and the Stage. The selections were
arranged under such headings as "hunters and fishermen,"
"doctors," "lawyers," "politicians," "preachers," "school-
masters and collegians," "the ladies--God bless them," and
many others. A full citation is given at the bottom of the
first page of each selection. In addition, the author provides
notes for names, events, scenes, customs, language, etc.,
in the selections. For selections with authors the editor supplies brief biographical information giving his source at the
bottom of the page. These biographical sketches are noteworthy for titles of books and for the names of periodicals
for which many authors wrote. Hudson says, for example,
that William Ward's poems were published mostly in the
Philadelphia American Courier, the Macon (Georgia) Beacon,
and the New Orleans Times-Picayune (page 485). Although
brief, the sketches contain miscellaneous information for the
scholar who is studying an author and his works. Mr. Hudson writes, for example, that Poems by Alfred W. Arrington
(1869) "contains a memoir by his wife which is said to be
the chief source of information about him" (page 417). For
the biographical sketch of "T. B. Thorpe and Mike Fink"
there is a footnote, page 297, referring the reader to Walter
Blair and Franklin J. Meine's Mike Fink, King of Mississippi
Keelboatmen (New York: Holt, 1933). The author of this superb collection was on the faculty of the University of North
Carolina at the time of publication.

A fair number of author bibliographies were published
as books and parts of books. They covered major and minor
writers of the nineteenth and twentieth century and were published by university and commercial presses and by bookshops. They vary in length from Oscar Wegelin's 20-page
bibliography of John Esten Cooke (1925) to John W. Robertson's two-volume bibliography of Edgar Allan Poe (1934).[77]
The latter is a remarkable work for its amount of commentary. The whole of volume two, 300 pages in length, is

composed of commentary on items in volume one, followed
by a 10-page index to both volumes. The commentary is
more biographical and literary than bibliographical because
it examines the conditions under which Poe wrote and published his poems and tales. Full collation and many notes
are given for titles in volume one. Although in two volumes,
the Poe bibliography is not nearly so long as Thomas F.
Currier's Bibliography of John Greenleaf Whittier (1937),
which has 692 pages set in small type, and remains even
today one of the most detailed bibliographies ever compiled
for an American author. [78] It gives very full collation and
full information on binding, on variant states and editions,
and on printing and publishing history, quoting from newspapers, auction catalogs, letters, biographies, and other
sources. For Whittier's Home Ballads and Poems (1860)
Currier writes that it was "entered for copyright and copy
deposited July 30, 1860, but not put on sale until October,
for reasons explained in the letter below" (page 86). On the
next page he gives the text of the letter in the Essex Institute. The compiler is very thorough when he is discussing
the scholarship relating to the date or textual variants of a
poem. He devotes four pages (50-53) to the pamphlet and
broadside printing of The Song of the Vermonters and the
text as given in Samuel T. Pickard's Life and Letters of
John Greenleaf Whittier (1894). [79] Two plates reproduce the
pamphlet and broadside texts, and eight lines of Pickard's
text are compared with those of the original reading that
Currier gives as the one found in the June 1833 issue of the
New England Magazine, where it was printed anonymously.
Currier quotes from a letter written by Whittier to the (Vermont) Free Press and Times, August 4, 1877, stating that
he wrote the poem in 1833 or 1844 (page 50).

Part 1 of this Whittier bibliography contains a list of
all his books and leaflets, alphabetic lists of his poems,
prose essays and tales, a chronological list of his letters to
the press, and titles of newspapers edited by Whittier. The
fifth section of this first part is a bibliography of biography
and criticism by Pauline F. Pulsifer (pages 485-546). The
appendices include "First Printings Within a Book or Pamphlet of Whittier's Prose and Verse," pages 607-628, a
"Chronology of Poems," pages 629-662, and "Poems Incor-
rectly Attributed to Whittier," pages 603-606. The detailed
index, pages 663-692, contains names of people, places, and
titles. Thomas F. Currier was a librarian at Harvard for
more than 40 years, working as a cataloger much of the
time and doing administrative work in his later years.

Two other major nineteenth-century writers were covered by scholarly bibliographies in the 1930's. Merle Johnson revised his 1910 bibliography of Mark Twain and Robert E. Spiller and Philip C. Blackburn did their bibliography of James Fenimore Cooper. [80] The Twain bibliography gives very full descriptions for the books, including collation, binding, paper, editions, issues, and original publication. Johnson took great care to establish the printing and the date of first publication of the books. The first edition of The Prince and the Pauper (1882) was printed by two presses, the Franklin Press and the John Wilson University Press. "A careful study of the plates indicates that the Franklin Press copies are the first printing. It is also noted that the gilt plate on the spine is about 3/8" from the top in the first state; in later bindings this was lowered" (page 40). Johnson lists the Boston 1882 edition as the first but notes that the English edition preceded the American by almost two weeks. He also states that the author confirmed the priority of the English edition when he lost a court action to get copyright protection for the Montreal edition based on his two-week residence in Canada before its appearance (page 41). Another interesting note for the same novel states that "A Boy's Adventure" was intended as a chapter for the novel. It was first published in the Bazaar Budget, June 4, 1880 (page 41).

The book has a very detailed index, pages 191-274, listing all the titles in the bibliography with cross references to facilitate use. The index also has entries for a great deal of information in the notes. The one major complaint about the book is that many of Twain's periodical publications are not listed, although many more have been added in this revised addition. Another fault is that some periodical citations lack page numbers.

The Cooper bibliography is especially good for Continental editions, information about the writer's publishing vicissitudes, and the appendix of letters dealing with the production of his books (pages 215-248). Illustrations for some title pages are included.

Doubleday, Doran and Random House both gave their attention to modern writers. Doubleday published a very fine bibliography of Christopher Morley. [81] It is a descriptive bibliography giving Morley's separate works and contributions to books. The book is especially good for printing and publishing information. About Morley's Mince Pie, Alfred P. Lee, the author of the bibliography, writes that it was "pub-

lished Dec. 17, 1919 in an edition of 3000." The first issue
has the last word on page vii misspelled "of." This was
later corrected to "on" (page 23). The book would be better
if it included Morley's periodical contributions. Barton Currie's Booth Tarkington (1932) is another descriptive bibliography which lacks periodical writings of the author.[82]

The Random House bibliographies vary in scope, some
containing all the writings of the author and some containing
only a selection. Sydney S. Albert's Bibliography of Robinson
Jeffers (1933) attempts to be complete and gives very full information for all books, including manuscripts, and often
quoting from the author on matters relating to content and
publication.[83] The bibliography has reproductions of title
pages, manuscript pages, and a long list of writings about
Jeffers, pages 181-228, an index of first lines, pages 239-
254, and a general index, pages 255-262, containing among
other entries all titles written by Jeffers. The Eugene O'Neill
bibliography lacks periodical publications and does not contain
manuscript information.[84] Like the Jeffers bibliography it
gives full bibliographic description for first editions and contains clear reproductions of title pages. It also has an anthology of O'Neill's early poems, pages 111-161, for the first
time collected with the permission of the author (page 110).

Bookshops were also active in turning out bibliographies. The Brick Row Book Shop published Lawson M.
Melish's bibliography of Edith Wharton, which includes her
books but omits periodical publications.[85] The Hampshire
Bookshop in Northampton, Massachusetts, published a short
bibliography of Emily Dickinson.[86] In Philadelphia the Centaur Bookshop published between 1922 and 1932 several bibliographies of modern authors, all of them small volumes,
neatly printed and carefully done. The Theodore Dreiser bibliography (1928) by Edward D. MacDonald contains a very
short foreword by Dreiser, collations for his books, and
separate lists for his contributions to books and periodicals.[87]
The last section of the book has biographical and critical
writings about Dreiser. The notes make delightful reading,
such as the one following the 1923 reissue of The Genius, one
of the author's suppressed novels. MacDonald says that "the
real immunity for babes and fools ... is the length of the
book. Unless the prurient minds were at the same time
strong, they, too, would probably cave in at the mere sight
of the book's 736 plus, closely printed pages" (page 61). The
compiler's introduction, pages 15-26, is also well worth reading for bibliographic information about Dreiser. MacDonald

states that the author was already familiar to many readers before Sister Carrie (1900) was published. He had already written almost 45 articles or poems for magazines, such as Cosmopolitan, Munsey's, Harper's, and a few others (page 21). The other volumes in the series, all intended for the book collector but of value to the scholar, are on such authors as Joseph Hergesheimer, Stephen Crane, and James B. Cabell.[88] Guy Holt's Cabell bibliography (1924) was much enlarged in 1932 by Isidore R. Brussel.[89]

Bibliographies in author biographies are a common feature, but many are short and incomplete, lacking all or many of the shorter works of the biographee. Some literary biographers give more time and thought to bibliography and prepare longer lists of an author's works in the hope that the biographies will serve more scholarly purposes. One such example is Amos L. Herold's James Kirke Paulding (1926), which lists Paulding's separate works in chronological order and arranges his contributions to periodicals under name of periodical by year and month.[90] In addition, he includes in chapter five, pages 88-92, a chronological list of the author's tales. Another long chronological list (pages 343-349) of an author's works is in Edward S. Bradley's George Henry Boker (1927).[91] Another bibliography carefully done is in Homer F. Barnes's Charles Fenno Hoffman (1930).[92] He is especially thorough in giving information about editions, listing, for example, four editions of The Vigil of Faith (1842, 1845, 1846, and one without a date). In a note to the fourth edition he writes that there is no evidence that a third edition was published (page 320). In the same note he suggests that the edition with no date is "probably counted as the second" (page 320). For another title, Greyslaer, Mr. Barnes writes on page 320 that after much searching he has not been able to locate an 1842 edition published by Baker and Scribner, although he did find it listed by Joseph Sabin in his Dictionary of Books Relating to America (1877) in volume eight, page 360. "Appendix B" of the volume contains the text of some uncollected poems of Hoffman with a complete citation to the original publication for most of the poems and a much abbreviated one for the others (pages 289-316).

What must surely be the longest bibliography in a short biography is found in Carl Van Doren's Sinclair Lewis (1933).[93] Compiled by Harvey Taylor, the bibliography begins on page 77 and ends on page 187. It lists writings by and about Lewis and gives a detailed description of the first editions of his books and a briefer description for books to which he contributed. The periodical publications are listed in chronological order beginning with the name of the periodical and location, then title of contribution, and designation as story, poem, or article. One major fault with this portion of the bibliography is that page references are omitted for many entries. All of Lewis's titles can be located quickly by the use of the index on pages 193-205.

The greater part of the bibliographic control in this period was achieved in those works which list belles lettres only by author and title. They list a great many, but they fall far short of recording all the imaginative literature of the United States. The reader will note that huge lists of 10,000 to 50,000 titles were not produced except for the CHAL. Even in that work there are no separate lists for fiction, poetry, and drama. While the work is comprehensive in the sense that it covers the literature of the whole country, it does so only to the extent that it does not purposely omit any historical period, nor geographic area, nor any one of the genre, nor many minor writers. The writers that are included are those that the editors and the authors of the essays consider as having some special significance for the student or researcher in American literature. Even among minor writers of special significance the editors had to make a selection. The work is a milestone of bibliography, though, for the great many titles that it does record.

* * *

An even greater number of titles are included in the separate national genre lists, the regional bibliographies and collections, the state and local genre compilations, the author bibliographies, and the anthologies. These publications plus the comprehensive national bibliographies make up the principal structure of the bibliographic organization that was established in this period. The reader who glances at the titles in Appendix A of the present book, and who reviews this Chapter 1, will see that more than a little bibliographic work was done on the national, regional, state, and local level. One will also remember that some of the bibliographic publications contain a small amount of information relating to the subject content of the titles listed or cited. These bibliographic works, which take the form of the annotated bibliography and the essay, are noteworthy because, while fairly few in number, together they represent a greater effort at subject analysis than had been attempted in previous years.

The masters' and doctoral essays begin in this period to make an important contribution to this effort.

Not all anthologies produced in these years are of course listed in the present work, but enough are given to show that they do contain a very large number of poems, short stories, and plays. Many of these literary selections were not to be listed, either in bibliographies produced in this period or in the two decades before 1920. Many may not even now be listed in a bibliography by author and title. The reader will also note that some of these anthologies do have bibliographies which list many belles-lettres titles that are in other publications. Some of them also have biographical sketches citing titles for the authors included. Many of these short sketches are for minor writers not covered by separate author bibliographies.

Many author bibliographies were compiled in this period, and some of them are among the best that have been done to date. Currier's Bibliography of John Greenleaf Whittier is the one that immediately comes to mind when one remembers the 1930's. For the major writers, and particularly those who were prolific, the author bibliographies have great importance, for only there can one expect a full and accurate listing of all publications of an author, both whole books and articles. Some of the author bibliographies are valuable tools for the research scholar who wants more than brief information about an author's works.

One final glance at the titles in Appendix A will reveal that authors of both the nineteenth and twentieth centuries were covered, and that two of the writers of this century, James B. Cabell and Edwin A. Robinson, are represented by two bibliographies. Modern authors received as much, if not more, attention than older writers.

Chapter 2

THE LITERARY HISTORY OF THE UNITED STATES, THE BIBLIOGRAPHY OF AMERICAN LITERATURE, AND OTHER BIBLIOGRAPHIC STUDIES

These twenty years from 1940 to 1960 constitute a period of great progress and growth in American bibliography. Many bibliographies were published as separates, many appeared as parts of books, and a great many were included in periodicals. They were compiled chiefly by college teachers, librarians, graduate students, and book dealers. Some of them are highly selective, while others are comprehensive, and a smaller number are very nearly complete. The two titles that stand out among all the others, and which are excellent examples of comprehensive bibliographies, are the bibliography volume of the Literary History of the United States [LHUS] (1948) and the Bibliography of American Literature [BAL] (1955 to date).[1]

The LHUS Bibliography was compiled and edited by Thomas H. Johnson, a Ph.D. from Harvard, who was chairman of the English Department at the Lawrenceville School, editor of The Poetical Works of Edward Taylor (1939), and author of a bibliography of Jonathan Edwards (1940).[2] The volume contains publications by and about many major and minor American writers and a large number of publications on many subjects relating to American literature, or useful for background reading in the study of American authors and their works. The volume is particularly valuable for listing books by American authors with dates. The book, however, cannot be used for shorter works that are not published as separates. Here it is important to recall that it is the author bibliography which often must be used to locate short stories, poems, one-act plays, and essays. The LHUS Bibliography gives titles of bibliographies, published letters, correspondence, and papers, and locates manuscripts in libraries and private collections. Bibliographic information

27

is also given for collected works, edited texts, and reprints. The notes for some of these titles are of great importance to the scholar. Concerning the 1890 Riverside Edition of the Writings of James Russell Lowell in ten volumes, the LHUS Bibliography states that it is "the first important edition of Lowell's collected works. The material was revised by the author" (page 629). The LHUS notes that as of 1948 "the text of Dickinson's poems has yet to be established. Only that in Bolts of Melody (1945) [edited by Mabel L. Todd and Millicent T. Bingham] approaches accuracy" (page 468). The first LHUS Bibliography Supplement (1959) mentions Thomas H. Johnson's three-volume variorum edition of 1955.

Some minor poets are not included in the author section of the Bibliography Supplement but in the earlier sections on individual periods. There are many notes here about books and authors, some of which give content information. William H. C. Hosmer (1814-1877) is described as a poet "who is at his best in nature descriptions of the country he knew in western New York.... A Collection was published as The Poetical Works of William H. C. Hosmer (2 vols., 1854)" (page 111). Elizabeth O. Smith (1806-1893) "made use of the frontier for The Western Captive (1842) and wrote a sentimental novel of slum life published as The Newsboy" (page 109).

The several published volumes of the BAL by Jacob Blanck constitute the most ambitious single attempt to provide bibliographic control for a great many important writers of American literature. Jacob Blanck conceived the idea for the bibliography in the 1930's and secured the support of the Lilly Endowment in 1942. The Bibliographical Society of America is supervising the work under the editorship of Mr. Blanck. The work covers only authors who died before 1930 and only those whose works were known or read in their own time. Because the work is concerned primarily with belles lettres, many American writers are not included. The bibliography is limited, according to the Preface, to "the material which constitutes the structure of American literature of the past one hundred and fifty years" (page xi). Works in subject fields are included but only if the authors also wrote imaginative literature. Historians and travel writers are included if their works have considerable literary interest. The bibliography lists all first editions, variant issues or states of the first edition, some reprints, later editions with important textual changes, and books containing the first appearance of any prose or poetry. Newspaper and

other periodical publications are not included except that some
of these publications later appeared as books or in books.[3]
When a periodical publication is reprinted in a published volume, the original source is given in a note. Don Byrne's
O'Malley of Shanganagh was published by Century Company in
1925. It originally appeared in Century Magazine between
December 1924 and February 1925 under the title of "An Untitled Story" (volume 1, page 465).

The BAL gives a full description for first editions:
signature collation, paper, binding, wrapper, inserted catalogs and ads, and illustrations. Many errors in authorship
made in older bibliographies of Americana have been corrected. Roorbach's Bibliotheca Americana (1855) covering
the period of October 1852 to May 1855 attributes the novel
The Flying Cloud (1854) to Joseph H. Ingraham (page 101).
Mr. Blanck writes that "No evidence [has been] found of
Ingraham's authorship" (volume 4, page 489). In the next
line he refers to entry 2671 in Lyle H. Wright's American
Fiction 1851-1875, which credits the title to Greenliffe Warren.

The BAL is a monument of scholarship and dedication
on the part of the editor, Jacob Blanck, and the many col-
laborators who assist in many ways to make the work complete and accurate. Donald Gallup, the distinguished bibliographer and curator of the Collection of American Literature
at Yale University Library, has contributed liberally to the
work. Others who have made valuable contributions include
Lawrence R. Thompson, William M. Gibson, George Arms,
and Norman Holmes Pearson. Paul Goren and Perry O'Neill
have been most cooperative in supplying information from the
collections in the New York Public Library. Librarians from
the Library of Congress, the Boston Public Library, the
Boston Athenaeum, the American Antiquarian Society, and
Harvard have also been helpful. Colin Clair and Simon
Nowell-Smith, two British scholars in bibliography, have supplied British publication information for many titles.[4]

Jacob Blanck was eminently qualified to undertake the
BAL. He had been rare book editor for Publishers' Weekly
and Antiquarian Bookman and had revised Merle Johnson's
American First Editions (1929) twice, once in 1936 and again
in 1942. Each time he made corrections and additions. For
many years this title was a standard reference work for
book collectors, librarians, and scholars.

Three other books on American literature became

standard reference works in the 1940's: American Authors
and Books, 1640-1940 (1943), the Oxford Companion to American Literature (1941), and Contemporary American Authors
(1940) by Fred B. Millett.[5] The first has authors in literature, history, art, science, and other subject fields. Brief
biographical information, principal titles with dates, and sometimes a very brief synopsis are given for each author. The
Oxford Companion concentrates much more on literary authors
and gives more information about them and their writings, including short stories and poems. Plot summaries are given
for many titles. The volume has some entries for people,
places, events, etc., that were significant in the cultural life
of America and which a student may find useful in his study
of American literature. At the end of the volume (pages 863-
888) there is a "Chronological Index," which gives a year-by-
year outline of the literary and social history of the United
States. Contemporary American Authors contains biobibliographies for 219 writers. It gives titles of separately-pub-
lished works by the writers, and studies and articles about
them. The work is valuable for the published volumes of the
authors, but it is much more useful for biographical information and literary criticism.

The later volumes of the Americana Annual contain
some good information about American literature.[6] The
volume published in 1940 contains some excellent descriptive
and critical comments for novels published in 1939. Paul
Corey's Three Miles Square is described as "an honest and
impressive picture of Midwest farm life" (page 458). Francis Griswold's A Sea Island Today is an "unusual and beauti-
ful novel about South Carolina" (page 458). More than a one-
line description is given for Walter Van Tilburg Clark's The
Track of a Cat in the 1950 volume:

> The year 1949 witnessed a flood of highly com-
> petent novels, difficult to classify, by members of the
> middle and younger generation of American writers.
> Walter Van Tilburg Clark's The Track of the Cat was
> the most powerful novel by a member of this mixed
> group. It was the apparently bare story of three
> brothers attempting to protect their livestock, huddled
> on the eastern slopes of the Sierra Nevada mountains
> during an early fall snow storm, from the attacks of
> a panther. Actually the novel was much more than
> this. It tapped reservoirs of deepest feeling in the
> reader by making him aware that each of the three
> brothers stood for a possible way of responding to

mortal destiny, and involving him completely in each of these ways. Rising above the merely excellent writing in his earlier works, The Ox-Bow Incident and The City of Trembling Leaves, Clark achieved major status as a writer in The Track of the Cat [page 30].

The article on the novel in this volume is more than two columns long (pages 30-31). The paragraphs on poetry cite six volumes in 1949 (page 31).

Lyle H. Wright continued his bibliographic work on fiction by revising his American Fiction 1774-1850 (1948).[7] It contains 600 more titles than the 1939 edition and gives authors for some anonymous and pseudonymous titles listed in the earlier edition. It contains a chronological index, pages 311-332, and a title index, pages 335-355. In 1957 he added a volume for 1851-1875 listing 2832 titles by 1193 authors.[8] Very brief notes giving locale or setting of the stories are given for many titles. The work contains a long index (pages 381-413) of all the titles in the bibliography.

Two other bibliographies are valuable for giving the geographical location of works of American fiction: the Newberry Library list of American novels (1941) and America in Fiction (1941), by Otis W. Coan and Richard G. Lillard.[9] The Newberry bibliography is a short checklist of American novels with an American setting printed before 1880. America in Fiction is a more lengthy work giving annotations for a rather large number of titles. The bibliography was compiled "to help readers understand their country better, by means of imaginative writing that presents specific human beings in realizable situations" (Preface, page iii). The titles are arranged by subject: pioneering, farm and village life, industrial America, politics, religion, the southern tradition, and minority ethnic groups. Although most of the annotations are brief, they do give some insight into setting and story. William Carlos Williams's White Mule (1937) is described as "a story of an immigrant couple, citizens by naturalization, and their struggles to manage on an average income in New York City" (pages 83-84). For students of American history the bibliography contains a number of very fine titles.

A long list of historical novels was compiled by Arthur T. Dickinson in 1958.[10] It contains brief annotations for 1224 novels published between 1917 and 1956. For more

information about plot, setting, history, and characters of
some of the historical novels listed in the above works, the
reader can consult studies on the historical novel by Ernest
E. Leisy, Robert A. Lively, and Joseph J. Waldmeir.[11]
Leisy's American Historical Novel (1950) comments on more
than 200 novels about colonial America, the American Revolution, the Westward movement, the Civil War and Reconstruction, and national expansion. The comments are critical, descriptive, and concise. To read them is to want to
run to the library shelves to borrow books. He has, for
example, great admiration for Conrad Richter's The Trees
(1940) and The Fields (1946):

> Conrad Richter's The Trees (1940), although it
> introduces no historical figures, is so well impreg-
> nated with the epic import of the pioneer's daily strug-
> gle for security that the reader feels the experiences
> of the Luckett family as his own. In the Ohio Valley
> at the close of the eighteenth century, the Lucketts
> find themselves in conflict not only with the forest
> primeval but with each other. The settler instinct of
> the wife clashes with the hunter instinct of the hus-
> band. She succumbs, but the daughter carries on,
> and, in the end, the husband hears his doom when the
> great hickories crash, marking the evolution of the
> pioneer from hunter to farmer. The Fields (1946)
> continues the story of the tilling, when towns are only
> beginning to appear, and when personal conflicts fur-
> ther reflect the conquest of the frontier. The author's
> lyric style takes its quality from the simple, primitive
> life in forest and field. Its idiom of the past is folk
> music, lovingly recorded. Quickened by humor and
> suspense, these quietly exciting and excellent novels
> wear lightly their author's extensive research on
> pioneer activities. Here is the living core of history
> [pages 124-125].

Additional historical novels with brief critical annotations are
listed in the bibliography (pages 219-259).

Robert A. Lively's Fiction Fights the Civil War (1957)
contains comments and quotes from many novels about the
Civil War. The bibliography (pages 199-217) lists more than
500 titles. The author's expressed intention is "to illustrate
their variety, their general tone, and their reliability as
sources of knowledge about the conflict" (page 5). In his
chapter "The Artist and the Past" he pauses to stress the

importance of the novels of John W. De Forest, Harold
Frederic, and Stephen Crane. He devotes six pages to a
discussion of three novels by these writers: Miss Ravenel's
Conversion from Secession to Loyalty by De Forest, The
Copperhead by Frederic, and The Red Badge of Courage by
Crane (pages 149-155). Mr. Lively makes the point that the
war outlined in these writings was "more a calamity in individual lives than a national or regional experience. Instead
of a gorgeously patterned epic of contending armies, battle
was here presented as a senseless denial of reason. Inter-
pretations of the war's meaning became exercises in abnormal
psychology, rather than explanations for the North's deci-
sions" (page 155).

Joseph H. Waldmeir's dissertation is on the ideology
of American novels of World War II. The main part of the
study is on the negative and positive aspects of this ideology.
A lengthy list (pages 181-191) of World War II novels written
by Americans concerning Americans is found at the end of
the essay.

William B. Dickens made a worthy contribution to
American bibliography when he completed his dissertation on
the American political novel between 1865 and 1910.[12] After
a short critical essay he provides a digest of 84 political
novels, giving for each one the title, author, imprint, type
and time of plot, locale, principal characters, a short critique, and a summary. The work concludes with an index
to novelists and novels, pages 392-402.

In 1942 a whole book on the American economic novel
was published.[13] The author, Walter F. Taylor, devotes
most of the book to Mark Twain, Hamlin Garland, Edward
Bellamy, and Frank Norris. Chapter two, pages 58-115, is
on the lesser novelists. The bibliography (pages 346-365)
gives titles by both the major and minor novelists discussed
in the text and includes a separate list (pages 354-355) of
novels not mentioned in the text. In 1944 Dr. Lisle A. Rose
made a list of additional titles for an article in American
Literature.[14]

Herbert R. Brown's The Sentimental Novel in America
(1940) is a well-documented essay on American fiction.[15]
The footnotes contain many fiction titles for the student who
is interested in American literature of the new American
nation. A separate bibliography of these titles at the end of
the volume would make the volume more useful for reference
purposes.

The magazine New Yorker achieves a certain amount of bibliographic control by collecting some of its short stories in two volumes, one published in 1940 and the other in 1949.[16] The volumes contain a total of 123 stories and include some of the finest writers of the period. Two anthologies of war stories were published.[17] The first collection by F. Van Wyck Mason contains fiction about American soldiers fighting in wars from the early colonial period through World War I. Most of the selections are from full-length novels according to the note at the bottom of the first page of each story. James F. Cooper, Walter D. Edmonds, Bruce Lancaster, Zane Grey, James Boyd, and Hervey Allen are among the authors. The other anthology, The Best Short Stories of World War II, contains 20 stories by writers such as Stephen Vincent Benét, William Faulkner, James Jones, Ralph Ellison, James Michener, Wallace Stegner, and Irwin Shaw. A short biographical sketch containing titles with dates precedes each selection.

No lengthy comprehensive list of American poems was compiled in this period. Some good bibliographic work was done, however, for the colonial period and the twentieth century. Milton H. Sugarman made a list of anonymous poetical pamphlets of the eighteenth century, and the University of Pennsylvania Library prepared a mimeographed list of poems published through the year 1865.[18] The latter includes 656 titles, including many not listed in other bibliographies.

Many individual poems and books of verse are cited in the text of Horace Gregory and Marya Zaturenska's History of American Poetry 1900-1940 (1942).[19] Dates are included in the text and the footnotes. The index gives titles under the names of the poets. Another useful list was published in 1945 by the Library of Congress under the title, Sixty American Poets 1896-1944.[20] The selection of poets was made by Allen Tate, who also wrote the critical notes and the preface. Frances Cheney compiled the checklist of titles. In 1954 the bibliography was revised by Kenton Kilmer.[21]

A number of people in this period did bibliographic work and wrote studies of the American drama. Arthur H. Quinn added 450 plays in his second edition (1943) of the History of the American Drama from the Beginning to the Civil War.[22] The University of Pennsylvania Library put out a checklist of early American drama containing 593 entries with full bibliographic information.[23] Joseph H. Weingarten covered only modern playwrights in his 1946 bibliog-

raphy.[24] From Native Roots (1948) by Felix Sper is a study
of regional drama containing a long list of plays found in collections and periodicals (pages 297-334).[25] Bibliographic information is adequate except for page numbers.

Five dissertations, all based on an examination of a
rather large number of plays, were written by Mary L. Andrews, Josef A. Elfenbein, Phyllis M. Ferguson, Caspar H.
Nannes, and John D. Reardon.[26] Josef A. Elfenbein studied
149 plays for his dissertation on socio-political thought in
American drama of 1782-1812. Phyllis M. Ferguson would
have studied many more plays for her dissertation if she
were able to locate them. She states in her essay for Dissertation Abstracts that "many of the plays of the first decade
[of this century] were neither published nor copyrighted."[27]

The Best American Plays series began in 1939 under
the title Twenty Best Plays of the Modern American Theatre.[28]
Beginning with the second series (1947) each volume contains
in full the best American plays for a six-year period. The
titles in these volumes would constitute a bibliography of the
best American drama of the twentieth century.

In 1944 a special volume in the Burns Mantle series
was published to cover the plays of 1899-1909.[29] Ten plays
are included, one for each year, and a complete list of
plays produced on the New York stage in that period (pages
346-584). Although the list contains no publication information, it is valuable for the names of authors and titles and
the dates of production. The volume ends with an index of
plays and cast (pages 612-624).

While not many comprehensive regional bibliographies
appeared in this period, three represent serious efforts to
list the literature of their respective regions.[30] The longest
was done on the South in 1954 by Jay B. Hubbell, professor
of American literature at Duke University. In separate essays for 115 writers he gives biographical information and
discusses their works. A long bibliography (pages 915-974)
is at the end of the volume. Richard B. Harwell's bibliography on Confederate belles lettres (1941) gives full bibliographic information for many novels, books of poetry, and
plays published in the South during the Civil War. South of
Forty from the Mississippi to the Rio Grande (1947) contains
a great many fiction and poetry entries. The author, Jesse
L. Rader, gives full description for many titles, including
size, illustrations, original publication, and editions. The

annotations are also useful for information about the content of the books.

Three other regional bibliographies of the West contain fiction and poetry titles. Kenneth Kurtz lists five pages of belles lettres, pages 28-29 and 39-41, in his Literature of the Southwest (1956).[31] Nellie Cliff did a bibliography for Ray B. West's Writing in the Rocky Mountains (1947).[32] She provides brief annotations for many fiction and poetry titles. David J. Harkness wrote a bibliographic essay for a number of Western writers in the October 1954 issue of the University of Tennessee Newsletter.[33]

Some of the best bibliographic work in this period was done on regional fiction.   John S. Hartin's dissertation on the Southeast in the novel (1957) is the most substantial study.[34] He annotates a great many novels in which the setting is the southeastern part of the United States.   His index groups the novels by state and provides separate lists for those novels in which the geographic area includes the Ohio and Mississippi rivers.   Janet Agnew's bibliography is on Southern historical novels published between 1929 and 1938.[35] She classifies the novels according to chronological period and provides brief annotations.   The long analytical index, pages 25-76, is especially good because it includes authors, titles, states, subjects, places, battles, and names of people.   A separate list of novels grouped by state follows the index.

Sheldon Van Auken wrote a very fine essay in 1948 on the Southern historical novel of the early twentieth century.[36] He gives brief information about 12 Southern writers "who constituted the most audible voice of the South for the majority of the nation since the Civil War" (page 165).   The writers include Thomas Dixon, Jr., F. Hopkinson Smith, and Maurice Thompson, and such well-known names as George W. Cable, Thomas Nelson Page, and Ellen Glasgow.   After the biographical sketches Van Auken makes brief descriptive and critical comments about their works.   Concerning Maurice Thompson's Alice of Old Vincennes (1900), he writes that it is "a vigorous tale of the capture of the key to the Northwest Territory by the British and its recapture by George Rogers Clark in 1778" (page 166).   In George W. Cable's The Grandissimes (1880) the author "devotes his chief attention to the creation of an authentic atmosphere" (page 166).   Van Auken finds Cable's criticism of slavery in the novel "fair and broadminded" (page 166).   Van Auken writes well and is able to give the essence of a novel in a few lines.   These brief notes

about the novels are about as good as one will find. He
writes one of his best descriptions for Ellen Glasgow's The
Battleground:

> In 1902 she published The Battleground, a careful and
> able chronicle of two country families in Virginia prior
> to and during the Civil War. It includes delightful
> scenes of the ante-bellum plantation as well as non-
> combatant and army life during the war. Her interest
> in the democracy of the Army of Northern Virginia,
> an army of caste contrasts, adds a vital and modern
> note to the romance. While it is not as panoramic as
> The Long Roll and Cease Firing, it is the best single
> book in this group on the war, both as a novel and as
> social history [page 171].

Another excellent bibliographic study is John T. Flanagan's essay on the Midwestern historical novel in the March
1944 issue of the Journal of the Illinois State Historical Society. [37] He cites many authors and titles and sometimes
gives a synopsis. Judging from his many fine critical comments, Flanagan has been a thoughtful and perceptive reader
of fiction. In comparatively few words he says a great deal
about some of the novels, and he says it very well. Two of
his finest descriptions are of Louis Bromfield's The Farm
(1933) and Joseph Kirkland's Zury: The Meanest Man in
Spring County (1887):

> Louis Bromfield's The Farm, 1933, is a fuller
> and more comprehensive attempt to chronicle the
> genesis of an Ohio farm, beginning with virgin soil
> in 1815 and ending with an industrial town obliterating
> the last vestiges of rural origin in 1914. Bromfield's
> story covers much more than mere farming since it
> includes religious growth, slavery, racial antipathies,
> politics; and the author insists that two basic traits--
> integrity and idealism--which explained the community's
> growth and have since vanished will reappear. But in
> essence it is a rather bitter saga of the utilization of
> the land.

> Central Illinois is the locale of one of the best of
> the novels portraying early farm life, Joseph Kirkland's
> Zury: The Meanest Man in Spring County, 1887. The
> characterization here is excellent. Zury's parsimony,
> his sharp bargaining, his industry and intelligence es-
> tablish him as a person, and Kirkland's care in re-
> cording the speech of his characters as well as in

describing the background makes for complete authenticity. It would have been easy to caricature Zury as
sordid and miserly; instead we are shown his fundamental honesty and a certain latent humanitarianism
[page 33].

Sometimes Professor Flanagan finds little or no value in a
novel, and he is not afraid to be blunt. In discussing A. G.
Riddle's The Tory's Daughter (1888) he writes that it is "a
confused and clumsy account of the war climaxed by the Battle of the Thames.... The romance itself is full of puerile
sentiment and vague rhetoric..." (page 19).

Nelle Dooley discusses about 35 short stories in her
1940 master's thesis.[38] The stories are about the Plains
states: Nebraska, Oklahoma, Kansas, Texas, and the Da-
kotas. The thesis is chronological beginning in 1870 and
ending with the depression years of the 1930's. She gives
synopses and quotes liberally from the stories to show local
color and sectionalism. About Frederick Bechdolt's "Tascosa" she writes: "Tascosa was the name of a ghost town
then located near Amarillo. It was a period when every man
made his own rules of conduct and enforced them if he was
able to do so" (page 23). One of her best discussions is of
the dust storm in John Hermann's "Two Days from the South,"
which appeared in Scribner's Magazine, May 1936, pages 277-
284. The story is about the Jasper family, who are living
near Dodge City, Kansas. She quotes several passages from
the story to show the effect of the 1936 dust storm on the
family. These are three of the best quotes:

> 'It's fun at school when they's a storm,' Jack
> said. 'Even if it did storm I could find my way
> home. I wouldn't care how hard it stormed. I
> wouldn't care if it was black as anything. I could
> find my way home' [page 279].

Little Freddie and the other brother younger than Jack said
they could, too.

> 'Well now. What a family I've got! They could
> find their way home from school, a mile away, in a
> storm like yesterday's. Why a bloodhound couldn't
> make its way through one of those howlers. The dust
> makes it so you can't draw a civilized breath of air
> into your lungs hardly, and your eyes smarting like
> you'd rubbed them with cactus' [page 279].

After the four children started for school, Caroline fed the baby.

> He coughed some but nothing like the day before when dust sifted in around the windows in spite of the strips of paper pasted on the cracks.--Caroline looked down at him, thinking of the dreaded dust pneumonia that had filled the hospitals and which the papers said was taking a life a day in Garden City. Her children must not get sick. It would be better to clear out of the country. Leave the farm and go east, as many of the landless tenant neighbors were doing and as those more favored wealthy folks were also doing [pages 279-280].

Another noteworthy thesis was done in 1954 by Lawana J. Shaul. [39] Her main subject is the treatment of the West in some short stories from the last part of the nineteenth century. The principal part of the thesis is a bibliography of stories arranged by subject or theme: Indians and soldiers, mining, railroading, religion, cowboys and ranch life, homesteading, and miscellaneous. The annotations are short, ranging from 50 to 100 words. She also includes in her thesis two other bibliographies: a list of 64 California stories not included in the annotated bibliography (pages 98-101) and a list of authors and stories arranged by states (pages 108-115).

Two short studies on the regional novel of the West were done in the 1950's by Helen Hitt and Harry H. Jones.[40] Helen Hitt wrote an essay about the historical novels of the Pacific Northwest that were published after 1920. Harry H. Jones did a six-page annotated bibliography of fiction about the Rocky Mountain mining area.

By comparison regional poetry received only scant attention. Harold S. Jantz made the most valuable bibliographic contribution when he compiled in 1943 a long list of early New England verse.[41] He includes all writers born up to 1670 and gives brief biographical information and full bibliographic description for the poems. He locates many poems in manuscripts, collections, authors' works, and almanacs. He often gives the number of lines and the subject of the poem. In 1945 he made a list of 24 unrecorded verse broadsides of the seventeenth century and locates them in libraries and private collections.[42]

Janet M. Agnew made a list in 1940 of volumes of poetry written by Southern poets between 1929 and 1938.[43] She arranges the titles in three separate lists: author, title, and state. Earl L. Rudolph made a long list of Confederate broadside verse.[44]

Signature of the Sun: Southwest Verse 1900-1950, edited in 1950 by Mabel Major and Thomas M. Pearce,[45] contains selections for 124 poets and notes about the authors. The notes are valuable for many book titles and dates of publication.

Many belles-lettres titles are listed in comprehensive state bibliographies. The Southern states have been particularly energetic in making bibliographies of their publications. Two of the best bibliographies were done for the two Carolinas. Robert J. Turnbull completed his monumental five-volume Bibliography of South Carolina in 1956.[46] The index volume, published in 1960, contains about 75 entries for novels, the same number for stories, and more than 75 for poetry. The index also contains entries for names of authors and titles of belles lettres and other writings. Complete bibliographic information is given for titles in the five volumes, including pages and size. Mary L. Thornton's bibliography of North Carolina is a shorter work, but it is also very useful for finding belles lettres.[47] Her fiction and drama index entries refer only to those titles with a North Carolina setting. For fiction more than 350 entries are given; for drama, more than 50; and for poetry, more than 300.

Barbara W. Greene did a master's thesis in 1959 on resources in Louisiana literature.[48] Near the end of the essay she made a list of writings by Louisiana authors and wrote brief annotations for the titles. Drama, poetry, and fiction are grouped separately.

Two other Southern states have identified their authors and their publications.[49] West Virginia Authors (1957) is a biobibliography giving very brief biographical information and a selection of titles. Sources of additional information in reference works and other books are noted. Georgia was one of the few states in the 1950's to make an annual list of books published by native writers. The list appeared each year in the winter issue of the Georgia Review beginning in 1950. For each title a brief annotation is given.

Richard E. Banta compiled what may very well be the

best state biobibliography ever done. Indiana Authors and
Their Books 1816-1916 was published in 1949 by Wabash
College in Crawfordsville, Indiana. Many of the biographical sketches are 100 words or more in length, and several
exceed 500 words. For the prolific writers many titles are
given with place of publication and date. The entry for
James Whitcomb Riley (pages 270-273) consists of an essay
of about 1000 words followed by a list of 49 titles. The
Booth Tarkington entry (pages 312-314) is also long and contains a list of 66 titles. Banta was for many years a book
dealer and a part-time assistant to the president of Wabash
College. He was also a writer of historical articles for
journals and encyclopedias. [50]

Lancaster Pollard did a long checklist of Washington
authors for the Pacific Northwest Quarterly in 1940. [51] The
list is arranged by author, and he identifies the titles as
fiction, drama, or verse. He gives the full names for the
authors, full imprint, and pages. He made additions and
corrections to the list in 1944. [52]

New Jersey is one of the few states in the Northeast
that has compiled a list of state authors. [53] Rudolf and Clara
Kirk made the Checklist in 1955. Maryland began to list its
authors in 1952 in the Maryland Historical Magazine. [54] It
has appeared annually in the March issue since then.

A very useful book for many names of Missouri
writers is the literary history of Missouri written in 1955
by Elijah L. Jacobs and Forrest E. Wolverton. [55] It is a
chronological history beginning with the pioneer period and
ending in 1955. It contains separate chapters on fiction,
poetry, and drama and cites many titles of poems, plays,
short stories, and novels. Synopses and critical comments
are given for many titles. Near the end of the volume (pages
339-347) there are separate lists giving the names of poets,
novelists, dramatists, and short story writers. The bibliography of primary sources (pages 349-360) gives the imprint
for the book titles discussed in the text.

State fiction received a great deal of attention in this
period. Both New Jersey and Delaware published bibliographic works about fiction with settings in their states. [56]
Augustus H. Able wrote a very readable essay about Delaware fiction that contains many titles with dates. He gives
critical comments as well as information about plots and
characters.

Again the South is outstanding in bibliographic works. Lawrence and Algernon Thompson did an annotated bibliography of full-length fiction in which the action takes place in Kentucky. [57] Their dual purpose in doing the work was "to examine Kentucky and Kentuckians as conceived in fiction and to present a case study of the use of regional themes in American fiction" (Preface, page v). The critical annotations are between 20 and 100 words in length. The book ends with two separate indexes, one for author and another for title. Hensley C. Woodbridge supplemented their bibliography in the Kentucky Historical Review by adding titles published between 1951 and 1957. [58] The North Carolina fiction list is similar to the Kentucky bibliography. [59] The work was done by the Joint Committee of the North Carolina English Teachers Association and the North Carolina Library Association, and was edited by William S. Powell. The list, which is briefly annotated, contains novels with a North Carolina setting. Florida is another state which did a fiction list. [60]

Georgia has a bibliographic essay on novels with a setting in the state written between 1926 and 1950. [61] Gertrude G. Odum, the author of the essay, comments on 50 novels, sometimes at some length. She devotes, for example, 26 lines (pages 244-245) to Gone with the Wind by Margaret Mitchell.

The Midwest also has bibliographic essays on the fiction of individual states. Alice L. Pearson wrote an article for Michigan History in 1940 about the Upper Peninsula in Michigan in which she comments on fiction with settings in that area in both the nineteenth and twentieth centuries. [62] Fuller comments are in her 1939 master's thesis. [63] Lucille B. Emch wrote a long essay on Ohio in the short stories of 1824-1839. [64] The essay gives much information about the content of the stories and Ohio life in that period. The end of the article has a four-page bibliography of short stories with Ohio locales.

John T. Frederick, a literary critic and professor of English, made a study of Iowa fiction and wrote three long articles for Palimpsest, a journal published by the State Historical Society of Iowa. [65] In his first article he writes about the farm in Iowa fiction published in the nineteenth and twentieth centuries. Although he does not cover a great many novels, he writes well and succinctly about several of the best. He gives just enough of the story of each novel to

make the reader want to read it. He is particularly concerned about characterization and the authenticity of the farm
experience. Professor Frederick has read his novels carefully and knows the farm country of Iowa from his early
childhood. One of his best descriptions of a farm novel is
for Don Jackson's Archer Pilgrim (1942):

> The ambition of farm parents for their children
> to have a life different from their own is a familiar
> theme in farm fiction--perhaps because it was a fre-
> quent phenomenon in farm homes in the years when
> most of our writers were growing up. In Don Jack-
> son's Archer Pilgrim (1942), this ambition is contrary
> to the desires of the child, a boy who has decided at
> the age of seven that he wants to be a farmer, and
> has never changed his mind. The resulting conflict
> and the boy's defeat--at the hands of the girl he thinks
> he loves, as well as those of his parents--send him
> to a college experience largely sterile, then to wasted
> years of work in a garage, until at last he finds his
> way back to the farm.

> The central figure of this story, whose name
> gives the book its title, is very finely drawn. He be-
> comes real for the reader, and highly interesting.
> His experience is authentic. When he goes out to
> shock oats, we are immediately sure that the writer
> not only knows how to shock oats, but how it feels to
> shock oats--which are slightly different matters. The
> one could be learned from watching; the other could
> not. The whole texture of farm experience is rendered
> with similar authority; and all the characters around
> Archer Pilgrim are presented with sympathy and con-
> sistency even in their opposition to him--his father
> most notably. But it is the reader's acceptance and
> liking of Arch himself, won in the first scene of his
> seven-year-old resolution, that gives the book strength
> and drive and weights its ending with meaning: 'What
> a fool thing you have done, Pilgrim, he told himself....
> Why have you done this. The answer was at his feet.
> As he tramped along the fence row with quick, alert
> steps, his shoes pressed into soft, brown soil.'[66]

His next article is on town and city in Iowa literature. Some
of his best writing relates the town to the farm, and this re-
lationship he finds particularly in Ruth Suckow's work:

> The close relation of town and farm is almost

universally present in Miss Suckow's work: as social
contrast or conflict, as economic interdependence, or
as mere physical nearness. Sarah, of The Bonney
Family, 'was possessed with a desire to get out to
the open road beyond the streetcar tracks, where she
could feel the wind cold against her face and see the
dark, moist country look of the shocked corn.' In
the two thousand words of the story, 'Retired' (Iowa
Interiors), she has achieved the finest portrayal of the
retired farmer in all American literature. She has
seen more clearly than any other writer the recurring
dramatic situation, within Iowa families, of contrasts
and conflicts between those who stay on the farm and
those who leave it, and has treated it more thoroughly,
with many variations of character and incident: most
fully in The Folks, but also with especial poignancy
in New Hope and in such stories as 'A Rural Community' and 'Four Generations' [page 73].

The third article is about the Iowa novels of Charlton Laird,
Phil Stong, Matthias M. Hoffman, and Johnson Brigham.

Harvey K. Jacobson wrote a short master's thesis in
1956 on the North Dakota novel.[67] He discusses rather
briefly 19 general novels, 15 historical novels, and eight
biographical novels. He is particularly interested in adventure stories and the novel of the farm.

Several Southern states supplemented their bibliographic
work by publishing collections of stories. The collections
from Alabama, Kentucky, Texas, and North Carolina are not
lengthy, but they are useful for locating stories by writers
of those states and about life and culture there.[68] The two
collections from South Carolina and Louisiana have more bibliographic value because they contain brief biographical sketches
giving titles and dates for books.[69]

Very little bibliographic work was done on state poetry.
One suspects that more lists were made but not published.
Even the Chicago Public Library seems not to have had the
funds to print its lengthy Bibliography of Illinois Poets Since
1900 (1942).[70] For each poet this mimeographed bibliography
gives three listings: collected poems, single poems in periodicals and outside collected works, and articles and books
about the poet. Full bibliographic information is given for
collections and single poems. The volume ends with a three-
page index of poems (pages 214-216).

State poetry collections continued to be published, and some of them came from the poetry societies. Richard G. Walser edited two volumes of North Carolina poetry, one in 1941 and the other ten years later.[71] The Poetry Society of Colorado put out a silver anniversary volume in 1946 containing poems by members of the Society.[72] A more lengthy collection was made by the South Dakota Poetry Society from poems written by its members between 1927 and 1949.[73] It contains 400 poems by 137 poets, an index of authors, and a separate index of titles of poems.

Local literary bibliographies and collections of literature may exist in a greater number than one might suppose, but they are difficult to locate. Short bibliographies and card files of local authors would be found in many public libraries in the country. Librarians in these libraries would not fail to note books written by local residents. One literary history for a city of some size was written by Marshall Wingfield in 1942.[74] The author writes in his Introduction, page 5, that his aim in writing the book is "to enlarge the acquaintance of Memphians with writers and writings of Memphis, and to show that the city is not a literary Sahara." The book has separate essays on historians, journalists, Memphis women, churchmen, Negroes, newspaper verse, book reviewers, educators, and other writers. The essay cites books and articles, sometimes with publisher, date, and content information. Grace Ross and Mabel Kuykendall edited a collection of Fort Worth poems in 1949.[75] It contains a list of volumes of verse (pages 177-183) by 50 of the city's authors. The poems in the anthology are arranged by subject: childhood, love, sorrow, social vision, philosophy, nature, Fort Worth, and Texas.

Gertrude Cone annotated a number of fiction titles in her bibliography of the Champlain Valley in New York State.[76] In Pennsylvania, both the Wyoming Valley and Somerset County put out small poetry collections in the 1940's.[77] Benton County in Oregon also published a poetry collection.[78]

Histories and historical bibliographies continued to list American literature in this period. Three of the best essays are in multi-volume histories of Delaware, Montana, and Ohio.[79] Harlan Hatcher wrote a whole chapter on Ohio in twentieth-century literature in volume six of the History of the State of Ohio (1942), edited by Carl F. Wittke. It is an excellent bibliographic essay on the subject with many titles and dates.

Three state historical bibliographies list belles lettres. [80] Writings on Pennsylvania History (1946) has a separate section listing Pennsylvania fiction, poems, tales, and
legends (pages 485-528). The titles are given with full imprint, pages, and brief annotations. J. Winston Coleman's
Bibliography of Kentucky History (1949) has a shorter list of
literature containing only historical fiction and legendary
stories (pages 280-286). The Subject Bibliography of Wisconsin History by Leroy Schlinkert has a three-page list of
fiction with a Wisconsin background (pages 160-162).

The American Guide Series refers to a group of state
guide books written by the federal WPA workers in the late
1930's and early 1940's. A guide book was done for all the
states and for some of the large cities. Almost all of them
have a section on literature varying in length between five
and 11 pages and containing titles with dates. A few of the
guide books were revised in the 1950's. The bibliographic
essays in these volumes do not add much to bibliographic
control, but they do identify some authors by state, and they
do contain some descriptive information about the contents of
titles. The essay in the Oklahoma guide book is 11 pages
long and contains the names of many writers but not many
titles. [81] It mentions detective novelists Todd Downing, Dorothy C. Disney, and Newton Gayle. It also gives the names
of 24 poets and four short story writers. Edward Donahue's
novel Madness in the Heart is described as "a dramatic re-
creation of the life of a boom oil town, and its social and
financial leeches" (page 91).

No bibliography of humor was published in this period,
but several anthologies containing many humorous selections
appeared. A Subtreasury of American Humor (1941) has parodies and burlesques, tall stories, reminiscence, stories from
politics and history, fables and other moral tales, and verse. [82]
The Pageant of American Humor (1946) has selections from 88
authors arranged chronologically. [83] Bennett Cerf's Encyclopedia of Modern American Humor (1954) classifies some of its
contents by geographical region, beginning with the country as
a whole and then such areas as New England, New York, the
South, Midwest, Southwest, and Far West. [84] The separate
section on verse has poems by T. A. Daly, Phyllis McGinley,
Ogden Nash, Dorothy Parker, Franklin P. Adams, and a few
other writers. Besides short stories the collection has excerpts from novels and plays. Bibliographic information is
given with the selections. Victor L. Chittick's collection of
tall tales of the American frontier has 36 stories and notes

about the authors and stories.[85] <u>Midland Humor</u>, edited by Jack Conroy, is a regional collection of Midwest humor containing 90 selections by 56 writers, including Ernest Hemingway, Carl Sandburg, James W. Riley, Booth Tarkington, Finley P. Dunne, Gwendolyn Brooks, and many more not so familiar.[86]

There was in this twenty-year period a great proliferation of author bibliographies. The book bibliographies came from commercial publishers, university presses, and libraries. Major and minor writers of the seventeenth through the first half of the twentieth centuries were covered by bibliographies that aimed to describe all their books, either in great detail or with sufficient information to identify first publication. Some of the bibliographies aim to be complete for all the writings of the authors, including essays, poems, and stories in periodicals and books. Some of these author bibliographies are very lengthy because they contain many notes, facsimile pages, quotations from the authors' works and from biographies and critical works. The longest bibliography of an American author is probably the three-volume work (1940) of Cotton Mather by Thomas J. Holmes.[87] It does not, however, fall within the scope of this study because the author wrote very little in belles lettres. A work which may be just as long because of the small type is Thomas F. Currier's <u>Bibliography of Oliver Wendell Holmes</u> (1953), edited by Eleanor M. Tilton.[88] It is much like his earlier bibliography of Whittier in that it gives very full information about first editions and a complete list of poetry and prose.[89] It contains letters, excerpts from letters, newspaper commentary, and remarks by acquaintances on Holmes's work. It contains portraits of the Autocrat at different ages, reproductions of title pages and covers of controversial issues, programs for special occasions, and many other illustrations. The bibliography also lists a large number of publications about Holmes. The index attempts to provide entries for the writings and all the miscellaneous information in the bibliography. The bibliography is a superb achievement!

Four very fine bibliographies were published by the Indiana Historical Society between 1944 and 1952.[90] They are on Indiana writers and they were all carefully done and neatly printed. They give full description of first editions, contents of collections, reprint editions, ephemeral publications, and books and periodical articles about the authors. Anthony and Dorothy Russo did the first one on James W. Riley, Dorothy did the second on George Ade, and Dorothy

Russo did the Booth Tarkington bibliography with the help of Thelma L. Sullivan. The fourth volume is on a group of writers of Crawfordsville, Indiana. Each volume is fully indexed in order to provide easy access to the quantity of publications and information in the volumes.

Three Whitman catalogs listing many publications of the poet appeared in this period.[91] Two of them are based on extensive library collections at Duke University and in the Library of Congress. The Library of Congress catalog gives information about manuscript collections, proofs and offprints, separate works, collections and selections, biography and criticism, translations, musical works based on or inspired by Whitman's writings, parodies and librettos, and bibliographies. The volume ends with a long index (pages 129-147) of names and titles. The third catalog is based on an exhibition held at the Detroit Public Library in 1955. The material for the exhibit was on loan from the famous Whitman collector, Charles E. Feinberg. It lists manuscripts, published books, and associated items.

The Yale University Library has done important bibliographic work on American authors. Between 1941 and 1959 it produced bibliographies of Gertrude Stein, William Faulkner, T. S. Eliot, Wallace Stevens, and Thornton Wilder.[92] Donald C. Gallup did the checklist of T. S. Eliot in 1947 and then revised it in 1953 for Harcourt, Brace. He also co-authored the exhibit catalog of Gertrude Stein. This catalog contains both published and unpublished writings of the author with contents notes. For an exhibit catalog the index has many entries (pages 56-64). The Wallace Stevens checklist by Samuel F. Morse celebrates the poet's 75th birthday.

The University of Virginia Press published a few bibliographies of American authors. The most outstanding one is on James B. Cabell in two volumes.[93] In the first volume Frances J. Brewer lists writings by and about him. In the second volume Matthew J. Bruccoli writes about the Cabell Collection at the University of Virginia. The University Press also published checklists of American authors in the Barrett Collection of the University of Virginia. Lucy T. Clark compiled the one of Bret Harte, and she and Fannie M. Elliott did the checklist of William D. Howells.[94] Both list printed and manuscript works.

Several short bibliographies were published in Heartman's Historical Series. Oscar Wegelin revised two of his

bibliographies, one of John Esten Cooke and the other of
William G. Simms.[95] Charles F. Heartman did a checklist
of the poet, Charles West Thomson, and he and James R.
Canny revised their 1932 bibliography of Edgar Allan Poe.[96]
Heartman was an internationally known rare book dealer who
lived for a while in Metuchen, N.J., then New Orleans, and
then in Hattiesburg, Mississippi. In the last location he had
a 500-acre farm called the Book Farm. He published, and
in part wrote, Heartman's Historical Series, which included
historical sketches and bibliographies.[97]

There had been author bibliographies in periodicals before 1940, but they were not nearly so numerous as those
which appeared after that year. Evidently the editors recog-
nized a need on the part of students and scholars for short
bibliographies listing writings by and about American writers.
The Bulletin of Bibliography is one of the leading journals for
author bibliographies. Many of them are on twentieth-century
writers, most of them are short, and most of them are valuable for the authors' works and for biography and criticism.
Some of these bibliographies are longer than one might suppose from the length as given in the citations because the
pages in the journal are printed double column and in small
type. The Ellen Glasgow bibliography by W. D. Quesenbery
in the summer and fall issues of 1959 is 13 pages long.[98]

The bibliographies in the Bulletin of the New York
Public Library are much longer and more scholarly. Some
of them give very full information about first editions and
about the contents of poetry and story collections. Probably
the longest author bibliography published in this journal is
the one on William D. Howells by William M. Gibson and
George Arms.[99] The bibliography began in the September
1946 issue and continued in eight later issues ending in
August 1947. It is arranged chronologically and attempts to
cover most of his books, periodical publications, and contributions to books. There is no separate listing by genre.
The bibliography was slightly revised and published as a book
in 1948 by the New York Public Library.[100]

Another admirable bibliography in the Bulletin of the
New York Public Library lists Katherine Anne Porter's
writings and the many critical articles about her.[101] Edward Schwartz compiled the bibliography and Robert Penn
Warren wrote a short introduction. Many entries have descriptive and critical notes and quotations from the story
writer and the critics.

The bibliography of Marianne Moore, which appeared in three successive issues of the Bulletin in 1958, contains not only a list of her poems but also an index of first lines. [102] A full description of first editions is given, including size and color of binding.

Another leading serial publication in American bibliography, Studies in Bibliography, began soon after its inception to publish bibliographies of American authors. J. Albert Robbins did a bibliography of some unrecorded poems of James Kirke Paulding for the 1950 volume. [103] The poems are located in a copy book in which Paulding transcribed in his 65th year poems which he had written in youth and middle age. Robbins gives number of lines, year, pages in the copy book, and first line. His notes contain information on content, title and textual changes, margin notes, excerpts, and additional locations. The copy book is in the Singer Memorial Collection of the University of Pennsylvania.

The checklist of John William De Forest in the 1956 volume of Studies in Bibliography contains separate lists for his novels, poems, short stories, and articles. [104] It contains many notes about changed titles and contents and often gives authority for those publications which were published anonymously. The compiler of the bibliography, E. R. Hagemann, writes, for example, that Poems; Medley and Palestrina (1902) contains "some of De Forest's fugitive verse, rewritten or revised..." (page 188).

The Princeton University Library Chronicle published several checklists of American authors between 1940 and 1960. Appendix B (q.v.) lists eight of them. The John Peale Bishop checklist was done with the help of scholars and poets, including Willard Thorp, Edmund Wilson, and Allen Tate. [105] The William Faulkner checklist is more lengthy than the others and contains the author's contributions to The Mississippian, a weekly student newspaper of the University of Mississippi. [106] The Fitzgerald checklist is intended to supplement the bibliography in Arthur Mizener's The Far Side of Paradise (1951). [107] The Benedict Thielen checklist is another bibliography of a Princeton alumnus. [108]

Biographies continued to be a source for a list of the publications of an author. One of the longest bibliographies (pages 418-480) is in Lewis Leary's That Rascal Freneau (1941). [109] It lists Freneau's publications in chronological order and includes reprints and changes in title. It is especially good in listing the poet's many periodical contributions. To locate these writings Professor Leary examined more than 300 newspapers and magazines. William Bartlett's biography of Jones Very is also outstanding for giving the poet's newspaper writings. [110]

Another long bibliography (pages 263-313) is in William P. Randel's biography of Edward Eggleston. [111] It lists his publications in chronological order and includes information about Eggleston's papers and manuscripts.

To look back at these twenty years from 1940 to 1960 is to remember the solid achievements, especially the comprehensive national bibliographies, the many lists of fiction, the state bibliographies, and the author bibliographies. The LHUS Bibliography, the first three volumes of the BAL, Burke and Howe's American Authors and Books, and the Oxford Companion to American Literature are landmark publications which have proved their worth many times over since their publication. The LHUS Bibliography Supplement (1959) and the new editions of the Oxford Companion represent a continuing effort to increase the coverage of authors and titles in comprehensive bibliographies.

The greatest amount of work--and the best--was done in the area of fiction. Lyle H. Wright's fiction bibliographies, the lists of historical fiction, the studies of regional fiction, the bibliographies and essays on state fiction, and the fiction collections--all of these together identify thousands of titles and provide information about American fiction. Such works as the Wright bibliographies, Dickinson's American Historical Fiction, Leisy's American Historical Novel, Taylor's The Economic Novel in America, and Waldmeir's dissertation on the ideology of World War II novels needed to be done, and they were done very well. The same is true for Flanagan's essay on the historical novel of the Midwest, Frederick's essays on Iowa fiction, The Kentucky Novel by the Thompsons, and North Carolina Fiction 1734-1957 by Powell. The last two titles contain annotations of sufficient length to make them models for other states to follow. These annotated bibliographies and the essays in periodicals and dissertations go beyond identifying titles and authors and attempt to give something of the essential content of the creative and imaginative literature of America.

The state bibliographies are outstanding in this period for the number of authors and titles they contain and for the

information some of them give about the authors. They are
especially valuable for the names of those authors who have
written only one or two books, or who have written only for
periodicals. Thornton's bibliography of North Carolina and
Banta's biobibliography of Indiana authors are among the
memorable achievements in bibliography.

Author bibliographies were produced in great numbers
in order to "catch up" with the many writers for whom there
were no bibliographies, or no adequate or complete bibliographies. Old bibliographies were revised and new ones were
compiled. Many were done for contemporary authors, and
many of these appeared in periodicals. Literary and bibliographic journals became an important location for bibliographies in American literature. These periodical bibliographies
were done with the same care as book-length bibliographies;
some were even published later as books. For scholarship
and length the bibliographies in the Bulletin of the New York
Public Library are among the best which have been done.
The one book-length bibliography which stands almost alone
as an example of prodigious industry and scholarship is A
Bibliography of Oliver Wendell Holmes by Thomas F. Currier
and edited by Eleanor Tilton.

Chapter 3

THE GOLDEN YEARS, 1960-1975

Bibliographic control was very much a subject of con-
cern in the years following World War II and all through the
1960's. The explosion of knowledge in this period made for
an increase in the number of books and articles published.
Libraries bought a huge quantity of printed material and increased their cataloging staffs. Periodical indexes increased
in size and many bibliographies were compiled on all subjects, including literature. There was a market for bibliographies that would list literature not included in local library
card catalogs. Scholars and graduate students wanted access
to all that has been written from the beginning of time. The
bibliographies that were compiled, therefore, were retrospec-
tive and current. The printed catalogs of the great national
libraries and those of many other research libraries made
the work somewhat easier and enabled the bibliographers to
find more publications with accurate bibliographic data. The
bibliographies in this period are not only more numerous but
many are lengthy lists of a wide variety of print and near-
print material.

Federal funds, larger book budgets, and an increase
in professional and clerical personnel helped many libraries
to expand and organize their collections, including research
material in rare book rooms. Many more American scholars
had the opportunity to see a large quantity of primary sources
either in the original or in microform in their own state or
section of the country. What they were not able to find in
their own geographic area they could borrow on interlibrary
loan or purchase on microfilm at small cost.

The two bibliography volumes of the LHUS that were
published in 1948 and 1959 pointed out gaps in the bibliography of belles lettres. Scholars and students of American
literature, and others interested in Americana, responded by

compiling many bibliographies of fiction, poetry, and drama. This is also the period in which three of the volumes of the BAL were published which supplement or supersede some of the separate bibliographies produced in earlier years. The new author bibliographies build on the old bibliographies and the BAL and add other publications and bibliographic information.

These fifteen years from 1960 to 1975 may be called the golden years for the bibliography of American belles lettres and for the bibliography of many other American publications for the sheer quantity of effort which has gone into the making of many bibliographic aids for all those people who need them for study and research.

Some of the comprehensive bibliographies in this period are either supplements, revisions, or indexes to earlier bibliographies. Bibliography Supplement II of the LHUS was published in 1972.[1] Like the other bibliography volumes it lists the published books of the authors, their collected works, collections of letters, and notebooks. It gives titles of biographies, critical works, and bibliographies, and locates manuscripts in libraries. This 1972 supplement adds 16 new authors and includes names like John Peale Bishop, John O'Hara, Arthur Miller, and Tennessee Williams.

Irving and Anne Weiss revised Burke and Howe's American Authors and Books, 1640 to the Present (1972).[2] This represents the third revised edition of what has become an increasingly useful identification and bibliographic tool for many librarians and bibliographers. It contains more than 700 pages of authors and titles of books, including a great many literary works.

In 1970 Arnold Rzepecki made an index to the literature and language bibliographies in 10 years (1910-1919) of the American Yearbook.[3] An index was also done for the writings in the volumes which Ralph Thompson gives in his catalog (pages 102-164) in his American Literary Annuals and Gift Books (1936).[4] Edward Kirkham and John Fink did the index in 1975. Gift books were a fashion for more than 30 years before the Civil War, and many American authors wrote for them.[5] Poe's "The Pit and the Pendulum" appeared for the first time in The Gift, A Xmas and New Year's Present (1843), pages 133-151. The Harbinger, A Maygift (1833) contains the first printing of Oliver Wendell Holmes's "The Dying Seneca."[6] Hawthorne wrote more than 20 stories for The Token.[7]

The Widener Library of Harvard University published its shelflist of American literature in 1970 in two large volumes.[8] Because the Widener Library has one of the best American literature collections in the world, the shelflist contains titles by a very large number of American writers, including many names that would not be in the BAL and the bibliography volumes of LHUS. For very brief information about many titles of belles lettres this work is a valuable source. For many scholarly purposes it has very limited value because the bibliographic information is not sufficient. Volume 1 has a classified listing by call number and a chronological list; volume 2 has an author and title list.

Occasionally a book dealer puts out a sales catalog that is acquired for reference use by a library because it has a quantity of good information about the titles in it. An example of this kind of catalog is First Books by American Authors 1765-1964 (1965) by the Seven Gables Bookshop. For each title the catalog gives imprint, pages, size, and binding. There are many notes giving information that can be used to identify first editions. Reproductions of title pages are given for some titles. The catalog lists 320 books, beginning with The Prince of Parthia (1765) by Thomas Godfrey and ending with Elliott Baker's Putnam Award Novel of 1964, A Fine Madness.

In 1964 the Readex Microprint Corporation published a microprint edition of an index of early American periodicals which had been done in the 1930's by WPA workers. Two of the five parts of the index are on fiction and poetry. The index has limited use because many entries are illegible, especially those which are handwritten.

Some major attempts were made in this period to list a very large portion of American fiction. Lyle H. Wright completed three more volumes of American fiction; one covers 1876-1900 (1966), and the other two are revisions: American Fiction 1774-1850 (1969) and American Fiction 1851-1875 (1965).[10] As long as these volumes are, they do not include all fiction published in those years. Wright omits publications of the American Tract Society, Sunday school unions, collections of anecdotes, juvenilia, jestbooks, folklore, and periodicals, including subscription series classed as periodicals, such as Belford, Clarke and Company's Household Library, a semi-weekly. Some entries have brief annotations giving locale, period, and subject or topic treated. Both volumes contain a complete title index. R. Glenn Wright's

multi-volume bibliography of English language fiction in the
Library of Congress (1973-74) supplements Lyle H. Wright's
works by bringing the historical record up to 1950.[11] R.
Glenn Wright's two sets of eight volumes each, one arranged
by author, and the other by chronology, were compiled from
the shelf list of fiction in the Library of Congress. Professor Wright, of Michigan State University, supplies place of
birth for all authors, American and foreign born.

The fifth edition of America in Fiction by Otis W.
Coan and Richard G. Lillard was published in 1967 by Pacific
Books in Palo Alto, California. Besides many new titles the
annotations are longer for many of the novels. A longer list
of novels about early America can be found in Jack VanDerhoof's Bibliography of Novels Related to American Frontier
and Colonial History (1971).[12] It contains 6439 entries and
has short annotations for some of them. Another annotated
list of American historical fiction is in McGarry and White's
Historical Fiction Guide (1963).[13] The list (pages 305-444)
is arranged by period beginning with the colonial and ending
with reconstruction and expansion. The 1973 edition of this
work is called World Historical Fiction Guide. The author
and title index is especially good because it lists titles separately and under the names of authors. For the reader who
is interested in the American pioneer there is a list of novels
(pages 299-311) in Nicholas J. Karolides's The Pioneer in the
American Novel (1967).[14] The list of World War II novels
(pages 168-177) in Joseph J. Waldmeir's American Novels of
the Second World War (1968) represents a revision of the bibliography in his 1959 dissertation on the subject.[15]

Two other fiction lists are worthy of note: one on the
political novel in Joseph Blotner's The Modern American Political Novel 1900-1960, pages 370-382, and the other on
satirical fiction in the second issue of the Satire Newsletter
for 1973.[16] The latter covers satires from 1637 to 1957.

An excellent work for verifying titles of poetry volumes is the Dictionary Catalog of the Harris Collection of
American Poetry and Plays published in 1972 in 13 volumes
by G. K. Hall in Boston. The catalog was prepared by the
Brown University Library, which has the collection. C. Fiske
Harris was a merchant and bibliophile who began to specialize
in American poetry in 1860. Within fifteen years he built up
a rather sizable collection. After his death in 1881 the
collection was bought by Henry B. Anthony, a Rhode
Island Senator, who in turn bequeathed the collection to Brown

University in 1884. Since then the University has added a
great many volumes.[17]

Roger E. Stoddard is an associate librarian at Harvard who is interested in the history of publishing, especially
concerning theater and poetry. In 1969 he made a long list
of books and pamphlets that supplement Oscar Wegelin's
Early American Poetry 1650-1820 (1930).[18] Two years later
he published another supplementary list in the April 1971
issue of the Papers of the Bibliographical Society of America.[19]

Another valuable work for locating early American
poetry is J. A. Leo Lemay's long list of periodical verse
which the American Antiquarian Society published in 1972.[20]
Lemay searched many colonial newspapers and magazines for
poetry written by Americans or which have American subject
matter. He also locates American poems in major English
periodicals of the seventeenth and eighteenth centuries. Many
of these poems appeared later in the American colonial periodicals (page xi).

Two bibliographic studies by Professor Eugene L.
Huddleston of Michigan State University are very useful for
information about early American poetry. The first is his
1965 dissertation, "Topographical Poetry in America 1783-
1812," which he completed at Michigan State University. The
essay is followed by a long list (pages 251-279) of topographical poems from early American books and magazines. A
topographical poem has as its fundamental subject a landscape,
such as a hill or a river. The list was later published in the
Bulletin of Bibliography in two successive issues of 1966 and
1967.[21] For the same publication Professor Huddleston prepared in 1975 a checklist of feminist verse satire in eighteenth-
century America.[22]

Two very substantial dissertations were done on American war poetry. James A. Hart's "American Poetry of the
First World War..." (1965) contains an essay and a long checklist of books and periodical verse.[23] The second is on World
War II and consists of summaries and commentaries of 583
poems written between 1939 and 1965.[24]

An outstanding biographical dictionary of contemporary
poets was published in 1970 by the St. James Press in London. The editor of Contemporary Poets, Rosalie Murphy,
made a selection of poets from many countries and gives

biographical and bibliographic data about them and their
works. Many major and minor American poets are represented with a full list of their published volumes. For Kenneth Patchen, for example, 29 poetry books are listed (page
838) with full imprint. Some of the anthologies in which his
work has appeared are also given (page 839). A second edition of Contemporary Poets was published in 1975.

In 1971 Galen Williams compiled a directory of American poets for the National Endowment for the Arts in Washington, D.C.[25] It arranges the poets by state and gives for
each poet the title of one book of verse and one other title
if the poet has also written fiction or drama. Another edition came out in 1973 listing 1300 poets.[26]

Scarecrow Press is filling a gap by publishing an index to American periodical verse.[27] The first volume, which
was issued in 1973, covers the 1971 output and indexes over
150 magazines; the coverage is annual since that time. Another publication of the Scarecrow Press is a checklist of
books of poetry by contemporary American poets.[28] The
volume is arranged by author and includes 3381 entries.

Because a number of poetry bibliographies now exist,
it is somewhat less necessary in this period to cite poetry
anthologies, but a few are worth noting. The Poetry Society
of America celebrated its 60th anniversary by publishing The
Diamond Anthology (1971).[29] It contains one poem from each
of 358 poets. The one poem is considered among the best
the poet has written, and it is one the poet has submitted.
The biographical notes (pages 272-321) for the authors contain titles of books, sometimes with dates.

Naked Poetry (1960) and The New Naked Poetry (1976)
are two collections of contemporary poetry that would contain many titles for a student who wanted to compile a bibliography of poems for the period 1945 through the early
years of the 1970's.[30] The second volume represents a new
anthology rather than a new edition for the first.

Three periodicals published collections of poems which
appeared in their pages.[31] The New Yorker Book of Poems
(1969) is a rather sizable volume (835 pages) containing
poems by many of the leading poets in contemporary American literature. The index is especially useful for the titles
of poems under the authors' names. The Virginia Quarterly
Review assembled some poems written between 1925 and 1967

which were published in its pages. Although more than 300 poets have published in the journal since 1925, only 50 are included in the collection. Among them are some of the finest writers of American poetry, such as Allen Tate, Robert Frost, and T. S. Eliot. New Southern Poets (1974) is a small volume of poems selected from Southern Poetry Review.

Two anthologies of war poems were published in the 1960's: The Poetry of the American Civil War (1960) by Lee Steinmetz and Where Is Vietnam?, edited by Walter Lowenfels and Nan Braymer.[32] The Civil War anthology has a fairly long bibliography (pages 257-264) listing books of poetry published in the 1860's. The Vietnam anthology has poems in which the poets respond to the war in Southeast Asia.

Bibliographic work in American drama continued in this period. The major achievement was the 13-volume Dictionary Catalog of the Harris Collection of American Poetry and Plays (1972) from the Brown University Library. C. Fiske Harris had also been a collector of plays. Since the Harris collection was given to Brown University, the Library has added a great many plays published in the past two hundred years. American plays written between 1714 and 1830 are listed in a title called Three Centuries of English and American Plays (1963) edited by G. William Bergquist.[33] The list was originally compiled for the Readex microprint edition (1952-56) of a large group of English and American plays. It gives plays published as separates and in collections. It is especially good for the many cross references to variant names, titles, and spellings. One fault with the bibliography is that the English and American plays are interfiled.

More plays for the period 1714-1830 can be found in Roger E. Stoddard's list in the Papers of the Bibliographical Society of America, third quarter 1971.[34] Stoddard made corrections and additions to Frank P. Hill's American Plays Printed 1714-1830 (1934). Stoddard made another list of old American plays for an article in the 1969 Proceedings of the American Antiquarian Society.[35] The plays were published between 1854 and 1862 by William V. Spencer, a Boston bookseller. For each play Stoddard gives title, author, date, collation by pages and signatures, and an analysis of preliminary texts.

Modern American plays were listed in several works.

Otis L. Guernsey did a cumulative index to the Best Plays Series, which began in 1920.[36] Linda Peavy lists 95 plays of the Provincetown Players in her article for the Papers of the Bibliographical Society of America, third quarter, 1975.[37] She lists the separate editions and locates other plays in anthologies and little magazines. She also gives author, title, and production date for unpublished plays.

Jane F. Bonin made a worthwhile contribution to bibliography when she completed her book on prize plays of the American theater.[38] She discusses briefly the major themes of 74 plays. The themes are women and marriage, work and material rewards, politics, and religion. Two lists at the end of the volume arrange the plays by author and year.

Caspar H. Nannes wrote a book (1960) on politics in the American drama in which he discusses plays produced in New York City between 1890 and 1959.[39] The Appendix lists the plays by decade. Two authors wrote books on the small town in American drama.[40] Ima H. Herron's study contains a bibliography (pages 527-550) in which she lists published and unpublished plays. James S. Douglas examined about 80 plays for his book.

Two doctoral dissertations were based on an examination of a rather large number of plays of the nineteenth century.[41] John D. Collins wrote "American Drama in Anti-Slavery Agitation 1792-1861," and William H. Wegner wrote "The Representation of the American Civil War on the New York Stage 1860-1900." Both essays contain general content information about the plays and bibliographies which list the plays discussed in the text.

A little was done in this period on regional bibliography. One very useful work is John M. Bradbury's Renaissance in the South (1963), which is a history of Southern literature from 1920 to 1960.[42] For a literary history it cites a large number of authors and titles and comments briefly on many of them. His description of Elizabeth Spencer's The Voice at the Back Door (1956) is one of his best:

> Miss Spencer's third novel, The Voice at the Back Door (1956), attacks boldly and directly the major problems of the modern South: the racial issue, corrupt politics, intolerance and resistance to change. Previously Negroes had appeared in her novels only as

superstitious, garrulous appurtenances; here she goes
so far as to adopt a dedicated worker for racial justice as one of her point of view characters and to turn
her story on the injustice done him. There is considerable of Warren's All the King's Men and Faulkner's Intruder in the Dust to be noted in Miss Spencer's plot and themes, but she handles them in her
own quiet, sensitive manner and with broad sympathy.
With a minimum of symbolic extension, she touches
intimate details of all her characters' lives with a
sure hand and brings them into revealing emotional
and ideological clashes.

   Idealist crusader Duncan Harper, cynical realist,
bootleg liquor operator, Jimmy Tallant, compromising
politician Willard Follansbee, Negro Beck Dozer, and
the women, Duncan's wife and his former girl, the
rebellious Marcia, project their clashing points of
view until all are caught in the swiftly developing cli-
max. Only Tallant is changed in the process--into a
militant supporter of equal rights--but the town's injustice and intolerance are manifest. The story, though
it rigidly adheres to its points of view, clearly indicts
the red necks and the upper levels of society for their
bigoted and inflexible inhumanity. Still, Miss Spencer's careful objectivity, in contrast to the too obviously weighted bias of so many liberal novelists of
her generation, preserves a rare artistic integrity
[page 119].

Briefer but equally good is his capsule synopsis of "Flowering
Judas" by Katherine Anne Porter:

   'Flowering Judas' itself, the first of her novellas,
sets Miss Porter's high standard in a beautifully con-
trolled, highly evocative account of a liberal American
girl's relations to revolutionary activity in Mexico
City. In her zeal to dedicate herself to a social ideal,
Laura finds herself deeply involved with the powerful
Braggioni, who is not only repulsive to her personally,
but essentially a perversion of the ideals themselves.
Wooed romantically also by a young Mexican, Laura
finds herself hopelessly confused; her revolutionary
sympathies confused with personal attachments and re-
pulsions, her sense of life involved with death, her
nights with days. Finally, through a nightmare sequence, she recognizes herself in the image of the
flowering judas tree as betrayer both of herself and
of the high purposes of the movement [pages 71-72].

Mabel Major and Thomas M. Pearce revised for the second time their literary history of the Southwest. [43] This third edition of Southwest Heritage (1972) is like previous editions in that it has separate chapters for fiction, poetry, and drama. A separate chapter covers the literature of 1948-1970. The long bibliography (pages 290-364) contains a great many new titles.

A bibliography listing current fiction and poetry is a regular feature of Great Lakes Review. The periodical, which began in the summer of 1974, is published twice a year by the departments of English and History of Northeastern Illinois University College in Chicago.

The South, Midwest, and West have been the focus of anthologies useful for locating fiction and poetry about those areas and by writers from those regions. [44] Two of the best are The Southwest in Life and Literature (1962) by Charles L. Sonnichsen and The Literature of the American West (1971) by J. Golden Taylor. The first has selections from 43 writers, including Paul Horgan, Oliver La Farge, Paul I. Wellman, and John C. Duval. The selections include 10 pages (pages 398-409) from Conrad Richter's Sea of Grass (1937) and 11 pages (pages 267-277) from Edna Ferber's Giant (1952). The collection contains short biographical sketches (pages 545-554) for the writers with titles and dates for some of their works. Taylor's Literature of the American West (1971) contains two novellas, 11 short stories, and 32 poems. The writings are about the West by western and nonwestern authors.

Only a few works published since 1960 contain regional fiction bibliography, and among these few the West and the Middle West are the areas that received the most study. "Appendix I" (pages 213-262) in Edwin Gaston's The Early Novel of the Southwest (1961) contains synopses for 40 novels ranging in length from one short paragraph to three pages. [45] Brief biographical information (pages 263-287) containing titles and dates is given for each author.

For farm novels of the Midwest a very long list (pages 200-242) can be found in Roy Meyer's Middle Western Farm Novel in the Twentieth Century (1965). [46] The annotations of 50-160 words are both descriptive and critical. Concerning Howard Erichsen's Son of Earth he writes that "the characters are largely caricatures, dialogue is wooden, and many events ... are overdrawn" (page 210). About Gerrard Harris's

The Treasure of the Land (1917) Meyer is quite devastating: "The novel has so many stereotypes and contrived situations, the propaganda is so blatant, and the farmer's problem is so grossly oversimplified that it is hard to take the book seriously" (page 217).

Patricia Kennedy is another author who has written about fiction in the Midwest. For her dissertation (1968) at the University of Illinois she studied the pioneer woman in novels written in the twentieth century with settings in the nineteenth. [47] The study is based on a survey of 100 novels.

Between 1953 and 1967 the Western Writers of America published 18 collections of stories written by members of the Association. [48] The Association, which has its headquarters in North Platte, Nebraska, is composed of freelance writers of fiction and nonfiction. It publishes a monthly called Roundup and presents awards each year for best books, film, and television scripts. The collections of stories, which vary in length from 200 to more than 400 pages, contain stories about the West.

A small amount of bibliographic work was done on regional poetry. Ray O. Hummel, Jr. made one of the most valuable contributions by listing a great many poetry broadsides in his Southeastern Broadsides Before 1877 (1971). [49] He gives 14 for Georgia, 23 for Louisiana, 14 for North Carolina, 39 for South Carolina, 91 for Virginia, and much smaller numbers for other Southern states. In a supplement to the Virginia section, which was published as a separate in 1975, he gives 37 more verse entries for that state. [50]

Lucien Stryk is the editor of two volumes of Midwest poetry: Heartland (1967) and Heartland II (1975). [51] They contain poems about the Midwest by living writers from the area or by writers who have had "firm ties with the area and ... have written a fair amount of poetry set in it" (Introduction to first volume, page xiii). Heartland (1967) has 29 poets with one to ten poems for each writer. Heartland II has twice as many poems as the first volume.

Several states published bibliographies of authors that give both biographical and bibliographic information. The Midwest has been particularly conscientious in compiling works of this kind. Donald E. Thompson did a very long supplement (688 pages) to Richard E. Banta's Indiana Authors and Their Books (1949). [52] The supplement (1974), which

covers 1917 through 1966, is like the first volume in that it
gives for many entries rather full information about the authors and their books. Another bibliography on Indiana is
the Catalog of the David Demaree Banta Indiana Collection
(1965). [53] It contains a separate section on literature (pages
35-48). David D. Banta (1833-1896) was a lawyer, judge,
and historian, and a great book collector. His collection,
which went to Franklin College in 1960, was much enlarged
by the College.

Ohio Authors and Their Books (1962), edited by William Coyle, is another long biobibliography. [54] It lists 4000
native and resident authors from 1796 to 1950. The Ohioana
Library Association sponsored the research. Another good
list is Frank Paluka's book on Iowa authors (1967). [55] It includes only native writers of five or more original books and
gives for some authors a quantity of information about them
and their writings. The biographical essays are more like
bibliographical essays. For some titles he gives such information as binding, illustrations, and number of copies of
first edition. The Michigan author list edited by Rachel Hilbert is a much shorter work, which is more valuable for
biographical information than for publication information about
titles. [56]

The Nebraska list (1964) by Alice G. Harvey has
separate lists for poetry, fiction writers, and dramatists
and gives for many titles full imprint information. [57] It also
contains biographical sketches (pages 3-41).

Kentucky has two biobibliographies, both published in
the 1960's, and both containing much information about books
and authors. [58] Ish Richey's list is composed of biographical
sketches containing comments on many literary works, particularly poems and novels. The sketch for Jesse Stuart is
15 pages long (pages 158-172) and includes the whole poem,
"Kentucky Is My Land." His synopsis for John Fox's Little
Shepherd of Kingdom Come is about 130 words long (pages
72-73). In about 200 words Richey describes Robert Penn
Warren's All the King's Men (1946):

> The great novel, All the King's Men, was pub-
> lished by Harcourt, Brace and Company in 1946, for
> which he received the Pulitzer Prize. This novel,
> also, was made into an Academy Award winning film.
> This powerful novel is the interlocked stories of three
> men and a woman. At its center is Willie Stark, a

young back-country lawyer in a Southern state, who
discovers that he has the gift for power, and follows
his star to become political boss of his state. His
compelling vitality draws to him Jack Burden, Anne
Stanton, and her brother, Adam. The three are childhood friends of aristocratic backgrounds, who live
under a sense of their own incompleteness.

From the moment that Stark gives Jack Burden
the job of digging up political dirt on a friend of the
Burden and Stanton families, the story weaves into a
single drama of ever mounting intensity. In Willie
Stark, Mr. Warren has added a notable figure to our
literature, a man of the people corrupted by success,
caught between his dreams of service and his ruthless
urge to power. In brilliant contrast are Adam Stanton, the man of ideas, Judge Irwin, the old-fashioned
man of honor, and Jack Burden, the uprooted seeker
for a faith [page 151].

Mary C. Browning's Kentucky Authors (1967) also
covers a great many writers of belles lettres. It has more
on dramatists than the book by Ish Richey. She has a separate section (pages 58-75) on the poets laureate of the State:
James T. C. Noe, Edwin C. Carlisle, and Jesse Stuart.
The next two long sections (pages 76-222) are also on poets.
For many of them she gives biographical information, quotes,
and selections. For Madison Cawein, for example, she gives
several quotes ranging in length from two to 16 lines (pages
133-137). In the pages on fiction Miss Browning is especially good in catching the joy and sorrow of living in many
of the Kentucky novels. One of her best descriptions is for
Harriette Arnow's Hunter's Horn (1958):

The setting of Hunter's Horn is situated in the
hills of Kentucky, where the scrub pine and sumac
are taking over and the people--no matter how ragged
and hungry at times--live with a zest and a dramatic
sense of both joy and sorrow unknown in more so-
phisticated places.

Over a brush fire in the dead of night, we listen
with Nunn Ballew to the baying of the hounds as they
follow the great red fox, King Devil. And we understand why Nunn must keep chasing the perverse crea-
ture, and must buy pedigreed puppies, though his
fences fall in ruin, his farm stock dwindles, and his
family goes in want.

> We go to school with the hill children in a one-
> room cabin that affords little in the way of educational
> materials. We share with young Suse her longing to
> go to high school, and her dreams of going to live in
> Detroit.
>
> We enjoy hunts, fires, dances, brawls, joy and
> pain in a book that makes the reader forget that he
> is in the modern industrial world, and places him in
> the mountains with the poor, but very proud, families
> [page 275].

Her excellent story description of The Dollmaker is somewhat
different, a little formal, less leisurely, but gives the same
sympathetic understanding of people and their feelings:

> In The Dollmaker we find that Gertie Nevels is
> a big, ugly, strong-willed and self-reliant woman who
> is capable and efficient as a wife and a mother in the
> hills of Kentucky. But when she is uprooted from her
> familiar surroundings and thrust into the confusion of
> wartime Detroit, her efficiency, her authority, and
> her way of life are all swept away. The government
> housing project where her husband has found a flat for
> her and their five children is strange and terrifying.
> Her neighbors only serve to increase this sense of
> strangeness. She is suddenly lost in misery and ter-
> ror. Her one consolation is the unfinished figure in
> the block of cherry wood which she has brought from
> Kentucky and which in moments of stress she whittles
> on with her knife.
>
> Gertie is intelligent enough to resist the sham
> and ugliness which surround her, but her innocence of
> spirit is not proof against the distorted values which
> eventually infect her husband and all but one of her
> children. In this lies the story. The story of Gertie's
> struggle to keep her simple moral principles in face
> of pressure from her family.
>
> Arnow has woven a story that seems to surpass
> her other books, before and after. It is filled with
> excitement, adventure, and fear that should keep any
> reader from wanting to put the book down, yet the
> reader will remain apprehensive about the end [page
> 276].

G. K. Hall in Boston published a long bibliography of
Alaska in 1974.[59] The subject index gives about 200 entries
for novels, 30 for short stories, and 100 for poems.

A few of the state literary histories published in this period are rich sources of information about books and authors. Arthur W. Shumaker's History of Indiana Literature (1962) is outstanding for the number of authors cited and discussed. [60] Even for a minor writer such as Frederick Landis (1872-1934) he devotes more than a page (pages 419-421) to two of his novels. For Caroline V. Krout (1852-1931), another novelist of small renown, he devotes six pages (pages 385-390) to her life and her four books. For a major author such as Booth Tarkington he writes fully about the man and his work (pages 350-385).

The Literary History of Iowa (1972) by Clarence A. Andrews might well serve as a model for similar works. [61] It is factual, interpretive, critical, and well-documented. Besides his own critical comments he quotes generously from the writings of scholars and contemporary critics. In one paragraph he is often able to summarize the whole of a literary work, as in his description of A Lantern in Her Hand (1928) by Bess Streeter Aldrich:

> A Lantern in Her Hand is the story of Abbie Mackenzie Deal from her pioneer childhood near Cedar Falls and Waterloo to her death in her farm home near Cedartown (Elmwood), Nebraska, at the age of eighty. Abbie's experiences as a child and through her marriage are those of Mary Anderson; the Deal and Mackenzie families are modeled after the Anderson and Streeter families. There is no plot to the novel as such--there is simply the slow roll of years, the cycles of crop failures and successes, the growth of towns and cities, the proliferation of families, the forestation of the bare land, the coming of the railroad, the building of schools and colleges. These are the background against which Abbie Deal constructs her life and the lives of her children. There is the building of the 'soddy,' (a cabin built of turf, in layers), death by rattlesnake, the inevitable blizzard and prairie fire, the grasshopper invasion. One of the novel's themes is the paradox of Nature--as provider, as giver of pleasant sensations, as destroyer--a theme which informs almost every novel of life on the Iowa prairie. A second theme is the conflict between the values of life on the prairie and life in the growing towns. A third theme is that of sacrifice for love-- and this one is present in several Aldrich novels [page 29].

The lengthy index (pages 267-287) lists titles separately and under the authors' names. The entry for Susan Glaspell (page 274) gives her drama titles first and then groups her other writings under the subheading "other works." Dr. Andrews is a professor of language and literature at Michigan Technological University.

Marilyn Jody's dissertation on Alaskan literature (1969) contains a long list of fiction written before 1920 and a list of novels written after that year.[62] The total list consists of 250 short stories, 100 dime novels and story papers, and 300 novels. The end of the study also has an annotated bibliography of the Alaskan writing of Jack London, Hamlin Garland, Joaquin Miller, John Muir, Frank Norris, and 12 other writers.

A few of the state literature collections serve as a bibliographic aid for belles lettres. Lee W. Storrs edited a California collection in 1968 that includes 80 writers, among them Walt Whitman, Robert Frost, Robinson Jeffers, Jack London, John Steinbeck, and Frank Norris.[63] Walt Whitman is represented by "Song of the Redtree" and Robert Frost, by "Once by the Pacific" and "A Peck of Gold." The fiction selections are from The Sea Wolf by Jack London, The Grapes of Wrath by John Steinbeck, and McTeague by Frank Norris. California Classics (1971) by Lawrence C. Powell has selections which treat of the State, not all of them by natives.[64] Most of the 31 selections are literary and were written by such writers as Bret Harte, John Steinbeck, Richard H. Dana, Nathanael West, and Aldous Huxley.

The University of South Carolina Press published a tricentennial anthology of South Carolina in 1971 in order "to demonstrate that South Carolina literature is of merit throughout her 300 years" (Introduction, page 4).[65] The writers and selections were chosen by Jay B. Hubbell, Louis D. Rubin, James B. Meriwether, C. Hugh Holman, and other scholars. Thirty-nine writers with one to four selections each are included. A separate list of sources for the writings is given on pages 576-580.

State fiction is listed in a few publications. One of the longest lists is that of Alaskan fiction (pages 322-341) in Hilton J. Wolfe's 1973 dissertation on Alaskan literature.[66] According to the author the list is "the most comprehensive ... in existence" (page 322). A list of novels with settings of New Jersey in the Revolution was published by the New

Brunswick Historical Club in 1964.[67]   The Michigan Council
of Teachers of English published a list of Michigan novels in
1963.[68]   The list contains 303 novels with annotations of 15
to 100 words.

Not much of a bibliographic nature was done on state
poetry.   The Michigan Association of School librarians published a list of 37 poets (pages 1-30) in Rachel M. Hilbert's
Michigan Poets with Supplement to Michigan Authors (1964).[69]
The list gives titles of books of poetry with dates and names
of anthologies and periodicals in which poems have appeared.
Elmer D. Johnson did a fairly long list of Louisiana poetry
for the January 1960 issue of Southwestern Louisiana Journal.[70]   Only books are included, and for each of them he
gives the full name of the author, title, and imprint.   A
three-page list of Minnesota North Country poetry is in the
spring 1974 issue of the Society for the Study of Midwestern
Literature Newsletter.[71]   The bibliography lists books of
poetry and writings about the poets.

The poetry societies continued to collect poetry written by their members.   Collections come from Alaska, Michigan, New Jersey, Pennsylvania, and Arizona.[72]   The volume
from Alaska contains many poems written before the Poetry
Society of Alaska was founded.   It has a number of selections
from poets who lived fifty or more years ago.   The volume
from Michigan is a fortieth anniversary anthology containing
117 poets.

Richard G. Walser edited another volume of North
Carolina poetry in 1963.[73]   This new collection contains only
living poets who wrote poems in the past dozen years (Preface, page xii).   The short biographical sketches give book
titles with dates.

Very little had been done before this period to list
plays by state.   Paul T. Nolan, professor of English at the
University of Southwestern Louisiana, is one of the few people in the country who did bibliographic work on state drama.
He and Amos E. Simpson did a checklist of Arkansas playwrights in 1963.[74]   The list includes 37 playwrights and
more than 100 copyrighted plays.   The footnotes in the bibliography give uncopyrighted plays and some miscellaneous
information about the authors.   Paul T. Nolan's list for Alabama covers only those plays written between 1870 and 1916.[75]

Edgar Heyl is another author of a list of state plays.

For several issues of the Maryland Historical Magazine between 1957 and 1969 he made a list of 600 plays by 275
Marylanders, both printed and typewritten.[76] The plays
were written between 1870 and 1916.

A number of works useful for locating the literature
of cities and towns were published. Perry G. Fisher's 1974
bibliography of Washington, D.C., contains a list of 58 novels (pages 49-55).[77] The annotations, which are factual and
critical, contain between 25 and 200 words. Thirty-eight
titles of fiction are included in John R. Adams's Books and
Authors of San Diego (1966).[78] Michael True wrote an essay
in 1972 about Worcester (Massachusetts) poets.[79] He includes 25 authors with titles of books and dates. John Aus-
ten, Esther Forbes, Stanley Kunitz, Elizabeth Bishop, and
Charles Olson are among the writers. A few poetry selections are also in the essay.

Local poetry anthologies were compiled for New York
City, Cape Cod, Charlotte and Greensboro (North Carolina),
Greenville (South Carolina), New Orleans, Milwaukee, and
other localities.[80] The New York City anthology is rather
lengthy and contains poems by 27 poets. The biographical
sketches (pages 545-571) give titles of books with imprint.
The Greensboro Reader (1968) contains poetry and fiction by
writers who received a degree from the University of North
Carolina at Greensboro or who have taught there in the English Department. The anthology includes 11 poets and 11
short-story writers. Randall Jarrell, Peter Taylor, and
Caroline Gordon are the most familiar names. Alfred S.
Reid compiled a short anthology of Greenville poets for the
November 1963 issue of Furman Studies. The biographical
sketches contain titles of books with dates.

State historical sources published in this period can
still be used for information about American literature.
Tennessee History: A Bibliography (1974) by Sam Smith and
Luke Banker has two separate lists of fiction: "Historical
and biographical fiction," pages 313-315, and "Social and cultural life in fiction," pages 315-318.[81] Sarah A. Rouse
wrote a 31-page essay on modern Mississippi literature for
A History of Mississippi, edited by Richard A. McLemore.[82]
It contains many titles with dates.

Two states observed the centennial of the Civil War by
publishing bibliographic works.[83] Michigan in the Civil War
(1965) by Helen H. Ellis is a guide to articles in Detroit

newspapers between 1861 and 1866. The entry in the index
for war poetry refers to 24 poems in the guide. Donald A.
Sinclair's Civil War and New Jersey (1968) lists poetry, fiction, and drama on pages 57-61. He gives full name of author, full imprint, and brief annotations.

Some authors and editors made a valuable contribution
to humor bibliography in the third period of this bibliographic
study. Brom Weber compiled an Anthology of American Humor (1962), which presents in historical sequence a selection
of American humor from Nathaniel Ward to Bernard Malamud.[84] "Richard Cory" by Edwin A. Robinson, "The Bear"
by Robert Frost, "The Deacon's Masterpiece" by Oliver W.
Holmes, and "I Taste a Liquor--Never Brewed" by Emily
Dickinson are among the poems in the anthology. The selections from novels are from William Faulkner's Sanctuary, F.
Scott Fitzgerald's The Great Gatsby, Herman Melville's Moby
Dick and White Jacket, Nathaniel Hawthorne's The House of
Seven Gables, and Henry Adams's Democracy. Some of the
short stories are "The Legend of Sleepy Hollow" by Washing-
ton Irving, "The Dulham Ladies" by Sarah O. Jewett, "The
Other Two" by Edith Wharton, "The Haircut" by Ring Lard-
ner, and "The Light of the World" by Ernest Hemingway.
The 71 writers represent some of the best authors in Ameri-
can literature, and the selections are among the best writings.
The anthology's editor, Brom Weber, was professor of English at the University of Minnesota at the time of publication.

Another excellent anthology is called With the Bark
On; Popular Humor of the Old South (1967).[85] Most of the
selections are from old newspapers of the period 1835 to
1860. Almost half are from the New Orleans Delta, the St.
Louis Reveille, the Louisville Daily Courier, and the Cham-
bers (Alabama) Tribune. The rest of the stories appeared
in the Richmond Compiler, the New Orleans Picayune, and
the New York Spirit of the Time. Most of the 70 sketches
are about the American backwoodsman and are classified as
follows: "The River," "The Backcountry," "Varmints and
Hunters," "Fun and Frolic," "The Professions," "Jokes and
Jokers," "Masculine Amusements," "Politicians," "Actors,"
and "Yokels in the City." The editor, John Q. Anderson, is
professor of English at the University of Houston.

In 1965 Wade H. Hall wrote a history of Southern
humor from 1865 to 1914.[86] There are many footnotes for
titles and quotes cited in the text. An alphabetic list of
titles is in the bibliography, pages 358-368. The author of

this volume, which is called The Smiling Phoenix, is a professor at Kentucky Southern College.

Tar Heel Laughter (1974) is an anthology of North Carolina writings of humor.[87] Among the selections are excerpts from several works of fiction, including Thomas Wolfe's Look Homeward Angel and The Hills Beyond and Guy Owen's The Ballad of the Flim-Flam Man. Richard G. Walser, an anthologist of other volumes of North Carolina literature, is also the editor of this collection.

Two anthologies for the West, The Home Book of Western Humor (1967) and Humor of the Old Southwest (1975), contain many selections for the student who wants to study the subject.[88] Both contain writings from books and periodicals. The second title is ably edited by Professor Hennig Cohen of the University of Pennsylvania and William B. Dillingham of Emory University. They found some of their selections from William T. Porter's Spirit of the Times, a very popular humor and sporting magazine (1831-1861) that contained original sketches and reprints of stories that first appeared in regional newspapers. Twenty-three writers are included, such as James K. Paulding, Joseph M. Field, George W. Harris, Johnson Hooper, John S. Robb, and Mark Twain. Biographical sketches for the authors include titles of books with dates.

The authors of the many bibliographies that were published after 1960 must have seen clearly that the way to achieve bibliographic control for the prolific writers is to compile separate bibliographies that would list all their writings and all or most of the writings about them. Both the writings and the scholarship were important, and the aim was to place them in one volume. Many book-length bibliographies were published with the idea that they would serve the needs of book collectors, students, librarians, and scholars. Without neglecting the old American writers the compilers looked more and more to the twentieth century for subjects, and they found a great many authors that needed to be covered. The contemporary authors received even more attention than the writers of the 1900-1940 period. Publishers responded with enthusiasm by printing the bibliographies, sometimes in rather handsome editions with illustrations, good paper, and attractive bindings.

For old American writers bibliographies were done for Edward Taylor, Herman Melville, Harold Frederic, Emily

Dickinson, William Dean Howells, Jack London, and Stephen
Crane. The Edward Taylor bibliography (1970) by Constance
J. Gefvert is a descriptive bibliography containing critical
annotations for many titles.[89] It includes both primary and
secondary sources and is an example of one of the fine bibliographies in the Serif Series by Kent State University Press.
The Melville bibliography (1973) by Beatrice Ricks and Joseph
D. Adams is especially good for giving later editions of the
author's prose writings and poetry collections.[90] Much of
the volume lists critical articles and books with brief annotations. The long subject index (pages 401-532) contains
entries for all his writings. The entry for "Benito Cereno"
begins with references to criticism and continues with editions,
character, and play. The play was written by Robert Lowell.
The bibliography is one of a series called Research Bibliographies in American Literature, published by G. K. Hall.
The fourth volume in this series is on Harold Frederic and
was published in 1975.[91] It is a checklist of writings by and
about the author. Besides the newspaper articles he wrote
as a journalist, it has two separate lists of his fiction books
and short fiction (pages 1-6, 8-10).

The bibliography of William Dean Howells includes for
the first time in one volume writings by and about the author.[92] It complements the chronological bibliography of
Gibson and Arms (1948) by listing his writings by form and
genre. The Jack London bibliography (1966) contains a list
of the author's books and a separate list of his short stories.[93] The bibliography is especially good for giving reprints and translations. Hensley C. Woodbridge did a long
supplement of more than a 100 pages for an enlarged edition
in 1973.[94] The Crane bibliography by Robert W. Stallman
includes the bibliography of Vincent Starrett and Ben Ames
Williams (1948) and adds a list of contemporary reviews
(pages 73-152) and a very long list (pages 237-620) of biography, bibliography, and critical writings.[95] Most of the
book is composed of annotations for the reviews and critical
articles. The annotations are particularly good because Professor Stallman knows Crane and his work very well after
many years of research for his 1968 biography of the author.

Two other bibliographies of nineteenth-century writers
need brief mention, one of a major writer and one of a minor
novelist. The Emily Dickinson bibliography (1972) by Willis
J. Buckingham is valuable for the critical writings about the
author.[96] The very short bibliography (9 pages) of the Barrett Library Collection of Edwin L. Bynner lists his writings

in chronological and alphabetic order.[97] Bynner was a Massachusetts lawyer who was best known for his novel Agnes Surriage (1886). Since 1960 the University of Virginia has published several lists of the writings of American authors in the collection which C. Waller Barrett gave to the University Library in 1952, 1958, and 1960. Mr. Barrett was a shipping executive and avid book collector.[98]

Bibliographies were done for some of the important fiction writers of the early part of the twentieth century. G. K. Hall published a bibliography of Theodore Dreiser in 1975, which is one of the best in its series of Research Bibliographies in American Literature.[99] It is a lengthy bibliography (515 pages) and aims to be complete for the author's writings. The long index (pages 445-515) has titles for all of them. For an author who is best known for his fiction there is no separate list of his novels and short stories. His writings are arranged in chronological order.

Matthew J. Bruccoli did bibliographies of F. Scott Fitzgerald (1972) and Ring Lardner (1975) for the University of Pittsburgh Series in Bibliography.[100] Both give very full descriptions of first editions and reproductions of title pages. He gives not only the name of the publisher but also the name of the printing press and the manufacturer of the plates. Besides collation he gives information about typography, paper, binding, and dust jacket. His description for Fitzgerald's The Great Gatsby is probably his longest (pages 59-71). He includes title entries in the indexes to both volumes. Mr. Bruccoli is professor of English at the University of South Carolina and a distinguished bibliographer. He is also the director of the Center for Editions of American Authors and the editorial director of the University of Pittsburgh Series in Bibliography. Besides Mr. Bruccoli the Editorial Board includes William R. Cagle, Charles W. Mann, and Fredson Bowers, the "Dean of American Bibliography."

The Ellen Glasgow bibliography (1964) by William W. Kelly is outstanding for the information which it gives about the impressions of her books.[101] He tries to list all the impressions and to describe the evidence on which they were based. Part two of the bibliography lists biography and critical writings with notes. In Part three he describes briefly the author's manuscripts at the University of Virginia.

The Edith Wharton bibliography (1966) by Vito J. Brenni represents a first attempt to list all of her writings

in one volume, both her books and her many periodical contributions.[102] Another aim of the bibliography is to include
in one book writings by and about her. Descriptive annotations are given for some of the entries.

The Upton Sinclair bibliography (1973) by Ronald Gottesman is one of the volumes in the Serif Series published by
Kent State University.[103] About twelve have been published
on American authors. The Sinclair bibliography is one of
the longer ones (544 pages) and attempts to be complete for
the author's writings. The main arrangement is chronological, and the appendix lists his major works in both alphabetic and chronological order. Part three of the book contains a long list (pages 389-476) of writings about him.

Many more bibliographies were done for fiction writers
of the past three or four decades. Audre Hanneman did a
comprehensive bibliography of Ernest Hemingway in 1967 and
made a supplement in 1975.[104] Tetsumaro Hayashi compiled
a bibliography of John Steinbeck in 1967, which contains separate lists for his novels, short stories, plays, and poetry.[105]
It also contains secondary material about the writer. The
new edition published in 1971 has a general index, a feature
which was lacking in the earlier work.[106] The William
Faulkner bibliography (1968) by Linton R. Massey is a catalog of the large Faulkner collection at the University of Virginia.[107] Part one has separate lists for his novels, short
stories, verse, essays, criticism, public addresses, letters,
interviews, and recordings. Part two has writings about him.
It has many reproductions of title pages. The volume was
published by the Bibliographical Society of Virginia in a rather
attractive format.

Bibliographies have been done for Gertrude Stein,
Robert Penn Warren, John O'Hara, and Katherine Anne
Porter.[108] The Stein bibliography by Robert A. Wilson gives
detailed information on first editions and also contains writings
about her. It is one of a small number of bibliographies published by the Phoenix Book Shop in New York City. Mary N.
Huff's bibliography of Robert Penn Warren is especially good
for listing his short stories and poems by title. The bibliography is a checklist rather than a descriptive bibliography.
It is one of the Fugitive Bibliographies published by David
Lewis. Matthew J. Bruccoli did a checklist for John O'Hara
that was published by Random House in 1972. Although the
arrangement is chronological, there are separate lists for
short stories and poetry.

Gale Research Company in Detroit published four bibliographies of contemporary novelists: James G. Cozzens (1973), Nelson Algren (1973), James Jones (1974), and Kurt Vonnegut (1972).[109] Each volume contains information about first editions and reproductions of title pages. James B. Meriwether's bibliography of Cozzens brings up to date the list which he did for the winter 1958 issue of Critique. The book contains separate lists of the author's short stories in periodicals and his poems. This bibliography of Cozzens follows by two years Pierre Michel's annotated checklist of the author which was published in the Serif Series by Kent State University.[110] The Serif Series also includes bibliographies of John Updike, Bernard Malamud, Thomas Wolfe, and Raymond Chandler.[111]

The Humanities Research Center at the University of Texas published a bibliography of Edward Dahlberg in its Tower Bibliography Series.[112] Dahlberg is the author of Bottom Dogs (1930), a story of the horror of orphanage, slum, and hobo experiences, and From Flushing to Calvary (1932), a novel about slum dwellers in New York City. The bibliography gives a full description of first American and English editions and uses reproductions of title pages instead of customary transcriptions. It also contains a list of book reviews and a short list of writings about him. Choice type has been used to print the volume.

Many bibliographies were compiled for poets of the twentieth century. Donald C. Gallup did a descriptive bibliography for Ezra Pound in 1963 and made corrections for the second impression of 1969.[113] The 1969 volume gives full information about first editions and notes special copies. The detailed index (pages 395-454) contains titles of all his writings, including short poems and essays. The volume belongs to the excellent Soho Bibliography Series of R. Hart-Davis in London. Mr. Gallup also made a thorough revision of his T. S. Eliot bibliography.[114]

Kent State University published in 1971 William White's bibliography of Edwin Arlington Robinson in the Serif Series.[115] It was compiled to serve as a supplement to Charles B. Hogan's Bibliography of Edwin Arlington Robinson (1936). The "Appendix" (pages 139-151) contains additions and corrections to the Hogan bibliography, and these were supplied by Mr. Hogan himself. A bibliography of Allen Tate was published in 1969 by David Lewis in the Fugitive Bibliography Series.[116] His books are listed with their contents, and a list of his poems is in a separate section.

Robert O. Lindsay did a descriptive bibliography for Witter Bynner (1967), giving very full information about his books and listing his individual poems in a separate section.[117] It contains translations, writings about the author, and an index that gives titles of all poems and proper names and titles of all works with which he was associated. The bibliography appeared as number two of the University of New Mexico Library Series.

Two other library bibliographies were published for American poets: the University of Virginia Library did a checklist of Robinson Jeffers (1960) in its Barrett Library Series and the Library of Congress did a bibliography of Carl Sandburg (1969).[118] The latter contains a lecture about the poet which Mark Van Doren gave in the Library on January 8, 1968. The lecture and bibliography were published "to reach a wider audience and as a contribution to literary history and criticism" (page iii).

Many more bibliographies were compiled for contemporary poets, and a fair number of these came from four publishers: the University of Pittsburgh, Kent State University, Gale Research Company, and the Phoenix Book Shop in New York City. The Wallace Stevens bibliography (1973) by Jerome M. Edelstein is one of the best because it gives very full information about first editions and contains excerpts from the author's letters.[119] The description for the poet's first book, Harmonium (1923), is five pages long. A reproduction of page two is given. The bibliography contains all his writings, translations, musical settings, and recordings. Writings about Stevens are also included. A full index (pages 401-429) with title entries concludes the work. The volume belongs to the University of Pittsburgh Series in Bibliography. A bibliography for John Berryman (1974) was also published in the same series.[120]

The volumes in the Serif Series of bibliographies from Kent State University vary in scope, descriptive detail, annotations, and form of entry. One of the best is Mary Novik's Robert Creeley: An Inventory 1945-1970 (1975).[121] It contains writings by and about the poet and gives the publishing history of individual writings (pages 80-136). It has two separate indexes, one for his poems (pages 187-204) and another for proper names in titles of poems and prose (pages 177-185). Another long bibliography (241 pages) in this series was done in 1973 for Theodore Roethke by James R. McLeod.[122] The index (pages 229-241) of this work includes all

the poet's poems and prose pieces.   Archibald MacLeish and
Richard Wilbur are two other poets in this series.[123]

Gale Research published a bibliography of James Dickey (1972) and Kenneth Millar (1971).[124]   They are somewhat like the other Gale bibliographies in that they give
brief information about first editions and reproductions of
title pages.   They lack an index.   The Millar bibliography
was done by Matthew J. Bruccoli.

The Phoenix Book Shop did bibliographies of Gregory
Corso (1966) and Charles Olson (1967).[125]   The Corso bibliography by Robert A. Wilson gives a small amount of information about first editions and contains a separate section
on contributions to periodicals.   The bibliography of Charles
Olson was done by George F. Butterick and Albert Glover.

William White, professor of journalism at Oakland
University and a prolific bibliographer of American literature, did two short bibliographies of contemporary poets,
one for John Ciardi (1959) and the other for William Snodgrass (1960).[126]   The Ciardi bibliography includes bibliographic descriptions of his books and material by the poet
in periodicals.   It has a list of critical articles and a list
of manuscripts in the Charles Feinberg collection.

Very few book-length bibliographies have been done
for playwrights.   The two that were done by the Humanities
Research Center of the University of Texas are most wel-
come contributions to the bibliography of American literature.
Manfred Triesch describes in his bibliography (1967) the
Lillian Hellman collection at the University of Texas.[127]
The collection consists mainly of manuscript material, such
as the extensive runs of various drafts of Miss Hellman's
dramas.   Mr. Triesch gives first the printed edition and
then describes the changes that were made in each draft.
For a student who is making a study of playwriting it is a
valuable source of information.   Laurence G. Avery compiled the Catalogue of the Maxwell Anderson Collection at
the University of Texas (1968).[128]

Jennifer M. Atkinson's Eugene O'Neill: A Descriptive Bibliography (1974) is the first descriptive bibliography
of the playwright.[129]   It lists his books and gives very full
information about first editions.   It gives his contributions
to books and periodicals and locates his plays in collections
and anthologies.   It omits writings about him.   The volume

was published in the University of Pittsburgh Series in Bibliography. The compiler is assistant director of the Center for Editions of American Authors of the Modern Language Association and adjunct professor of English at the University of South Carolina.

David Kherdian's Bibliography of William Saroyan 1934-1964 (1965) is another noteworthy bibliography of a playwright.[130] It is not a complete bibliography because it omits writings in periodicals. Reproductions of title pages and dust jackets are assembled on pages 73-89. The index contains all title entries, proper names, periodicals, and publishers.

Periodicals devoted even more space to author bibliographies than in the years preceding 1960. The Bulletin of Bibliography published a good many, especially for modern and contemporary writers. Some of the authors are Sara Teasdale, Flannery O'Connor, James Purdy, Jessamyn West, Shirley Grau, LeRoi Jones, Gore Vidal, Philip Roth, John Berryman, Joseph Hergesheimer, and Richard Wright.[131] The Teasdale bibliography contains a chronological list of her poems in periodicals and gives the first line of each poem. The first line helps to identify poems that have changed title. The Jessamyn West bibliography gives separate lists for short stories and poems that have not appeared in collections. The John Berryman checklist contains a separate list of all the poems that have appeared in periodicals. One of the best bibliographies to appear in the Bulletin is Dean Sherman's list of Owen Wister's writings.[132] The annotations are remarkably informative and range in length from 10 to 200 words.

Besides the author bibliographies in the Papers of the Bibliographical Society of America, the journal also includes some short articles giving information about entries in the Lyle Wright fiction volumes and in the BAL. For entry number 165 in Wright's American Fiction 1851-1875 a note in the first issue of the journal for 1970 supplies the name of the author.[133] The name, as it turns out, is very different from the initials which Wright gives. The author of the note, James Lawton, found the name in a letter which Daniel Mann wrote to Rufus W. Griswold in which he states that he wrote Wolfsden. Wright used the initials "J.B.," which appeared on the title page of the novel.

Proof, a new annual in American bibliography, contains

two bibliographies of American authors in the first volume
(1971).[134] The Theodore Dreiser checklist (pages 247-292)
by Donald Pizer builds on previous bibliographies, adds new
items, and discards ghosts. The Faulkner short-story list
(pages 293-329) by James B. Meriwether lists published, unpublished, and lost short stories. The annotations contain
information relating to dates, titles, and relationships. A
title index is included. The 1973 volume of Proof has a
long bibliography of Frank Norris (pages 155-220).[135]

Serif, a bibliographic journal from Kent State University, has published bibliographies of several American authors. An Edward Albee checklist appeared in the September
1969 issue and a supplement was published four years later.[136]
William White did a checklist of Robinson Jeffers covering the
years 1959 to 1965 for the June 1966 issue.[137] He also did
a list of Walt Whitman's periodical poetry for the summer
1974 issue.[138]

Between 1961 and 1976 Edgar M. Branch published
three bibliographies of James T. Farrell in the American
Book Collector.[139] They are supplements to his 1959 bibliography of the author. In 1965 the American Book Collector published a bibliography of William Inge.[140]

Early American Literature, which began publication in
the middle 1960's, evidently intends to include bibliographies
of early American authors. A few were published in its
first ten volumes. Ann Stanford did an annotated checklist
of Anne Bradstreet for the winter 1968/69 issue, and Paul
Witherington wrote a bibliographic essay on Charles Brockden Brown for the fall of 1974 issue.[141] The essay cites
writings by and about him.

American Literary Realism publishes bibliographies
of nineteenth-century writers of realism. It has already
brought out lists for Harold Frederic, Harris M. Lyon,
Abraham Cahan, Sherwood Bonner, Mary N. Murfree, and
Henry B. Fuller.[142] The Frederic checklist lists only his
short fiction. The bibliography of Harris M. Lyon contains
only a partial listing of his writings. The lists for Abraham
Cahan and Mary N. Murfree are annotated.

Twentieth Century Literature is one of the leading
literary journals for author bibliographies. It has published
bibliographies of Frederick Manfred, Elizabeth Bishop, Theodore Roethke, Edward Albee, and John Dos Passos.[143] The

bibliography of Dos Passos supplements previous bibliographies by covering his writings from 1950 to 1966.

Critique is another literary journal which has from its very beginning published bibliographies of modern authors. It has published bibliographies of John Barth, Allan Seager, Peter Taylor, and John Fowles.[144] It published two bibliographies of John Barth, one in 1963 and the second in 1972. Both contain writings by and about him.

A few author biographies are still sources for bibliographies. Jean Holloway's Hamlin Garland (1960) has a long chronology (pages 314-332) of the author's publications.[145] Mark Schorer's Sinclair Lewis (1961) also has a chronological checklist (pages 815-826) of publications of the author.[146]

The remarkable achievement in this period was the publication of many bibliographies on the national level. The second bibliography supplement of the LHUS (1972), the new editions of American Authors and Books (1972) and the Oxford Companion to American Literature (1965), and the appearance of three more volumes of the BAL are among the comprehensive works that made a significant contribution to bibliographic control. Even more noteworthy are the many bibliographies that list novels, poems, and plays by author, title, subject, and chronology. The lists of fiction by Lyle Wright and R. Glenn Wright give scholars a much greater access to the published novels and stories of American writers. The appearance of Brown University's Dictionary Catalog of the Harris Collection (1972) is a major event for literary students, for in this one work they are able to locate the titles of a large portion of the poetic and dramatic talent of America. Lemay's Catalog of American Poetry in the Colonial Newspapers and Magazines (1972) rescues many poems from oblivion and serves as a key to some of the life and thought of early America. Another title of great value to the historian of this period is VanDerhoof's Bibliography of Novels Related to American Frontier and Colonial History (1971). Stoddard's supplements in 1969 and 1971 to Wegelin's Early American Poetry (1930) and Hill's Early American Plays (1934) are important for increasing the value of those earlier works. The Index of American Periodical Verse (1973) is noteworthy, for it marks a new attempt to list current poetry on a regular basis. One other volume which stands out among these genre lists is Guernsey's Directory of the American Theater 1894-1971 (1971). As an index to the Burns Mantle Series of Best Plays it is a long list of some of the best American drama of the past 77 years.

The effort to achieve bibliographic control on the state and local level is second only to that which was expanded on the national level. Thompson's Indiana Authors and Their Books 1917-1966 (1974), Coyle's Ohio Authors and Books (1962), and the two bibliographic studies of Kentucky by Richey and Browning are examples of what three states have done to identify their authors. Next to Indiana and Kentucky the state that received the most study was Alaska. Tourville's Alaskan bibliography (1974) and two dissertations, Jody's in 1969 and Wolfe's in 1973, list books of fiction. The many state and local poetry anthologies identify many authors and titles not found in the state bibliographies.

Very significant progress was made in these years to list all the publications of those authors of reputation and excellence who constitute the main portion of study for many students and scholars in American literature. Bibliographies were done for such major writers as Herman Melville (1973), Emily Dickinson (1970), William D. Howells (1973), Theodore Dreiser (1975), Edith Wharton (1966), Wallace Stevens (1973), Ezra Pound (1963), Ernest Hemingway (1967 and 1975), John Steinbeck (1963 and 1973), Eugene O'Neill (1974), William Faulkner (1968), and F. Scott Fitzgerald (1972). Minor writers received an equal amount of attention and include such names as Ring Lardner (1975), Witter Bynner (1967), Harold Frederic (1975), Richard Wilbur (1971), Allen Tate (1969), John Berryman (1974), James Dickey (1972), Bernard Malamud (1969), James Gould Cozzens (1971 and 1973), and Nelson Algren (1973). The many short author bibliographies in periodicals would seem to indicate an awareness on the part of the editors and scholars that the writings of many American authors need to be listed fully and accurately and that the task of bibliographic control is an ongoing search for all the belles lettres of the United States.

Chapter 4

A BACKWARD GLANCE
AND SOME RECOMMENDATIONS

The bibliographic control of American literature increased with each decade since 1920, the year with which
this study begins. Between 1920 and 1975 bibliographies
of American belles lettres were published on the national,
regional, state, and local level. On the national level the
three great achievements are the bibliographies in the Cambridge History of American Literature, the three bibliography volumes of the LHUS, and the six volumes of the BAL.
In fiction the leading works were those of Lyle H. Wright
and R. Glenn Wright.[1] In poetry the 1930 edition of Wegelin's Early American Poetry, Stoddard's supplements to it,
Brown University's Dictionary Catalog of the Harris Collection (1972), Irish's Modern American Muse (1950), and the
three volumes of the Index of American Periodical Verse
(1973, 1974, 1975) are among the important titles for locating books and individual poems.[2] In drama, the Dictionary Catalog of the Harris Collection (1972), Frank P. Hill's
American Plays (1934), and Arthur H. Quinn's bibliographies
in his History of the American Drama (1923, 1927, 1936,
1951) make a significant contribution to the bibliography of
American drama.[3] Other titles could be cited which are as
important, or only a shade less important, than those named
above, but these suffice to recall some of the milestones on
the road to full bibliographic control on the national level.

On the regional level the achievement was nowhere
near that of the national bibliographies, but in this summary
review it cannot be slighted because some excellent work was
done. Southwest Heritage (1938 and later editions), The South
in American Literature 1607-1900 (1954) by Jay B. Hubbell,
The Early Novels of the Southwest (1961) by Edwin W. Gaston, The Middle Western Farm Novel in the Twentieth Century (1965) by Roy W. Meyer, Southeastern Broadsides Before

1877 (1971) by Ray O. Hummel, and "Bibliography of Early New England Verse" by Harold S. Jantz are among the more notable titles in regional bibliography. [4]

A very large contribution to bibliographic control was made by the individual states. Among the bibliographic aids that they produced, the comprehensive bibliography, the bio-bibliography, the fiction lists, and the poetry anthologies are the most important. Together they record the titles of a huge number of literary works. Thornton's Bibliography of North Carolina 1589-1956 (1958), Banta's Indiana Authors and Their Books (1949), Marable and Boylan's Handbook of Oklahoma Writers (1939), Powell's North Carolina Fiction (1958), Black's Michigan Novels (1963), Walser's three volumes of North Carolina poetry, and Harrison's long collection of California poetry (1932) are just a few examples of the bibliographic aids that were prepared for the literature of individual states. [5] If state literary histories, fiction collections, and bibliographic essays are added to these aids, the amount of bibliographic control would be considerably increased. The essays achieve a remarkable quantity of subject analysis of state literature, especially fiction. The three articles on Iowa fiction by John T. Frederick in Palimpsest and Clarence A. Andrews's Literary History of Iowa (1972) make many good statements about the belles lettres of one state. [6]

A little work of a bibliographic nature has been done for cities. Adams's Books and Authors of San Diego (1966) and Fisher's Materials for the Study of Washington (1974) are good for fiction titles of those cities. [7] Ross and Kuykendall's collection of Fort Worth poems (1949) has a bibliography of poetry books by fifty writers of the city. [8] Padgett and Shapiro's Anthology of New York Poets (1970) gives titles of volumes of verse by New York City writers in the biographical sketches at the end of the volume. [9] One of the best volumes for the literature of a city is Wingfield's Literary Memphis (1942), which is a history of the writers and writings of a cultural center in Tennessee. [10]

By far the greatest boon to local bibliography has been the anthology. A fair number of cities, counties, and other portions of states are represented by literary collections. Many cities have poetry anthologies, and a smaller number have anthologies which include prose and poetry. Ross and Kuykendall's collection of Fort Worth poems (1949), A Century of Benton County [Oregon] Poetry (1957), Lewis's Poets and Poetry of Wyoming Valley [Pennsylvania] Poetry (1940), and

Weston's <u>Baltimore in Verse and Prose</u> (1936) are some
examples.[11]

The bibliographic work in humor is not so surprising
as it is pleasing to the historian who is studying American
bibliography. He meets familiar titles and authors and laughs
or smiles once more. The two best lists of titles are in
Blair's <u>Native American Humor</u> (1937) and Hall's <u>The Smiling
Phoenix</u> (1965).[12] Some of the collections of humor make up
to some extent for more extensive bibliographies. Seaver's
<u>Pageant of American Humor</u> (1948) and Weber's <u>Anthology of
American Humor</u> (1962) are valuable for the student who wants
to make a chronological study of the subject.[13] Bennett Cerf's
<u>Encyclopedia of Modern American Humor</u> (1954) has a re-
gional arrangement.[14] Some of the very best anthologies
were done for the South, Midwest, and West. Hudson's <u>Hu-
mor of the Old Deep South</u> (1936) and Anderson's <u>With the
Bark On</u> (1967) have many selections from books and periodicals.[15] By searching many old newspapers the compilers
were able to locate some of the most amusing and hilarious
stories in southern literature. These are scholarly collections containing miscellaneous information about the selections
and the authors. Cohen and Dillingham's <u>Humor of the Old
Southwest</u> (1975) and Conroy's <u>Midland Humor</u> (1947) contain
many humorous writings for those geographic areas.[16]

So many author bibliographies were compiled that one
might be inclined to think that if no other bibliographies were
published, they would be sufficient for the bibliographic control of belles lettres. The truth is that they would be entirely
adequate for many of the authors which are studied in the tra-
ditional high school and college literature program. By the
end of 1975 these authors were covered by bibliographies,
sometimes two, three, and four times. Louis H. Cohn did
a bibliography of Hemingway in 1931; Lee Samuels, in 1951;
and Audre Hanneman, in 1967.[17] Donald C. Gallup did four
bibliographies of T. S. Eliot between 1937 and 1969, each
time adding titles and making corrections.[18] Even writers
of less renown were covered more than once. Two bibliographies were done for Booth Tarkington (1932, 1949) and two
for Carl Van Vechten (1924, 1955).[19]

Many author bibliographies aim to be complete for all
writings, but some contain only published books, or only
writings in books. Some have only a chronological arrangement, while others are arranged by genre, and a relatively
few have both arrangements. Indexes vary, but in general

they are adequate. Some of them are so complete that they include all titles in the bibliography. Some of them include subject entries for titles, notes, and any other information contained in the descriptions of the titles.

Most of the author bibliographies are checklists in the sense that they aim to give lists of publications with only brief information. Because these checklists are so numerous, they make the greater contribution to bibliographic control. The bibliographies which give full descriptions do make some corrections in the checklists and are valuable for those times when first issues of first editions differ in some one or more important ways from later issues. These descriptive bibliographies are particularly important when no other bibliography exists. Some of them aim to be just as complete for periodical publications as the checklists.

No discussion of author bibliographies can fail to take into account the notes which contain miscellaneous information about the publications, including the brief statements made about the subject matter. While such statements are all too infrequent, they do occur in some bibliographies that attempt to give the scholar additional information which may be useful.

The many author bibliographies in periodicals cover new and old writers. For contemporary writers the bibliographies serve until a book-length bibliography is compiled. The periodical bibliographies for the old writers are valuable for supplementing existing bibliographies and, not infrequently, for providing for the first time a fairly long list of publications for an author who has received nothing like careful bibliographic study. Some periodical bibliographies are for old authors whose writings were scattered in so many publications that many eluded earlier bibliographers. The great increase in periodical author bibliographies after 1940 would seem to suggest that scholarly journals in bibliography and literature had taken seriously the responsibility and the challenge to make a substantial contribution to bibliographic control.

Some author biographies have lengthy bibliographies. The biographies listed in the Appendices give not only the published volumes of the authors but also the many publications which they wrote for books by other writers, for collections, and for magazines, journals, and newspapers. Two biographies containing very long lists of publications are

Lewis Leary's <u>That Rascal Freneau</u> (1941) and William Bartlett's <u>Jones Very</u> (1942).[20] Both biographers spent many
hours searching old newspapers for the writings of these authors.

To review the history of author bibliography is to recall the many teachers, librarians, book dealers, book collectors, and others who compiled the bibliographies that are
now used by students of American literature all over the
world. To remember the bibliographers is to think of such
names as Thomas F. Currier, Donald C. Gallup, William
White, and Matthew Bruccoli for the quantity and quality of
their work. Currier's bibliographies of Whittier and Holmes
and Gallup's bibliographies of Eliot and Pound are among the
truly excellent author bibliographies in American literature.[21]
Perhaps of all the bibliographers William White has compiled
the greatest number of single-author bibliographies. He began many years ago and has not stopped his bibliographic
labors. With reference to him and his many bibliographies
one can say--as librarians like to say as they walk by the
shelves of bibliographies in libraries--"there is no end to
bibliography." Matthew Bruccoli has done some very fine
bibliographic work and he is helping others to do the same.
As editor of both the Pittsburgh Series in Bibliography and
the series from Gale Research Company he reviews the work
of other bibliographers to insure high standards and consis-
tent format.

Much has been accomplished, and more remains to be
done before all, or even most, of the belles lettres of the
United States is listed with accurate bibliographic information.
Very lengthy lists of American short stories, plays, and
poems are needed. Selective national and regional lists are
needed for the genres with long, descriptive, and critical
annotations. Some of the state biobibliographies which have
been done need to be updated, and new ones for other states
need to be compiled. Many states need literary histories,
separate fiction and play lists, and bibliographies of poetry.
They need comprehensive literary anthologies with notes
about the selections and the authors. Many states also need
separate anthologies carefully edited for fiction, poetry, plays,
and humor. Both historical and subject anthologies would be
useful. More needs to be known about the subject content of
the creative literature of each state before definitive state
histories can be written. Bibliographic essays about the
literature of a state during particular periods would be helpful to the literary and cultural historian, especially if the

essays relate the literature to the reading of books by the people of the state.

Local bibliography is very much an area that needs to be developed. The big states need bibliographies which list the literature about particular regions. Cities and counties also should compile lists of local color writings. All the larger cities of the country should have literary histories that focus on the special contribution of the writings to the cultural and social life of the people. The histories should have separate lists of fiction arranged by author, title, and subject. Anthologies arranged by historical period and by subject would also have value. Anthologies which include poetry from local newspapers would preserve some of the better poems for posterity. The anthologies might even reveal a poet of some distinction.

Much also needs to be done for humor. A long bibliography should be compiled listing writings from the colonial period to the present. It should contain regional lists and a fairly detailed subject index. A separate biographical dictionary would also be useful. More anthologies are needed for regions and states. Besides the selections these anthologies should have bibliographies and brief biographical information about the authors.

Many of the author bibliographies that have been done need to be checked for errors and lacunae, and revised. The compilers often confess, in their introductions and prefaces, to incompleteness and probable errors. Their indexes could also be improved by including entries for all belles lettres and subject entries for all other writings. For all authors of belles lettres separate genre lists should follow the chronological list of publications. A separate list of poems, for example, would facilitate the use of the bibliography for the student who is studying only an author's poems and not his other writings. For narrative poems, short stories, fiction, and plays a brief synopsis would also be useful.

If the years 1920 through 1975 were very fruitful for American bibliography, the likelihood is that an even greater period will follow. The computer and new printing methods will enable scholars to do far more than those early pioneers of bibliography who did everything themselves but set their own type. The student of American literature can expect to see more bibliographies in the future and more of a size approaching the 13-volume Dictionary Catalog of the Harris Collection of American Poetry and Plays (1972) from Brown University. For those bibliographies the various regional union catalogs of the United States will be tapped for titles that were never known to exist except by a few people. The future bibliographies of belles lettres will very probably open up fresh areas of research for young scholars who want to study new authors and subjects. The new bibliographies may even be a subject of study for some librarian and student of literature, as this essay is for a number of bibliographies of the past.

CHAPTER NOTES

CHAPTER 1

[1]Samuel Kettell, ed., Specimens of American Poetry with Critical and Biographical Notices (3 vols. Boston: S. G. Goodrich, 1829); John Keese, ed., The Poets of America (2 vols. N. Y.: Samuel Colman, 1840-42); Rufus W. Griswold, Poets and Poetry of America With an Historical Introduction (Phila.: Carey and Hart, 1842); Female Poets of America (Phila.: Carey and Hart, 1849).

[2]Leon and Brother, Catalog of First Editions of American Authors (N. Y.: Leon and Brother, 1885); Beverly Chew, Longfellow Collectors' Handbook; A Bibliography of First Editions (N. Y.: William Evarts Benjamin, 1885).

[3]Oscar Wegelin, Early American Fiction 1774-1830... (Stamford, Conn.: The Compiler, 1902); 2d ed. (1913); Early American Plays 1714-1830. Publications of the Dunlap Society, new series, no. 10 (N. Y.: Dunlap Society, 1900); 2d ed. (N. Y.: Literary Collector Press, 1905); Early American Poetry... (2 vols. N. Y.: the Compiler, 1903-07).

[4]Nina E. Browne, Bibliography of Nathaniel Hawthorne (Boston: Houghton Mifflin, 1905); George W. Cook, A Bibliography of James Russell Lowell (Boston: Houghton Mifflin, 1906); Le Roy Phillips, A Bibliography of the Writings of Henry James (Boston: Houghton Mifflin, 1906); George B. Ives, A Bibliography of Oliver Wendell Holmes (Boston: Houghton Mifflin, 1907); George W. Cooke, Bibliography of Ralph Waldo Emerson (Boston: Houghton, 1908); Francis H. Allen, A Bibliography of Henry David Thoreau (Boston: Houghton Mifflin, 1908).

[5]Cambridge History of American Literature, ed. by William P. Trent and others (4 vols. N. Y.: Putnam, 1917-21): hereafter referred to as the CHAL.

[6]Bradford M. Fullerton, Selective Bibliography of American Literature, 1775-1900 (N.Y.: W. F. Payson, 1932).

[7]Merle Johnson, ed., American First Editions; Bibliographical Checklists of the Works of One Hundred and Five American Authors (N.Y.: Bowker, 1929).

[8]Stephen H. Wakeman, The Stephen H. Wakeman Collection of Books of 19th Century American Writers (N.Y.: American Art Association, 1924).

[9]John M. Manly and Edith Rickert, Contemporary American Literature (N.Y.: Harcourt, Brace, 1922).

[10]John M. Manly and Edith Rickert, Contemporary American Literature..., introduction and revision by Fred B. Millett (N.Y.: Harcourt, Brace, 1929).

[11]William Rose Benét and Norman H. Pearson, eds., The Oxford Anthology of American Literature (N.Y.: Oxford Univ. Press, 1938).

[12]The American Yearbook; A Record of Events and Progress (N.Y.: American Yearbook Corp., 1910-50).

[13]Jonathan Nield, A Guide to the Best Historical Novels and Tales, 5th ed. (N.Y.: Macmillan, 1929).

[14]N. J. Thiessen, An Annotated Bibliography of American Historical Fiction (Emporia: Kansas State Teachers College, 1938); Rebecca W. Smith, "Of the Chief Novels and Short Stories by American Authors Dealing with the Civil War and Its Effects," Bulletin of Bibliography 16 (1939), 193-94; 17 (1940), 10-12, 33-35, 53-55, 72-75.

[15]Lisle A. Rose, "A Descriptive Catalog of Economic and Politico-Economic Fiction in the U.S. 1902-1909" (Ph.D. dissertation, Univ. of Chicago, 1935).

[16]Robert L. Shurter, "The Utopian Novel in America 1865-1900" (Ph.D. dissertation, Western Reserve Univ., 1936).

[17]Claude R. Flory, "Economic Criticism in American Fiction 1792 to 1900" (Ph.D. dissertation, Univ. of Pennsylvania, 1935).

[18]Dorothy E. Wolfe, "An Annotated Bibliography of the

Short Story" (M.S. thesis, Kansas State Teachers College, 1932).

[19]The O. Henry Memorial Award Prize Stories (Garden City, N.Y.: Doubleday, Page, 1920 to date); Best Short Stories of [year] and the Yearbook of the American Short Story (Boston: Houghton Mifflin, 1915 to date).

[20]Best Short Stories of 1915 (Boston: Small, Maynard, 1916), p. 7-8.

[21]Best Short Stories of 1921 (Boston: Small, Maynard, 1922), p. xv-xvi.

[22]Oscar Wegelin, Early American Poetry..., 2d ed. (N.Y.: Peter Smith, 1930); Ola E. Winslow, American Broadside Verse from Imprints of the 17th and 18th Centuries (New Haven, Conn.: Yale Univ. Press, 1930).

[23]Roger E. Stoddard, "Oscar Wegelin, Pioneer Bibliographer of American Literature," Papers of the Bibliographical Society of America 56 (1962), 241.

[24]The Biographical Dictionary of Contemporary Poets; The Who's Who of American Poets (N.Y.: Avon House, 1938).

[25]William S. Braithwaite, Anthology of Magazine Verse (N.Y.: Gomme, 1913-29).

[26]New Yorker, New Yorker Book of Verse; An Anthology of Poems First Published in the New Yorker 1925-1935 (N.Y.: Harcourt, Brace, 1935).

[27]Davis's Anthology of Newspaper Verse, ed. by Athie S. Davis (N.Y.: Harrison, 1918-?).

[28]Edith Warren, ed., Important American Poets (N.Y.: Valiant House, 1938).

[29]Thomas Del Vecchio, ed., Contemporary American Men Poets (N.Y.: Henry Harrison, 1937); Tooni Gordi, ed., Contemporary American Women Poets (N.Y.: Henry Harrison, 1936).

[30]Burton E. Stevenson, ed., Poems of American History, rev. ed. (Boston: Houghton Mifflin, 1936).

[31]Arthur H. Quinn, A History of the American Drama from the Beginning to the Civil War (New York: Harper, 1923); A History of the American Drama from the Civil War to the Present Day (2 vols. N. Y.: Harper, 1927); A History of American Drama from the Civil War to the Present Day, rev. ed. (N. Y.: F. S. Crofts, 1936).

[32]Frank P. Hill, American Plays Printed 1714-1830; A Bibliographical Record (Palo Alto, Calif.: Stanford Univ. Press, 1934).

[33]Margaret G. Mayorga, A Short History of the American Drama; Commentaries on Plays Prior to 1920 (N. Y.: Dodd, Mead, 1932); Allan G. Halline, ed., American Plays (N. Y.: American Book Co., 1935).

[34]Best Plays Series (N. Y.: Dodd, Mead, 1919 to date).

[35]The Best Plays of 1909-1919 and the Yearbook of the Drama of America, ed. by Burns Mantle and Garrison P. Sherwood (N. Y.: Dodd, Mead, 1933).

[36]Yearbook of Short Plays, ed. by Claude M. Wise and Lee O. Snook, first to sixth series (Evanston, Ill.: Row, Peterson, 1931-40); Best One-Act Plays 1937-1960 (N. Y.: Dodd, Mead, 1938-61); One-Act Plays for Stage and Study, first to ninth series (N. Y.: Samuel French, 1925-38).

[37]Mabel Major et al., Southwest Heritage; A Literary History with a Bibliography (Albuquerque: Univ. of New Mexico, 1938).

[38]Rowena Longmire, "Dictionary Catalog of the Short Stories of Arkansas, Missouri, and Iowa from 1869 to 1900" (Ph.D. dissertation, Univ. of Chicago, 1932).

[39]Carl B. Spotts, "The Development of Fiction on the Missouri Frontier," Missouri Historical Review 28 (1934), 195-205, 275-86; 29 (1934-35), 17-26, 100-08, 186-94, 279-94.

[40]Carl B. Spotts, "The Development of Fiction on the Missouri Frontier" (Ph.D. dissertation, Penn State Univ., 1934).

[41]Levette J. Davidson, "Early Fiction of the Rocky Mountain Region," Colorado Magazine 10 (1933), 161-72.

[42]Hilton R. Greer, ed., Best Short Stories from the Southwest (Dallas, Texas: Southwest Press, 1928; 2d series, 1931).

[43]B. S. Ivey, ed., Pirate Gold; An Anthology of Southwestern Verse 1898-1928 (Austin, Texas: Morgan Printing Co., 1928); Benjamin Botkin, ed., The Southwest Scene; An Anthology of Regional Verse (Oklahoma City: The Economy Co., 1931).

[44]Janet Agnew, "A Southern Bibliography: Fiction 1929-1938," Louisiana State University Bulletin, n. s. 30, no. 7, Library School Bibliography Series, no. 1 (Baton Rouge: Louisiana State Univ. Press, 1939); William Y. Elliott, "Local Color in Southern Literature: A Bibliography" (M. A. thesis, Univ. of Alabama, 1929).

[45]Edd W. Parks, ed., Southern Poets; Representative Selections, with Introduction, Bibliography, and Notes (N. Y.: American Book Co., 1936).

[46]Bertha S. Hart, Introduction to Georgia Writers (Macon, Ga.: J. W. Burke, 1929).

[47]Mary H. Marable and Elaine Boylan, A Handbook of Oklahoma Writers (Norman: Univ. of Oklahoma Press, 1939).

[48]Edgar J. Hinkel, ed., Bibliography of Fiction, Poetry, Drama. Produced on a WPA Project. Sponsored by the Alameda County Library, Oakland, Calif. (Oakland: 1938).

[49]Mary E. Hazeltine, One Hundred Years of Wisconsin Authorship, 1836-1937; A Contribution to a Bibliography of Books by Wisconsin Authors (Madison: Wisconsin Library Association, 1937).

[50]Madge K. Goodrich, A Bibliography of Michigan Authors (Richmond, Va., Richmond Press, 1928).

[51]Alexander N. DeMenil, "A Century of Missouri Literature," Missouri Historical Review 15 (October 1920), 74-125.

[52]"North Carolina Bibliography," North Carolina Historical Review, April issue, beginning 1935.

[53]Mary G. Boyer, Arizona in Literature (Glendale,

Calif.: Arthur H. Clark, 1935).

[54]Bernice M. Foster, Michigan Novelists (Ann Arbor: George Wahr, 1928).

[55]Lizzie C. McVoy and Ruth B. Campbell, A Bibliography of Fiction by Louisianians and on Louisiana Subjects, Louisiana State University Studies, no. 18 (Baton Rouge: Louisiana State Univ. Press, 1935).

[56]Worthington C. Ford, Broadsides, Ballads, etc., Printed in Massachusetts 1639-1800 (Boston: Massachusetts Historical Society, 1922).

[57]Gertrude F. Jacobi, "Minor Poets of South Carolina" (M.A. thesis, Univ. of Florida, 1937); Venice Wallenberg, "A Bibliography of Texas Poetry" (M.A. thesis, Texas Christian Univ., 1927).

[58]Minnie M. Brashear, "Missouri Verse and Verse Writers," Missouri Historical Review 18 (1924), 315-44; 19 (1924), 36-93.

[59]Armistead C. Gordon, Virginia Writers of Fugitive Verse (N.Y.: James T. White, 1923).

[60]Walter J. Coates, Favorite Vermont Poets, series 1-4 (North Montpelier, Vt.: 1928-31).

[61]Harrison R. Merrill and Elsie T. Brandley, eds., Utah Sings: An Anthology of Contemporary Verse (3 vols. Provo: Utah Academy of Sciences, Arts and Letters, 1934-42).

[62]Philip Graham, ed., Early Texas Verse (1835-1850) Collected from the Original Newspapers (Austin, Texas: Steck Co., 1936); Poetry Society of Texas, Book of the Year (Dallas, Texas: The Society, 1925); Pearle M. Stevens, ed. Greater Texas Anthology of Verse with Poets of the Southwest (San Antonio, Texas: Naylor, 1939).

[63]Florida Poets; An Anthology of Contemporary Verse (Laramore, N.Y.: Henry Harrison, 1931); Georgia Poets; An Anthology of 33 Contemporaries (N.Y.: Harrison, 1932); Michigan Poets; An Anthology of 36 Contemporaries (N.Y.: Henry Harrison, 1936).

[64]Henry Harrison, ed., California Poets: An Anthology of 244 Contemporaries (N.Y.: Henry Harrison, 1932).

[65]Poetry Society of Georgia, Prize Poems, Poetry Society of Georgia 1924-1925 (Savannah: Poetry Society of Georgia, 1925).

[66]Poetry Society of Georgia, 25th Anniversary 1923-1948 (Athens: Univ. of Georgia, 1949).

[67]Poetry Society of Oklahoma, State Anthology (Oklahoma City: Times-Journal Pub. Co., 1936).

[68]Battle Creek Scribblers' Club, Battle Creek Writers, Poems and Prose (Battle Creek, Mich.: 1927); Charles M. Elam, ed., Cincinnati Poetry of the Nineteenth Century (Cincinnati: Open Sesame Press, 1928); Pliny L. Harwood, eds., The Poets of New London: An Anthology (New London, Conn.: 1933); Peoria Book of Verse (Peoria, Ill.: Published for the Peoria Allied English Interests by the Manual Arts Press, 1922); Latrobe Weston, Baltimore in Verse and Prose (Baltimore: H. G. Roebuck, 1936); National League of American Pen Women, N.Y.C. Branch, Anthology of Modern Poetry by Members of the League (N.Y.: Hogan-Paulus Corp., 1926); National League of American Pen Women, San Diego Branch, Wind in the Palms; Anthology of San Diego Verse, 1932 (San Diego, Calif.: Press of the City Print Co., 1932).

[69]C. H. Hanford, ed., Seattle and Environs 1852-1924 (3 vols. Chicago: Pioneer Historical Pub. Co., 1924).

[70]Lester J. Cappon, Bibliography of Virginia History Since 1865 (Charlottesville, Va.: The Institute for Research in the Social Sciences, University of Virginia, 1930).

[71]Stanley T. Williams, "The Literature of Connecticut," History of Connecticut in Monographic Form, ed. by Norris G. Osborn (N.Y.: States History Co., 1925), vol. 2, p. 483-537.

[72]Irving S. Kull, ed., New Jersey: A History (4 vols. N.Y.: American Historical Society, 1930).

[73]Edwin C. Torrey, "Early Poets of South Dakota," Early Days in Dakota (Minneapolis: Farnham Printing and Stationery Co., 1925), p. 65-74.

[74]Walter Blair, Native American Humor (1800-1900) (N.Y.: American Book Co., 1937).

[75]Howard S. Mott, Jr., Three Hundred Years of American Humor (1637-1936) (N. Y.: the Author, 1937).

[76]Franklin J. Meine, Tall Tales of the Southwest; An Anthology of Southern and Southwestern Humor 1830-1860 (N. Y.: Knopf, 1930); Arthur P. Hudson, ed., Humor of the Old Deep South (N. Y.: Macmillan, 1936).

[77]Oscar Wegelin, A Bibliography of the Separate Writings of John Esten Cooke, Heartman's Historical Series, no. 43 (Metuchen, N. J.: C. F. Heartman, 1925); John W. Robertson, Bibliography of the Writings of Edgar Allan Poe (San Francisco: Grabhorn Press, 1934).

[78]Thomas F. Currier, Bibliography of John Greenleaf Whittier (Cambridge, Mass.: Harvard Univ. Press, 1937).

[79]Samuel T. Pickard, Life and Letters of Whittier (Boston: Houghton Mifflin, 1894), vol. 1, p. 68-70.

[80]Merle D. Johnson, A Bibliography of the Work of Mark Twain, Samuel Langhorne Clemens, rev. ed. (N. Y.: Harper, 1935); Robert E. Spiller and Philip C. Blackburn, A Descriptive Bibliography of James Fenimore Cooper (N. Y.: R. R. Bowker, 1934).

[81]Alfred P. Lee, A Bibliography of Christopher Morley (Garden City, N. Y.: Doubleday, Doran, 1935).

[82]Barton Currie, Booth Tarkington: A Bibliography (Garden City, N. Y.: Doubleday, Doran, 1932).

[83]Sydney S. Alberts, A Bibliography of the Works of Robinson Jeffers (N. Y.: Random House, 1933).

[84]Ralph Sanborn and Barrett H. Clark, A Bibliography of the Works of Eugene O'Neill (N. Y.: Random House, 1931).

[85]Lawson M. Melish, A Bibliography of the Collected Writings of Edith Wharton (N. Y.: Brick Row Book Shop, 1927).

[86]Alfred L. Hampson, Emily Dickinson: A Bibliography (Northampton, Mass.: Hampshire Bookshop, 1930).

[87]Edward D. MacDonald, A Bibliography of the Writings of Theodore Dreiser (Phila: Centaur Book Shop, 1928).

[88]Guy Holt, A Bibliography of the Writings of James Branch Cabell (Phila.: Centaur Book Shop, 1924); Vincent Starrett, Stephen Crane: A Bibliography (Phila.: Centaur Book Shop, 1923); Herbert L. Swire, A Bibliography of the Works of Joseph Hergesheimer (Phila.: Centaur Book Shop, 1922).

[89]Isidore R. Brussel, A Bibliography of the Writings of James Branch Cabell: A Revised Bibliography (Phila.: Centaur Book Shop, 1932).

[90]Amos L. Herold, James Kirke Paulding: Versatile American (N.Y.: Columbia Univ. Press, 1926).

[91]Edward S. Bradley, George Henry Boker: Poet and Patriot (Phila.: Univ. of Pennsylvania Press, 1927).

[92]Homer F. Barnes, Charles Fenno Hoffman (N.Y.: Columbia Univ. Press, 1930).

[93]Carl Van Doren, Sinclair Lewis: A Biographical Sketch with a Bibliography by Harvey Taylor (N.Y.: Doubleday, Doran, 1933).

CHAPTER 2

[1]Literary History of the United States, ed. by Robert E. Spiller and others. Bibliography, ed. by Thomas H. Johnson (N.Y.: Macmillan, 1948): hereafter referred to as the LHUS Bibliography; Jacob Blanck, Bibliography of American Literature Compiled ... for the Bibliographical Society of America (New Haven: Yale Univ. Press, 1955-): hereafter referred to as the BAL.

[2]Who's Who in America 1974-75, vol. 1, p. 1605.

[3]Information on the scope of the BAL is taken from its Preface.

[4]Most of the acknowledgments in BAL are in vol. 4, p. xiii-xiv and vol. 5, p. xiii-xiv.

[5]William J. Burke and Will D. Howe, American Authors and Books, 1640-1940 (N.Y.: Gramercy Pub. Co.,

1943); James D. Hart, Oxford Companion to American Litera-
ture (N. Y.: Oxford Univ. Press, 1941); Fred B. Millett,
Contemporary American Authors; A Critical Survey and 219
Bio-Bibliographies (N. Y.: Harcourt, Brace, 1940).

[6]Americana Annual (N. Y.: Americana Corp., 1923-).

[7]Lyle H. Wright, American Fiction 1774-1850; A Contribution Toward a Bibliography, rev. ed. (San Marino,
Calif.: 1948).

[8]Lyle H. Wright, American Fiction 1851-1875 (San
Marino, Calif.: Huntington Library, 1957).

[9]Newberry Library, Chicago, American Novels with
an American Setting Printed Before 1880; A Checklist of
Books in the Library, Aug. 1941 (Chicago, 1941); Otis W.
Coan and Richard G. Lillard, America in Fiction (Palo Alto,
Calif.: Stanford Univ. Press, 1941).

[10]Arthur T. Dickinson, American Historical Fiction
(N. Y.: Scarecrow Press, 1958).

[11]Leisy, Ernest E., The American Historical Novel
(Norman: Univ. of Oklahoma Press, 1950); Robert A. Lively,
Fiction Fights the Civil War; An Unfinished Chapter in the
Literary History of the American People (Chapel Hill: Univ.
of North Carolina Press, 1957); Joseph J. Waldmeir, "Ideo-
logical Aspects of the American Novels of World War II"
(Ph. D. dissertation, Michigan State Univ., 1959).

[12]William B. Dickens, "A Guide to the American Political Novel 1865-1910" (Ph. D. dissertation, Univ. of Michigan, 1954).

[13]Walter F. Taylor, The Economic Novel in America
(Chapel Hill: Univ. of North Carolina Press, 1942).

[14]Lisle A. Rose, "A Bibliographic Survey of Economic
and Political Writings 1865-1900," American Literature 15
(1944), 381-410.

[15]Herbert R. Brown, The Sentimental Novel in America 1789-1860 (Durham, N. C.: Duke Univ. Press, 1940).

[16]New Yorker, Short Stories from the New Yorker
(N. Y.: Simon & Schuster, 1940); New Yorker, 55 Short

Stories from the New Yorker (N. Y.: Simon & Schuster, 1949).

[17]F. Van Wyck Mason, ed., The Fighting American; A War Chest of Stories of American Soldiers from the French and Indian Wars Through the First World War (N. Y.: Reynal and Hitchcock, 1943); Charles A. Fenton, ed., The Best Short Stories of World War II; An American Anthology (N. Y.: Viking Press, 1957).

[18]Milton H. Sugarman, "A Bibliography of a Collection of Anonymous Poetical Pamphlets of the 18th Century in the Library of the University of Cincinnati" (Ph. D. dissertation, Univ. of Cincinnati, 1953).

[19]Horace Gregory and Marya Zaturenska, A History of American Poetry 1900-1940 (N. Y.: Harcourt, Brace, 1942).

[20]U. S. Library of Congress, General Reference and Bibliography Division, Sixty American Poets, 1896-1944; Selected with Preface and Critical Notes by Allen Tate; A Preliminary Checklist by Frances Cheney (Washington, D. C.: 1945).

[21]U. S. Library of Congress, General Reference and Bibliography Division, Sixty American Poets 1896-1944; Selected with Preface and Notes by Allen Tate, rev. by Kenton Kilmer (Washington, D. C., 1954).

[22]Arthur H. Quinn, A History of the American Drama from the Beginning to the Civil War, 2d ed. (N. Y.: Appleton-Century-Crofts, 1951).

[23]University of Pennsylvania Library, Checklist of American Drama Published in the English Colonies of North America and the United States Through 1865 in the Possession of the Library, University of Pennsylvania, Compiled by Albert Von Chorba, Jr. (Phila.: 1951).

[24]Joseph A. Weingarten, Modern American Playwrights: A Bibliography (N. Y.: 1946).

[25]Felix Sper, From Native Roots; A Panorama of Our Regional Drama (Caldwell, Idaho: Caxton Printers, 1948).

[26]Mary L. Andrews, "Modern Poetic Drama in America, 1900-1924" (Ph. D. dissertation, New York Univ., 1943);

Josef A. Elfenbein, "American Drama 1782-1812 as an Index
to Socio-Political Thought" (Ph. D. dissertation, New York
Univ., 1951); Phyllis M. Ferguson, "Women Dramatists in
the American Theatre 1901-1940" (Ph. D. dissertation, Univ.
of Pittsburgh, 1957); Caspar H. Nannes, "Politics in the
American Drama as Revealed by Plays Produced on the New
York Stage 1890-1945" (Ph. D. dissertation, Univ. of Pennsylvania, 1949); John D. Reardon, "Verse Drama in America
from 1765 to the Civil War" (Ph. D. dissertation, Univ. of
Kansas, 1958).

27Phyllis M. Ferguson, "Women Dramatists in the
American Theatre 1901-1940," Dissertation Abstracts 18
(1958), 231.

28Best American Plays (N. Y.: Crown Publishers,
1939-).

29The Best Plays of 1899-1909 and the Yearbook of
the American Drama, ed. by Burns Mantle and Garrison P.
Sherwood (N. Y.: Dodd, Mead, 1944).

30Jay B. Hubbell, The South in American Literature
1607-1900 (Durham, N. C.: Duke Univ. Press, 1954); Richard
B. Harwell, Confederate Belles-Lettres; A Bibliography and
a Finding List of Fiction, Poetry, Drama, Songsters, and
Miscellaneous Literature Published in the Confederate States
of America (Hattiesburg, Miss.: Book Farm, 1941); Jesse L.
Rader, South of Forty from the Mississippi to the Rio Grande;
A Bibliography (Norman: Univ. of Oklahoma Press, 1947).

31Kenneth Kurtz, Literature of the American Southwest; A Selective Bibliography (Los Angeles: Occidental College, 1956).

32Ray B. West, Writing in the Rocky Mountains with
a Bibliography by Nellie Cliff (Lincoln: Univ. of Nebraska
Press, 1947).

33David J. Harkness, "The Southwest and West Coast
in Literature," Univ. of Tennessee Newsletter 33 (Oct. 1954),
1-55.

34John S. Hartin, "The Southeastern United States in
the Novel Through 1950; A Bibliographic Review" (Ph. D.
dissertation, Univ. of Michigan, 1957).

[35]Janet Agnew, A Southern Bibliography: Historical Fiction 1929-1938, Louisiana State University Bulletin n. s. 32, no. 8, Library School Bibliography Series, no. 2 (Baton Rouge: Louisiana State Univ. Press, 1940).

[36]Sheldon Van Auken, "The Southern Historical Novel in the Early Twentieth Century," Journal of Southern History 14 (1948), 157-91.

[37]John T. Flanagan, "The Middle Western Historical Novel," Journal of the Illinois State Historical Society 37 (March 1944), 7-47.

[38]Nelle Dooley, "Sectionalism and Local Color in the Short Stories of the Plains States, 1870-1938" (Master's thesis, Fort Hays Kansas State College, 1940).

[39]Lawana J. Shaul, "Treatment of the West in Selected Magazine Fiction, 1870-1900; An Annotated Bibliography" (M.A. thesis, Univ. of Wyoming, 1954).

[40]Helen Hitt, "History in Pacific Northwest Novels Written Since 1920," Oregon Historical Quarterly 51 (Sept. 1950), 180-206; Harry H. Jones, "Fiction of the Rocky Mountain Mining Area," Univ. of Wyoming Publications 20, no. 1 (1956), 124-29.

[41]Harold S. Jantz, "Bibliography of Early New England Verse," Procs. of the American Antiquarian Society, n. s. 53 (1943), 391-508.

[42]Harold S. Jantz, "Unrecorded Verse Broadsides of Seventeenth Century New England," Papers of the Bibliographical Society of America 39 (First Quarter 1945), 1-19.

[43]Janet M. Agnew, A Southern Bibliography: Poetry 1929-1938. Louisiana State University Bulletin n. s. 32, no. 11, Library School Bibliography Series, no. 3 (Baton Rouge, 1940).

[44]Earl L. Rudolph. Confederate Broadside Verse; A Bibliography and Finding List of Confederate Broadside Ballads and Songs (New Braunfels, Texas: Book Farm, 1950).

[45]Mabel Major and Thomas M. Pearce, eds., Signature of the Sun; Southwest Verse 1900-1950 (Albuquerque: Univ. of New Mexico Press, 1950).

[46]Robert J. Turnbull, Bibliography of South Carolina 1563-1950 (5 vols. Charlottesville: Univ. of Virginia Press, 1956).

[47]Mary L. Thornton, A Bibliography of North Carolina 1589-1956 (Chapel Hill: Univ. of North Carolina Press, 1958).

[48]Barbara W. Greene, "Resources in Louisiana Literature; Affective Writers" (M.A. thesis, Southwestern Louisiana Institute, 1959).

[49]Vito J. Brenni, West Virginia Authors: A Biobibliography (Morgantown: W. Va. Library Assoc., 1957); John W. Bonner, "Bibliography of Georgia Authors," Georgia Review, winter issue, beginning 1950.

[50]Donald E. Thompson, Indiana Authors and Their Books 1917-1966 (Crawfordsville, Ind.: Wabash College, 1974), p. 28.

[51]Lancaster Pollard, "A Checklist of Washington Authors," Pacific Northwest Quarterly 31 (1940), 3-96.

[52]Lancaster Pollard, "A Checklist of Washington Authors," Pacific Northwest Quarterly 35 (1944), 233-66.

[53]Rudolf Kirk and Clara M. Kirk, Authors of New Jersey: A Checklist (Trenton: Division of the State Library, Archives and History, 1955).

[54]"Maryland Bibliography," Maryland Historical Magazine, March issue of each year, beginning 1952.

[55]Elijah L. Jacobs and Forrest E. Wolverton, Missouri Writers; A Literary History of Missouri, 1780-1955 (St. Louis: State Pub. Co., 1955).

[56]Horace G. Richards, One Hundred South Jersey Novels; A Bibliography of Fiction with a Southern New Jersey Setting (Trenton: New Jersey Folklore Society, 1947); Augustus H. Able, "Fiction as a Mirror of Delaware Life," Delaware History 3 (1948), 37-53.

[57]Lawrence S. Thompson and Algernon D. Thompson, The Kentucky Novel (Lexington: Univ. of Kentucky Press, 1953).

[58]Hensley C. Woodbridge, "The Kentucky Novel, 1951-5," Kentucky Historical Society Review 54 (April 1956), 134-36; "The Kentucky Novel, 1956-57," Kentucky Historical Society Review 56 (April 1958), 156-64.

[59]William Powell, ed., North Carolina Fiction 1734-1957 (Chapel Hill: Univ. of North Carolina Library, 1958).

[60]Mary O. McRory. Florida in Fiction: A Bibliography (Tallahassee, Fla.: State Library, 1958).

[61]Gertrude G. Odum, "Georgia Fiction: 1926-1950," Georgia Review 5 (Summer 1951), 244-57.

[62]Alice L. Pearson, "The Upper Peninsula in Fictional Literature," Michigan History 24 (1940), 329-38.

[63]Alice L. Pearson, "The Upper Peninsula of Michigan in Literature" (M.A. thesis, Univ. of Colo., 1939).

[64]Lucille B. Emch, "Ohio in Short Stories 1824-1839," Ohio Archeological and Historical Quarterly 53 (July-Sept. 1944), 209-50.

[65]John T. Frederick, "The Farm in Iowa Fiction," Palimpsest 32 (Mar. 1951), 121-52; "Town and City in Iowa Literature," Palimpsest 35 (Feb. 1954), 49-96; "Early Iowa in Fiction," Palimpsest 36 (Oct. 1955), 389-420.

[66]Frederick, "The Farm in Iowa Fiction," p. 145-46.

[67]Harvey K. Jacobson, "A Study of Novels about North Dakota" (Master's thesis, Univ. of North Dakota, 1956).

[68]Hudson Strode, ed., Spring Harvest; A Collection of Stories from Alabama (N.Y.: Knopf, 1944); Hollis S. Summers, ed., Kentucky Story; A Collection of Short Stories (Lexington: Univ. of Kentucky Press, 1954); William Peery, ed., 21 Texas Short Stories (Austin: Univ. of Texas Press, 1954); Richard G. Walser, ed., North Carolina in the Short Story (Chapel Hill: Univ. of North Carolina Press, 1948).

[69]Katharine M. Jones and Mary V. Schlaefer, South Carolina in the Short Story (Columbia: Univ. of South Carolina Press, 1952); Lizzie C. McVoy, ed., Louisiana in the Short Story, Louisiana State Univ. Studies, no. 41 (Baton Rouge: Louisiana State Univ. Press, 1940).

[70]Chicago Public Library Omnibus Project, Bibliography of Illinois Poets Since 1900 (Chicago: 1942).

[71]Richard G. Walser, ed., North Carolina Poetry (Richmond: Garrett and Massie, 1941; rev. ed., 1951).

[72]Poetry Society of Colorado, Silver Souvenir 1921-1946 (Denver: Sage Books, 1946).

[73]Adeline M. Jenney, ed., Prairie Poets; An Anthology of Verse of the South Dakota Poetry Society 1927-1949 (Minneapolis: Lund Press, 1949).

[74]Marshall Wingfield, Literary Memphis; A Survey of Its Writers and Writings (Memphis: West Tennessee Historical Society, 1942).

[75]Grace Ross and Mabel Kuykendall, eds., Poetry Out Where the West Begins; A Collection of Poems by Fort Worth Authors (Dallas: Kaleidograph Press, 1949).

[76]Gertrude Cone, A Selective Bibliography of Publications on the Champlain Valley (Plattsburg? N. Y.: 1959).

[77]Victor E. Lewis, ed., Poets and Poetry of Wyoming Valley [Pa.]; A Collection of Selected Contemporary Verse, Rhymes, and Poems (Wilkes Barre, Pa.: Llewellyn Bros., 1940); A Little Book of Somerset County [Pa.] Verse (Somerset, 1945).

[78]A Century of Benton County Poetry (Roseburg, Oregon: Poetry Clinic, 1957).

[79]Augustus H. Able, "Delaware Literature," Delaware: A History of the First State, ed. by Henry C. Reed (N. Y.: Lewis Historical Pub. Co., 1947), vol. 2, p. 935-66; Harold G. Merriam, "Montana Writing," A History of Montana, by Merrill G. Burlingame and K. Ross Toole (N. Y.: Lewis Historical Pub. Co., 1957), vol. 2, p. 265-90; Harlan Hatcher, "Ohio in the Literature of the Twentieth Century," The History of the State of Ohio, ed. by Carl F. Wittke (Columbus: Ohio State Archeological and Historical Society, 1942), vol. 6, p. 267-93.

[80]Arthur C. Bining et al., Writings on Pennsylvania History: A Bibliography (Harrisburg: Pennsylvania Historical and Museum Commission, 1946); J. Winston Coleman, A

Bibliography of Kentucky History (Lexington: Univ. of Kentucky Press, 1949); Leroy Schlinkert, Subject Bibliography of Wisconsin History (Madison: State Historical Society of Wisconsin, 1947).

[81] Federal Writers' Program, Oklahoma; A Guide to the Sooner State (Norman: Univ. of Oklahoma Press, 1941).

[82] Elwyn B. White and Katharine S. White, eds., A Subtreasury of American Humor (N.Y.: Coward-McCann, 1941).

[83] Edwin Seaver, ed., Pageant of American Humor (Cleveland: World, 1948).

[84] Bennett Cerf, ed., An Encyclopedia of Modern American Humor (Garden City, N.Y.: Hanover House, 1954).

[85] Victor L. Chittick, ed., Ring-Tailed Roarers; Tall Tales of the American Frontier 1830-1860 (Caldwell, Idaho: Caxton Printers, 1941).

[86] Jack Conroy, ed., Midland Humor (N.Y.: Current Books, 1947).

[87] Thomas J. Holmes, Cotton Mather: A Bibliography of His Works (3 vols. Cambridge, Mass.: Harvard Univ. Press, 1940).

[88] Thomas F. Currier, A Bibliography of Oliver Wendell Holmes, ed. by Eleanor M. Tilton (N.Y.: New York Univ. Press, 1953).

[89] Thomas F. Currier, Bibliography of John Greenleaf Whittier (Cambridge: Harvard Univ. Press, 1937).

[90] Anthony J. Russo and Dorothy R. Russo, A Bibliography of James Whitcomb Riley (Indianapolis: Indiana Historical Society, 1944); Dorothy R. Russo, A Bibliography of George Ade, 1866-1944 (Indianapolis: Indiana Historical Society, 1947); Dorothy R. Russo and Thelma L. Sullivan, A Bibliography of Booth Tarkington 1869-1946 (Indianapolis: Indiana Historical Society, 1949); Dorothy R. Russo and Thelma L. Sullivan, Bibliographic Studies of Seven Authors of Crawfordsville, Indiana: Lew and Susan Wallace, Maurice and Will Thompson, Mary Hannah and Caroline Virginia Krout, and Meredith Nicholson (Indianapolis: Indiana Historical Society, 1952).

[91]Duke University Library, Catalog of the Whitman Collection in the Duke University Library being a Part of the Trent Collection..., compiled by Ellen F. Frey (Durham, N.C.: Duke Univ. Library, 1945); U.S. Library of Congress, Reference Dept., Walt Whitman: A Catalog Based Upon the Collections of the Library of Congress... (Washington, D.C.: 1955); Charles E. Feinberg, Walt Whitman: A Selection of the Manuscripts, Books, and Association Items Gathered by Charles E. Feinberg; Catalog of an Exhibition held at the Detroit Public Library, Detroit, Mich., 1955 (Detroit, 1955).

[92]Robert B. Haas and Don C. Gallup, A Catalog of the Published and Unpublished Writings of Gertrude Stein Exhibited in the Yale University Library, 22 Feb. to 29 Mar. 1941 (New Haven, Conn.: Yale Univ. Library, 1941); Robert W. Daniel, A Catalog of the Writings of William Faulkner (New Haven, Conn.: Yale Univ. Library, 1942); Don C. Gallup, A Bibliographical Checklist of the Writings of T. S. Eliot (New Haven, Conn.: Yale Univ. Library, 1947); Don C. Gallup, T. S. Eliot: A Bibliography (N.Y.: Harcourt, Brace, 1953); Jerome M. Edelstein, A Bibliographical Checklist of the Writings of Thornton Wilder (New Haven, Conn.: Yale Univ. Library, 1959); Samuel F. Morse, Wallace Stevens: A Preliminary Checklist of His Published Writings, 1898-1954; Published in Connection with an Exhibition Held in Honor of the Poet's 75th Birthday, 2 Oct. 1954 (New Haven, Conn.: Yale Univ. Library, 1954).

[93]Frances J. Brewer and Matthew J. Bruccoli, James Branch Cabell (Charlottesville: Univ. of Virginia Press, 1957).

[94]University of Virginia Library, The Barrett Library: Bret Harte: A Checklist of Printed and Manuscript Works, compiled by Lucy T. Clark (Charlottesville: Univ. of Virginia Press, 1957); The Barrett Library: W. D. Howells: A Checklist of Printed and Manuscript Works..., compiled by Fannie Mae Elliott and Lucy Clark (Charlottesville: Univ. of Virginia Press, 1959).

[95]Oscar Wegelin, A Bibliography of the Separate Writings of John Esten Cooke, 2d ed., Heartman's Historical Series, no. 43 (Hattiesburg, Miss.: Book Farm, 1941); A Bibliography of the Separate Writings of W. G. Simms of South Carolina 1806-1870, 3rd ed. (Hattiesburg, Miss.: Book Farm, 1941).

[96]Charles F. Heartman, Bibliographical Checklist of

the Writings of the Poet, Charles West Thomson, Heartman's
Historical Series, no. 60 (Hattiesburg, Miss.: Book Farm,
1941); Charles F. Heartman and James R. Canny, A Bibliog-
raphy of First Printings of Edgar Allan Poe..., rev. ed.,
Heartman's Historical Series, no. 53 (Hattiesburg, Miss.:
Book Farm, 1943).

[97]"Charles F. Heartman," New York Times, Mar.
10, 1953, p. 88, column 4.

[98]W. D. Quesenbery, Jr., "Ellen Glasgow: A Critical
Bibliography," Bulletin of Bibliography 22 (1959), 201-06,
230-36.

[99]William M. Gibson and George Arms, "A Bibliography of William Dean Howells," Bulletin of the New York
Public Library 50 (1946), 675-98, 857-68, 51 (1947), 49-56,
91-105, 213-48, 341-45, 384-88, 431-57, 486-512.

[100]William M. Gibson and George Arms, A Bibliography of William Dean Howells (N.Y.: New York Public Library, 1948).

[101]Schwartz, Edward, "Katherine Anne Porter: A
Critical Bibliography," Bulletin of the New York Public Library 57 (1953), 211-47.

[102]Eugene P. Sheehy and Kenneth A. Lohf, "The
Achievement of Marianne Moore," Bulletin of the New York
Public Library 62 (1958), 131-49, 183-90, 249-59.

[103]J. Albert Robbins, "Some Unrecorded Poems of
James Kirke Paulding: An Annotated Checklist," Studies in
Bibliography 3 (1950), 229-40.

[104]E. R. Hagemann, "A Checklist of the Writings of
John William De Forest (1826-1906)," Studies in Bibliography
8 (1956), 185-94.

[105]J. Max Patrick and Robert W. Stallman, "John
Peale Bishop: A Checklist," Princeton University Library
Chronicle 7 (Feb. 1946), 62-79.

[106]James B. Meriwether, "William Faulkner: A Checklist," Princeton University Library Chronicle 18 (Spring
1957), 136-58.

[107]Henry D. Piper, "F. Scott Fitzgerald: A Checklist," Princeton University Library Chronicle 12 (1951), 196-208; Arthur Mizener, The Far Side of Paradise: A Biography (Boston: Houghton Mifflin, 1951).

[108]Eric W. Carlson, "Benedict Thielen: An Introduction and a Checklist," Princeton University Library Chronicle 13 (Spring 1952), 143-55.

[109]Lewis Leary, That Rascal Freneau: A Study in Literary Failure (New Brunswick, N.J.: Rutgers Univ. Press, 1941).

[110]William I. Bartlett, Jones Very, Emerson's "Brave Saint" (Durham, N.C.: Duke Univ. Press, 1942).

[111]William P. Randel, Edward Eggleston: Author of The Hoosier School-Master (N.Y.: King's Crown Press, 1946).

CHAPTER 3

[1]Literary History of the United States, ed. by Robert E. Spiller and others. Bibliography Supplement II (N.Y.: Macmillan, 1972).

[2]William J. Burke and Will D. Howe, American Authors and Books, 1640 to the Present, 3rd rev. ed., rev. by Irving and Anne Weiss (N.Y.: Crown, 1972).

[3]Literature and Language Bibliographies from the American Yearbook 1910-1919, Introduction and Indexes by Arnold N. Rzepecki (Ann Arbor, Mich.: Pierian Press, 1970).

[4]Ralph Thompson, American Literary Annuals and Gift Books 1825-1865 (N.Y.: H. W. Wilson, 1936); Edward Kirkham and John W. Fink, Indices to American Literary Annuals and Gift Books 1825-1865 (New Haven, Conn.: Research Publications, 1975).

[5]Thompson, p. 1, 23.

[6]Thompson, p. 128.

[7]Thompson, p. 23-24.

[8]Harvard University, Widener Library, Wiedener Library Shelflist, 26: American Literature (2 vols. Cambridge, Mass.: Harvard Univ. Library, 1970).

[9]Index to Early American Periodicals to 1850 (N.Y.: Readex Microprint Corp., 1964-).

[10]Lyle H. Wright, American Fiction 1876-1900 (San Marino, Calif.: Huntington Library, 1966); American Fiction 1774-1850, 2d rev. ed. (San Marino, Calif.: 1969); American Fiction 1851-1875 (San Marino, Calif.: Huntington Library, 1965).

[11]R. Glenn Wright, ed., Author Bibliography of English Language Fiction in the Library of Congress Through 1950 (8 vols. Boston: G. K. Hall, 1973); Chronological Bibliography of English Language Fiction in the Library of Congress Through 1950 (8 vols. Boston: G. K. Hall, 1974).

[12]Jack VanDerhoof, A Bibliography of Novels Related to American Frontier and Colonial History (Troy, N.Y.: Whitston Pub. Co., 1971).

[13]Daniel D. McGarry and Sarah H. White, Historical Fiction Guide (N.Y.: Scarecrow Press, 1963).

[14]Nicholas J. Karolides, The Pioneer in the American Novel 1900-1950 (Norman: Univ. of Oklahoma, 1967).

[15]Joseph J. Waldmeir, American Novels of the Second World War (The Hague: Mouton, 1968).

[16]Joseph Blotner, The Modern American Political Novel 1900-1960 (Austin: Univ. of Texas Press, 1966); John C. McCloskey, "American Satires, 1637-1957; A Selective Checklist, Part II: Fiction; Augmented and Updated by Carol and Donald Kay," Satire Newsletter 10, no. 2 (1973), 97-122.

[17]Roger E. Stoddard, "C. Fiske Harris, Collector of American Poetry and Plays," Papers of the Bibliographical Society of America 57 (first quarter 1963), 14-32.

[18]Roger E. Stoddard, "A Catalogue of Books and Pamphlets Unrecorded in Oscar Wegelin's Early American Poetry 1650-1820," Books of Brown 23 (1969), 1-84.

[19]Roger E. Stoddard, "Further Addenda to Wegelin's Early American Poetry," Papers of the Bibliographical Society of America 65 (1971), 169-72.

[20]J. A. Leo Lemay, A Calendar of American Poetry in the Colonial Newspapers and Magazines and in Major English Magazines Through 1765 (Worcester, Mass.: American Antiquarian Society, 1972).

[21]Eugene L. Huddleston, "Topographical Poetry in America: A Checklist 1783-1812," Bulletin of Bibliography 25 (Sept.-Dec. 1966), 8-13; 25 (Jan.-Apr. 1967), 35-36, 39.

[22]Eugene L. Huddleston, "Feminist Verse Satire in America: A Checklist 1700-1800," Bulletin of Bibliography 32 (July 1975), 115-21.

[23]James A. Hart, "American Poetry of the First World War 1914 to 1920; A Survey and Checklist" (Ph.D. dissertation, Duke Univ., 1965).

[24]Charles R. Andrews, "A Thematic Guide to Selected American Poetry About the Second World War" (Ph.D. dissertation, Case Western Reserve Univ., 1967).

[25]Galen Williams, A Partial Directory of American Poets (N.Y.: Poets and Writers, 1971).

[26]A Directory of American Poets (N.Y.: Poets and Writers, 1973).

[27]Sander W. Zulauf and Irwin H. Weiser, Index of American Periodical Verse: [year] (Metuchen, N.J.: Scarecrow Press, 1973-).

[28]Lloyd Davis and Robert Irwin, Contemporary American Poetry: A Checklist (Metuchen, N.J.: Scarecrow, 1975).

[29]Poetry Society of America, The Diamond Anthology, ed. by Charles Angoff et al. (South Brunswick, N.J.: A. S. Barnes, 1971).

[30]Stephen Berg and Robert Mezey, eds., Naked Poetry; Recent American Poetry in Open Forms (Indianapolis: Bobbs-Merrill, 1969); The New Naked Poetry; Recent American Poetry in Open Forms (Indianapolis: Bobbs-Merrill, 1976).

[31]New Yorker, The New Yorker Book of Poems, Selected by the Editors of the New Yorker (N. Y.: Viking Press, 1969); Virginia Quarterly Review, Poems from the Virginia Quarterly Review 1925-1967 (Charlottesville: Univ. Press of Virginia, 1969); Guy Owen and Mary C. Williams, eds., New Southern Poets; Selected Poems from Southern Poetry Review (Chapel Hill: Univ. of North Carolina Press, 1974).

[32]Lee Steinmetz, ed., The Poetry of the American Civil War (East Lansing: Michigan State Univ. Press, 1960); Walter Lowenfels and Nan Braymer, eds., Where Is Vietnam? American Poets Respond; An Anthology of Contemporary Poems (N. Y.: Doubleday, 1967).

[33]G. William Bergquist, ed., Three Centuries of English and American Plays; A Checklist: England 1500-1800; United States 1714-1830 (N. Y.: Hafner Pub. Co., 1963).

[34]Roger E. Stoddard, "Some Corrigenda and Addenda to Hill's American Plays Printed 1714-1830," Papers of the Bibliographical Society of America 65 (1971), 278-95.

[35]Roger E. Stoddard, "A Guide to 'Spencer's Boston Theatre,' 1855-1862," Papers of the Bibliographical Society of America 79 (1969), 45-98.

[36]Otis L. Guernsey, ed., Directory of the American Theater 1894-1971 (N. Y.: Dodd, Mead, 1971).

[37]Linda Peavy, "A Bibliography of Provincetown Players' Dramas, 1915-1922," Papers of the Bibliographical Society of America 69 (1975), 569-74.

[38]Jane F. Bonin, Major Themes in Prizewinning American Drama (Metuchen, N.J.: Scarecrow Press, 1975).

[39]Caspar H. Nannes, Politics in the American Drama (Washington, D.C.: Catholic University of America Press, 1960).

[40]Ima H. Herron, The Small Town in American Drama (Dallas, Texas: Southern Methodist Univ. Press, 1969); James S. Douglas, "The Small Town in American Drama, 1900-1940" (Ph.D. dissertation, Washington State Univ., 1970).

[41]John D. Collins, "American Drama in Anti-Slavery Agitation 1792-1861" (Ph. D. dissertation, Iowa State Univ., 1963); William H. Wegner, "The Representation of the American Civil War on the New York Stage 1860-1900" (Ph. D. dissertation, New York Univ., 1966).

[42]John M. Bradbury, Renaissance in the South; A Critical History of the Literature 1920-1960 (Chapel Hill: Univ. of North Carolina Press, 1963).

[43]Mabel Major and Thomas M. Pearce, Southwest Heritage; A Literary History with Bibliographies, 3d ed. (Albuquerque: Univ. of New Mexico Press, 1972).

[44]Walter Havighurst, ed., The Great Lakes Reader (N. Y.: Macmillan, 1966); John Corrington and Miller Williams, eds., Southern Writing in the Sixties (2 vols. Baton Rouge: Louisiana State Univ., 1966-67); Charles N. Sonnichsen, ed., The Southwest in Life and Literature (N. Y.: Devin-Adair, 1962); Martin Shockley, ed., Southwest Writers Anthology (Austin, Texas: Steck-Vaughn, 1967); J. Golden Taylor, ed., The Literature of the American West (N. Y.: Houghton Mifflin, 1971).

[45]Edwin W. Gaston, Jr., The Early Novel of the Southwest (Albuquerque: Univ. of New Mexico Press, 1961).

[46]Roy W. Meyer, "An Annotated Bibliography of Middle Western Farm Fiction 1891-1962," The Middle Western Farm Novel in the Twentieth Century (Lincoln: Univ. of Nebraska, 1965), p. 200-42.

[47]Patricia Kennedy, "The Pioneer Woman in Middle Western Fiction" (Ph. D. dissertation, Univ. of Illinois, 1968).

[48]Western Writers of America, Bad Men and Good; A Roundup of Western Stories (N. Y.: Dodd, Mead, 1953), Holsters and Heroes (N. Y.: Macmillan, 1954), Wild Streets; Tales of the Frontier Towns (Garden City, N. Y.: Doubleday, 1958), Spurs West (Garden City, N. Y.: Doubleday, 1960), and Legends and Tales of the Old West (Garden City, N. Y.: Doubleday, 1962). Only five volumes are cited here to give some idea of the titles.

[49]Ray O. Hummel, Jr., ed., Southeastern Broadsides Before 1877: A Bibliography (Richmond: Virginia State Library, 1971).

[50]Ray O. Hummel, Jr., More Virginia Broadsides Before 1877 (Richmond: Virginia State Library, 1975).

[51]Lucien Stryk, ed., Heartland: Poems of the Midwest (De Kalb: Northern Illinois Univ. Press, 1967); Heartland II: Poets of the Midwest (De Kalb: Northern Illinois Univ. Press, 1975).

[52]Donald E. Thompson, Indiana Authors and Their Books 1917-1966 (Crawfordsville, Ind.: Wabash College, 1974).

[53]Robert Y. Coward and Hester H. Coward, Catalog of the David Demaree Banta Indiana Collection, 2d ed. (Menasha, Wis.: George Banta Co., 1965).

[54]William Coyle, ed., Ohio Authors and Their Books (Cleveland: World, 1962).

[55]Frank Paluka, Iowa Authors; A Biobibliography of Sixty Native Writers (Iowa City: Friends of Univ. of Iowa Libraries, 1967).

[56]Rachel M. Hilbert, ed., Michigan Authors (Ann Arbor: Michigan Association of School Librarians, 1960).

[57]Alice G. Harvey, Nebraska Writers, rev. ed. (Omaha, Neb.: The Author, 1964).

[58]Ish Richey, Kentucky Literature 1784-1963 (Tompkinsville, Ky.: Monroe County Press, 1963); Mary Carmel Browning, Kentucky Authors: A History of Kentucky Literature (Owensboro, Ky.: Brescia College Bookstore, 1968).

[59]Elsie A. Tourville, Alaska: A Bibliography 1570-1970 (Boston: G. K. Hall, 1974).

[60]Arthur W. Shumaker, A History of Indiana Literature (Indianapolis: Indiana Historical Bureau, 1962).

[61]Clarence A. Andrews, A Literary History of Iowa (Iowa City: Univ. of Iowa Press, 1972).

[62]Marilyn Jody, "Alaska in the American Literary Imagination" (Ph.D. dissertation, Indiana Univ., 1969).

[63]W. Storrs Lee, ed., California: A Literary Chronicle (N.Y.: Funk & Wagnalls, 1968).

[64]Lawrence C. Powell, California Classics; The Creative Literature of the Golden State (Los Angeles: Ward Ritchie Press, 1971).

[65]Richard J. Calhoun and John C. Guilds, eds. A Tricentennial Anthology of South Carolina Literature 1670-1970 (Columbia: Univ. of South Carolina Press, 1971).

[66]Hilton J. Wolfe, "Alaskan Literature: the Fiction of America's Last Frontier" (Ph.D. dissertation, Michigan State Univ., 1973).

[67]Oral S. Coad, New Jersey in the Revolution: A Bibliography of Historical Fiction 1784-1963 (New Brunswick, N.J.: New Brunswick Historical Club, 1964).

[68]Albert G. Black, Michigan Novels; An Annotated Bibliography (Ann Arbor: Michigan Council of Teachers of English, 1963).

[69]Rachel M. Hilbert, ed., Michigan Poets with Supplement to Michigan Authors (Ann Arbor: Michigan Association of School Librarians, 1964).

[70]Elmer D. Johnson, "A Preliminary Checklist of Louisiana Poetry in English," Southwestern Louisiana Journal 4 (Jan. 1960), 43-60.

[71]William Elliott, "Minnesota North Country Poetry: A Bibliography," Society for the Study of Midwestern Literature Newsletter 4, no. 1 (1974), 8-10.

[72]Poetry Society of Alaska, One Hundred Years of Alaska Poetry (Denver: Big Mountain Press, 1966); Poetry Society of Michigan, Forty Salutes to Michigan Poets; Fortieth Anniversary Anthology (Poetry Society of Michigan, 1975); Vivian M. Meyer et al., eds., Cosmic Cadence (Pitman, N.J.: New Jersey Poetry Society, 1971); Pennsylvania Poetry Society, Prize Poems 1969; 20th Anniversary Year (Harrisburg, Pa.: Keystone Press, 1969); Mabelle A. Lyon et al., eds., Sing, Naked Spirit; A Compilation of Verse from Members of the Arizona Poetry Society (Mesa, Ariz.: Printed by P. Gillespie, 1970).

[73]Richard G. Walser, ed., Poets of North Carolina (Richmond: Garrett and Massie, 1963).

[74]Paul T. Nolan and Amos E. Simpson, "Checklist of Arkansas Playwrights," Arkansas Historical Quarterly 22 (Spring 1963), 67-75.

[75]Paul T. Nolan, "Alabama Drama, 1870-1916: A Checklist," Alabama Review 18 (1965), 65-72.

[76]Edgar Heyl, "Plays by Marylanders 1870-1916," Maryland Historical Magazine 62 (1967), 438-47; 63 (1968), 70-77, 179-87, 420-26; 64 (1969), 74-77, 412-19.

[77]Perry G. Fisher, Materials for the Study of Washington; A Selected Annotated Bibliography (Washington, D.C.: George Washington Univ., 1974).

[78]John R. Adams, Books and Authors of San Diego (San Diego: San Diego State Collect Press, 1966).

[79]Michael True, Worcester Poets, With Notes Toward a Literary History (Worcester: Worcester County Poetry Assoc., 1972).

[80]Ron Padgett and David Shapiro, eds., An Anthology of New York Poets (N.Y.: Random House, 1970); John V. Hinshaw, ed., East of America; An Anthology of Cape Cod Poets (Chatham, Mass.: Chatham Press, 1969); Charleen Whisnant and Robert W. Grey, eds., Eleven Charlotte Poets (Charlotte, N.C.: Red Clay Publishers, 1971); Robert Watson and Ruark Gibbons, eds., The Greensboro Reader (Chapel Hill: Univ. of North Carolina Press, 1968); Alfred S. Reid, "Poets of Greenville," Furman Studies n.s. 11 (Nov. 1963), 1-44; Joe Ireland and Ann Gallmeyer, eds., New Orleans Anthology (New Orleans: New Orleans Public Library, 1972); Martin J. Rosenblum, ed., Brewing; 20 Milwaukee Poets (Lyme Center, N.H.: Giligia Press, 1972).

[81]Sam B. Smith and Luke H. Banker, eds., Tennessee History: A Bibliography (Knoxville: Univ. of Tennessee Press, 1974).

[82]Sarah A. Rouse, "Literature 1890-1970," A History of Mississippi, ed. by Richard A. McLemore (Hattiesburg: Univ. and College Press of Mississippi, 1973), vol. 2, p. 446-76.

[83]Helen H. Ellis, Michigan in the Civil War; A Guide

to the Material in Detroit 1861-1866 (Lansing: Michigan Civil War Centennial Observance Commission, 1965); Donald A. Sinclair, The Civil War and New Jersey: A Bibliography (New Brunswick: Published by Friends of the Rutgers University Library for New Jersey Civil War Centennial Commission, 1968).

[84]Brom Weber, ed., An Anthology of American Humor (N.Y.: Crowell, 1962).

[85]John Q. Anderson, ed., With the Bark On; Popular Humor of the Old South (Nashville, Tenn.: Vanderbilt Univ. Press, 1967).

[86]Wade H. Hall, The Smiling Phoenix; Southern Humor from 1865 to 1914 (Gainesville: Univ. of Florida Press, 1965).

[87]Richard Walser, ed., Tar Heel Laughter (Chapel Hill: Univ. of North Carolina Press, 1974).

[88]Philip H. Ault, ed., The Home Book of Western Humor (N.Y.: Dodd, Mead, 1967); Hennig Cohen and William B. Dillingham, eds., Humor of the Old Southwest, 2d ed. (Athens: Univ. of Georgia Press, 1975).

[89]Constance J. Gefvert, Edward Taylor: An Annotated Bibliography 1668-1970, Serif Series: Bibliographies and Checklists, no. 19 (Kent, Ohio: Kent State Univ. Press, 1971).

[90]Beatrice Ricks and Joseph D. Adams, Herman Melville; A Reference Bibliography, 1900-1972 (Boston: G. K. Hall, 1973).

[91]Thomas F. O'Donnell et al., A Bibliography of the Writings by and About Harold Frederic, Research Bibliographies in American Literature, no. 4 (Boston: G. K. Hall, 1975).

[92]Vito J. Brenni, William Dean Howells: A Bibliography (Metuchen, N.J.: Scarecrow Press, 1973).

[93]Hensley C. Woodbridge et al., Jack London: A Bibliography (Georgetown, Calif.: Talisman Press, 1966).

[94]Hensley C. Woodbridge et al., Jack London: A

Bibliography, enl. ed. (Millwood, N.Y.: Kraus Reprint Co., 1973).

[95]Robert W. Stallman, Stephen Crane: A Critical Bibliography (Ames: Iowa Univ. Press, 1972).

[96]Willis J. Buckingham, ed., Emily Dickinson: An Annotated Bibliography (Bloomington: Indiana Univ. Press, 1970).

[97]University of Virginia Library, The Barrett Library: Edwin Lasseter Bynner: A Checklist of Printed and Manuscript Works, comp. by Lucy T. Clark (Charlottesville: Univ. of Virginia Press, 1961).

[98]"Clifton Waller Barrett," Current Biography, 1965, p. 15-18.

[99]Donald Pizer et al., Theodore Dreiser: A Primary and Secondary Bibliography (Boston: G. K. Hall, 1975).

[100]Matthew J. Bruccoli, F. Scott Fitzgerald: A Descriptive Bibliography (Pittsburgh: Univ. of Pittsburgh Press, 1972); Ring W. Lardner: A Descriptive Bibliography (Pittsburgh: Univ. of Pittsburgh Press, 1975).

[101]William W. Kelly, Ellen Glasgow: A Bibliography (Charlottesville: Printed for Bibliographical Society of Virginia by Univ. Press of Virginia, 1964).

[102]Vito J. Brenni, Edith Wharton: A Bibliography (Morgantown: West Virginia Univ. Library, 1966).

[103]Ronald Gottesman, Upton Sinclair: An Annotated Checklist (Kent, Ohio: Kent State Univ. Press, 1973).

[104]Audre Hanneman, Ernest Hemingway: A Comprehensive Bibliography (Princeton, N.J.: Princeton Univ. Press, 1967).

[105]Tetsumaro Hayashi, John Steinbeck: A Concise Bibliography, 1930-1965 (Metuchen, N.J.: Scarecrow Press, 1967).

[106]Tetsumaro Hayashi, A New Steinbeck Bibliography, 1929-1971 (Metuchen, N.J.: Scarecrow Press, 1973).

[107]Linton R. Massey, William Faulkner, "Man Working," 1919-1962; A Catalog of the William Faulkner Collections at the University of Virginia (Charlottesville: Bibliographic Society of Univ. of Virginia, 1968).

[108]Robert A. Wilson, Gertrude Stein: A Bibliography (N. Y.: Phoenix Bookshop, 1974); Mary N. Huff, Robert Penn Warren: A Bibliography (N. Y.: David Lewis, 1968); Matthew J. Bruccoli, John O'Hara: A Checklist (N. Y.: Random House, 1972); Louise Waldrip and Shirley A. Bauer, A Bibliography of the Works of Katherine Anne Porter (Metuchen, N. J.: Scarecrow Press, 1969).

[109]James B. Meriwether, James Gould Cozzens: A Checklist (Detroit: Gale Research Co., 1973); Kenneth G. McCollum, Nelson Algren: A Checklist (Detroit: Gale Research Co., 1973); John R. Hopkins, James Jones; A Checklist (Detroit: Gale Research Co., 1974); Betty L. Hudgens, Kurt Vonnegut, Jr.: A Checklist (Detroit: Gale Research Co., 1972).

[110]Pierre Michel, James Gould Cozzens: An Annotated Checklist, Serif Series: Bibliographies and Checklists, no. 22 (Kent, Ohio: Kent State Univ. Press, 1971).

[111]C. Clarke Taylor, John Updike, Serif Series: Bibliographies and Checklists, no. 4 (Kent, Ohio: Kent State Univ. Press, 1968); Rita N. Kosofsky, Bernard Malamud: An Annotated Checklist, Serif Series: Bibliographies and Checklists, no. 7 (Kent, Ohio: Kent State Univ. Press, 1969); Elmer D. Johnson, Tom Wolfe: A Checklist, Serif Series: Bibliographies and Checklists, no. 12 (Kent, Ohio: Kent State Univ. Press, 1970); Matthew J. Bruccoli, Raymond Chandler: A Checklist, Serif Series: Bibliographies and Checklists, no. 2 (Kent, Ohio: Kent State Univ. Press, 1968).

[112]Harold W. Billings, A Bibliography of Edward Dahlberg (Austin: Humanities Research Center, Univ. of Texas, 1971).

[113]Donald C. Gallup, A Bibliography of Ezra Pound (London: R. Hart-Davis, 1963); 2d impression, corrected, 1969.

[114]Donald C. Gallup, T. S. Eliot: A Bibliography, new ed. (London: Faber, 1969).

[115]William White, Edwin Arlington Robinson; A Supple-

mentary Bibliography, Serif Series: Bibliographies and Checklists, no. 17 (Kent, Ohio: Kent State Univ. Press, 1971).

[116]Marshall Fallwell, Jr., et al., Allen Tate: A
Bibliography (N.Y.: David Lewis, 1969).

[117]Robert O. Lindsay, Witter Bynner: A Bibliography
(Albuquerque: Univ. of New Mexico Press, 1967).

[118]University of Virginia Library, The Barrett Li-
brary: Robinson Jeffers: A Checklist of Printed and Manu-
script Works, comp. by Anita Rutman and Lucy Clark, the
Manuscripts by Marjorie Carver (Charlottesville: Univ. of
Virginia Press, 1960); Mark Van Doren, Carl Sandburg,
With a Bibliography of Sandburg Materials in the Library of
Congress (Washington, D.C.: Library of Congress, 1969).

[119]Jerome M. Edelstein, Wallace Stevens: A Descriptive Bibliography (Pittsburgh; Univ. of Pittsburgh Press,
1973).

[120]Ernest C. Stefanik, John Berryman: A Descriptive
Bibliography (Pittsburgh: Univ. of Pittsburgh Press, 1975).

[121]Mary Novik, Robert Creeley: An Inventory 1945-
1970, Serif Series: Bibliographies and Checklists, no. 28
(Kent, Ohio: Kent State Univ. Press, 1975).

[122]James R. McLeod, Theodore Roethke: A Bibliography, Serif Series: Bibliographies and Checklists, no. 27
(Kent, Ohio: Kent State Univ. Press, 1973).

[123]Edward J. Mullaly, Archibald MacLeish: A Check-
list, Serif Series: Bibliographies and Checklists, no. 26
(Kent, Ohio: Kent State Univ. Press, 1973); John P. Field,
Richard Wilbur: A Bibliographical Checklist, Serif Series:
Bibliographies and Checklists, no. 16 (Kent, Ohio: Kent State
Univ. Press, 1971).

[124]Franklin Ashley, James Dickey: A Checklist (Detroit: Gale Research, 1972); Matthew J. Bruccoli, Kenneth
Millar/Ross MacDonald (Detroit: Gale Research Co., 1971).

[125]George F. Butterick and Albert Glover, Bibliography of Works by Charles Olson (N.Y.: Phoenix Book Shop,
1967); Robert A. Wilson, A Bibliography of Works by Gregory
Corso, 1954-1965 (N.Y.: Phoenix Book Shop, 1966).

126William White, John Ciardi: A Bibliography (Detroit: Wayne State Univ. Press, 1959); W. D. Snodgrass: A Bibliography (Detroit: Wayne State Univ. Press, 1960).

127Manfred Triesch, The Lillian Hellman Collection at the University of Texas (Austin: Humanities Research Center, Univ. of Texas, 1967).

128Laurence G. Avery, A Catalog of the Maxwell Anderson Collection at the University of Texas, Tower Bibliographical Series, no. 6 (Austin: Humanities Research Center, Univ. of Texas, 1968).

129Jennifer M. Atkinson, Eugene O'Neill: A Descriptive Bibliography (Pittsburgh: Univ. of Pittsburgh Press, 1974).

130David Kherdian, A Bibliography of William Saroyan, 1934-1964 (San Francisco: Roger Beacham, 1965).

131Vivian Buchan, "Sara Teasdale, 1884-1933," Bulletin of Bibliography 25 (1967), 94-97, 120-23; Joan T. Brittain, "Flannery O'Connor," Bulletin of Bibliography 25 (1967-68), 98-100, 123-24, 142; George E. Bush, "James Purdy," Bulletin of Bibliography 28 (1971), 5-6; Margaret S. Grissom, "Shirley Ann Grau," Bulletin of Bibliography 28 (1971), 76-78; Stanley Schatt, "LeRoi Jones," Bulletin of Bibliography 28 (1971), 55-57; Loretta Gilliam, "Gore Vidal: A Checklist," Bulletin of Bibliography 30 (1973), 1-9, 44; John N. McDaniel, "Philip Roth: A Checklist," Bulletin of Bibliography 31 (1974), 51-53; Ernest C. Stefanik, "A John Berryman Checklist," Bulletin of Bibliography 31 (1974), 1-4, 28; James J. Napier, "Joseph Hergesheimer: A Selected Bibliography 1913-1945," Bulletin of Bibliography 24 (1963-64), 46-48, 52, 69-70; Michel Fabre and Edward Margolies, "Richard Wright (1908-1960): A Bibliography," Bulletin of Bibliography 24 (1965); 131-33, 137; Alfred S. Shivers, "Jessamyn West," Bulletin of Bibliography 28 (1971), 1-3.

132Dean Sherman, "Owen Wister: An Annotated Bibliography," Bulletin of Bibliography 28 (1971), 7-16.

133James N. Lawton, "The Authorship of Item 165 in Lyle Wright's American Fiction 1851-1875," Papers of the Biographical Society of America 64 (1970), 83.

134Donald Pizer, "The Publications of Theodore Dreiser:

A Checklist," Proof 1 (1971), 247-92; James B. Meriwether, "The Short Fiction of William Faulkner: A Bibliography," Proof 1 (1971), 293-329.

[135]Joseph Katz, "The Shorter Publications of Frank Norris," Proof 3 (1973), 155-220.

[136]Philip C. Kolin, "A Classified Edward Albee Checklist," Serif 6 (Sept. 1969), 16-32; "A Supplementary Edward Albee Checklist," Serif 10 (Spring 1973), 28-39.

[137]William White, "Robinson Jeffers: A Checklist 1959-1965," Serif 3 (June 1966), 36-39.

[138]William White, "Walt Whitman's Poetry in Periodicals," Serif 11 (Summer 1974), 31-38.

[139]Edgar M. Branch, "A Supplement to the Bibliography of James T. Farrell's Writings," American Book Collector 11 (Summer 1961), 42-48; Supplements in American Book Collector 17 (May 1967), 9-19 and in 26 (Jan-Feb. 1976), 17-22.

[140]Francis Manley, "William Inge: A Bibliography," American Book Collector 16 (Oct. 1965), 13-21.

[141]Ann Stanford, "Anne Bradstreet: An Annotated Checklist," Early American Literature 3 (Winter 1968/69), 217-28; Paul Witherington, "Charles Brockden Brown: A Bibliographic Essay," Early American Literature 9 (Fall 1974), 164-87.

[142]Robert H. Woodward and Stanton Garner, "Frederic's Short Fiction: A Checklist," American Literary Realism 1 (1968), 73-76; Clayton L. Eichelberger and Zoë Lyon, "A Partial Listing of the Published Work of Harris M. Lyon," American Literary Realism 3 (1970), 41-52; Stanford E. Marovitz and Lewis Fried, "Abraham Cahan (1860-1951): An Annotated Bibliography," American Literary Realism 3 (1970), 197-243; Jean N. Biglane, "Sherwood Bonner: A Bibliography of Primary and Secondary Material," American Literary Realism 5 (1972), 39-60; Reese M. Carleton, "Mary Noailles Murphree (1850-1922): An Annotated Bibliography," American Literary Realism 7 (1974) 293-378; Jeffrey Swanson, "A Checklist of the Writings of Henry Blake Fuller," American Literary Realism 7 (1974), 211-43.

[143]George Kellogg, "Frederick Manfred: A Bibliography," Twentieth Century Literature 11 (1965), 30-35; Nancy L.

McNally, "Checklist of Elizabeth Bishop's Published Writings,"
Twentieth Century Literature 11 (1966), 201; Susan W. Hollen-
berg, "Theodore Roethke: A Bibliography," Twentieth Century
Literature 12 (1967), 216-22; Margaret W. Rule, "An Edward
Albee Bibliography," Twentieth Century Literature 14 (1968),
35-44; Virginia S. Reinhart, "John Dos Passos 1950-1966:
Bibliography," Twentieth Century Literature 13 (1966), 167-78.

144Jackson R. Bryer, "John Barth," Critique 6, no.
2 (1963), 86-89; Joseph N. Weixlmann, "John Barth: A Bibliography," Critique 13, no. 3 (1972), 45-56; Allan Hanna,
"An Allan Seager Bibliography," Critique 5, no. 3 (1963),
75-90; Jackson R. Bryer, "John Hawkes," Critique 6, no. 2,
(1963), 89-94; James P. Smith, "A Peter Taylor Checklist,"
Critique 9, no. 3 (1967), 31-36; Prescott Evarts, Jr., "John
Fowles: A Checklist," Critique 13, no. 3 (1972), 105-07.

145Jean Holloway, Hamlin Garland: A Biography (Austin: Univ. of Texas Press, 1960).

146Mark Schorer, Sinclair Lewis: An American Life
(N. Y.: McGraw-Hill, 1961).

CHAPTER 4

1Lyle H. Wright, American Fiction 1774-1850 (San
Marino, Calif.: 1939); rev. ed., 1948; 2d rev. ed., 1969;
American Fiction 1851-1875 (San Marino, Calif.: 1957); new
ed., 1965; American Fiction 1876-1900 (San Marino, Calif.:
Huntington Library, 1966); R. Glenn Wright, Author Bibliography of English Language Fiction in the Library of Congress
Through 1950 (8 vols. Boston: G. K. Hall, 1973); Chronological Bibliography of English Language Fiction in the Library
of Congress Through 1950 (8 vols. Boston: G. K. Hall, 1974).

2Oscar Wegelin, Early American Poetry, 2d ed. (N. Y.:
Peter Smith, 1930); Roger E. Stoddard, "A Catalog of Books
and Pamphlets Unrecorded in Oscar Wegelin's Early American
Poetry 1650-1820," Books of Brown 23 (1969), 1-84; "Further
Addenda to Wegelin's Early American Poetry," Papers
of the Bibliographical Society of America 65 (April 1971) 169-
72; Brown University Library, Dictionary Catalog of the
Harris Collection of American Poetry and Plays (13 vols.
Boston: G. K. Hall, 1972); Wynot R. Irish, Modern American

Poetry: A Complete Bibliography of American Verse 1900-
1925 (Syracuse, N.Y.: Syracuse Univ. Press, 1950); Sander
W. Zulauf and Irwin H. Weiser, Index of American Periodical Verse: [year] (Metuchen, N.J.: Scarecrow Press, 1973
to date).

[3]Brown University Library, Dictionary Catalog of the
Harris Collection of American Poetry and Plays (13 vols.
Boston: G. K. Hall, 1972); Frank P. Hill, American Plays
Printed 1714-1830 (Palo Alto, Calif.: Stanford Univ. Press,
1934); Arthur H. Quinn, A History of the American Drama
From the Beginning to the Civil War (N.Y.: Harper, 1923);
2d ed., 1951; A History of the American Drama From the
Civil War to the Present Day (N.Y.: Harper, 1927); rev. ed.,
1936.

[4]Mabel Major et al., Southwest Heritage (Albuquerque:
Univ. of New Mexico, 1938); 3d ed., rev. and enl., 1972;
Jay B. Hubbell, The South in American Literature 1607-1900
(Durham: Duke Univ. Press, 1954); Edwin W. Gaston, The
Early Novel of the Southwest (Albuquerque: Univ. of New
Mexico Press, 1961); Roy W. Meyer, The Middle Western
Farm Novel in the Twentieth Century (Lincoln: Univ. of
Nebraska, 1965); Ray O. Hummel, ed., Southeastern Broad-
sides Before 1877: A Bibliography (Richmond: Virginia State
Library, 1971); Harold S. Jantz, "Bibliography of Early New
England Verse," Procs. of the American Antiquarian Society
n.s. 53 (1943), 391-508.

[5]Mary L. Thornton, A Bibliography of North Carolina
1589-1956 (Chapel Hill: Univ. of North Carolina Press, 1958);
Richard E. Banta, Indiana Authors and Their Books 1816-
1916 (Crawfordsville, Ind.: Wabash College, 1949); Mary H.
Marable and Elaine Boylan, A Handbook of Oklahoma Writers
(Norman: Univ. of Oklahoma Press, 1939); William S. Powell,
ed., North Carolina Fiction 1734-1957 (Chapel Hill: Univ. of
North Carolina Library, 1958); Albert G. Black, Michigan
Novels: An Annotated Bibliography (Ann Arbor: Michigan
Council of Teachers of English, 1963); Richard G. Walser,
ed., North Carolina Poetry (Richmond, Va.: Garrett and
Massie, 1941); rev. ed., 1951; Poets of North Carolina (Rich-
mond, Va.: Garrett and Massie, 1963); Henry Harrison, ed.,
California Poets; An Anthology of 244 Contemporaries (N.Y.:
Henry Harrison, 1932).

[6]John T. Frederick, "The Farm in Iowa Fiction,"
Palimpsest 32 (March 1951), 121-52; "Town and City in Iowa

Literature," Palimpsest 35 (Feb. 1954), 49-96; "Early Iowa in Fiction," Palimpsest 36 (Oct. 1955), 389-420; Clarence A. Andrews, A Literary History of Iowa (Iowa City: Univ. of Iowa Press, 1972).

[7]John R. Adams, Books and Authors of San Diego (San Diego: San Diego State College Press, 1966); Perry G. Fisher, Materials for the Study of Washington: A Selected Annotated Bibliography (Washington, D.C.: George Washington Univ., 1974).

[8]Grace Ross and Mabel Kuykendall, eds., Poetry Out Where the West Begins; A Collection of Poems by Fort Worth Authors (Dallas, Texas: Kaleidograph Press, 1949).

[9]Ron Padgett and David Shapiro, eds., An Anthology of New York Poets (N.Y.: Random House, 1970).

[10]Marshall Wingfield, Literary Memphis: A Survey of Its Writers and Writings (Memphis: West Tennessee Historical Society, 1942).

[11]A Century of Benton County Poetry; A Collection of Original Poetry (Roseburg: Oregon Poetry Clinic, 1957); Victor E. Lewis, ed., Poets and Poetry of Wyoming Valley: A Collection of Selected Contemporary Verse, Rhymes, and Poems (Wilkes Barre, Pa.: Llewellyn Bros., 1940); Latrobe Weston, Baltimore in Verse and Prose (Baltimore: H. G. Roebuck, 1936).

[12]Walter Blair, Native American Humor (1800-1900) (N.Y.: American Book Company, 1937); Wade H. Hall, The Smiling Phoenix: Southern Humor from 1865 to 1914 (Gainesville: Univ. of Florida Press, 1965).

[13]Edwin Seaver, ed., Pageant of American Humor (Cleveland: World, 1948); Brom Weber, ed., An Anthology of American Humor (N.Y.: Crowell, 1962).

[14]Bennett Cerf, ed., An Encyclopedia of Modern American Humor (Garden City, N.Y.: Hanover House, 1954).

[15]Arthur P. Hudson, ed., Humor of the Old Deep South (N.Y.: Macmillan, 1936); John Q. Anderson, ed., With the Bark On; Popular Humor of the Old South (Nashville, Tenn.: Vanderbilt Univ. Press, 1967).

[16]Hennig Cohen and William B. Dillingham, eds., Humor of the Old Southwest (Athens: Univ. of Georgia Press, 1964); Jack Conroy, ed., Midland Humor (N. Y.: Current Books, 1947).

[17]Louis H. Cohn, A Bibliography of Works of Ernest Hemingway (N. Y.: Random House, 1931); Lee Samuels, A Hemingway Checklist (N. Y.: Scribner's 1951); Audre Hanneman, Ernest Hemingway: A Complete Bibliography (Princeton, N.J.: Princeton Univ. Press, 1967).

[18]Donald C. Gallup, A Catalog of English and American First Editions of Writings of T. S. Eliot Exhibited in the Yale University Library (New Haven, Conn.: Yale Univ. Library, 1937); A Bibliographical Checklist of the Writings of T. S. Eliot (New Haven, Conn.: Yale Univ. Library, 1947); T. S. Eliot: A Bibliography (N. Y.: Harcourt, Brace, 1953); new ed., 1969.

[19]Barton Currie, Booth Tarkington: A Bibliography (Garden City, N. Y.: Doubleday, Doran, 1932); Dorothy Russo and Thelma Sullivan, A Bibliography of Booth Tarkington 1869-1946 (Indianapolis: Indiana Historical Society, 1949): Scott Cunningham, A Bibliography of the Writings of Carl Van Vechten (Phila.: Centaur Book Shop, 1924); Klaus W. Jonas, Carl Van Vechten: A Bibliography (N. Y.: Knopf, 1955).

[20]Lewis Leary, That Rascal Freneau; A Study in Literary Failure (New Brunswick, N.J.: Rutgers Univ. Press, 1941); William I. Bartlett, Jones Very, Emerson's "Brave Saint" (Durham, N.C.: Duke Univ. Press, 1942).

[21]Thomas F. Currier, Bibliography of John Greenleaf Whittier (Cambridge, Mass.: Harvard Univ. Press, 1937); A Bibliography of Oliver Wendell Holmes, ed. by Eleanor M. Tilton (N. Y.: New York Univ. Press, 1953); Donald C. Gallup, T. S. Eliot: A Bibliography, new ed. (London: Faber, 1969); A Bibliography of Ezra Pound (London: R. Hart-Davis, 1963).

Appendices:
Bibliographic Control of American Literature

APPENDIX A 1920-1939

COMPREHENSIVE NATIONAL BIBLIOGRAPHY

The American Yearbook; A Record of Events and Progress,
1910-1919, 1925-50. N.Y.: Nelson, 1929-1950. 36
vols.

Benét, William R., and Pearson, Norman H., eds. The
Oxford Anthology of American Literature. N.Y.: Oxford Univ. Press, 1938. 1697p.

Cambridge History of American Literature. Ed. by William
P. Trent and others. N.Y.: Putnam, 1917-21. 4 vols.

Fullerton, Bradford M. Selective Bibliography of American
Literature, 1775-1900; A Brief Estimate of the More
Important American Authors and a Description of Their
Representative Works. N.Y.: W. F. Payson, 1932.
327p.

Johnson, Merle, ed. American First Editions; Bibliographic
Checklists of the Works of One Hundred and Five
American Authors. N.Y.: Bowker, 1929. 242p.

Manly, John M., and Rickert, Edith. Contemporary American Literature. N.Y.: Harcourt, Brace, 1922. 188p.

_____, and _____. Contemporary American Literature;
Bibliographies and Study Outlines. Introduction and revision by Fred B. Millett. N.Y.: Harcourt, Brace,
1929. 378p.

Wakeman, Stephen H. The Stephen H. Wakeman Collection
of Books of 19th Century American Writers. N.Y.:
American Art Association, 1924. 258p.

NATIONAL FICTION BIBLIOGRAPHY

Best American Short Stories of [year] and the Yearbook of
the American Short Story. Boston: Houghton Mifflin,
1915- (annual).

Flory, Claude R. Economic Criticism in American Fiction
1792 to 1900. Phila.: Univ. of Pennsylvania Press,
1937. 261p.

Nield, Jonathan. A Guide to the Best Historical Novels and
Tales. 5th ed. N. Y.: Macmillan, 1929. 424p.

The O'Henry Memorial Prize Stories, 1919- . Garden City,
N. Y.: Doubleday, Page, 1920- (annual).

Rose, Lisle A. "A Descriptive Catalogue of Economic and
Politico-Economic Fiction in the United States, 1902-
1909." Ph. D. dissertation, Univ. of Chicago, 1935.
315p.

Shurter, Robert L. "The Utopian Novel in America 1865-
1900." Ph. D. dissertation, Western Reserve Univ.,
1936.

Smith, Rebecca W. "The Civil War and Its Aftermath in
American Fiction 1861-1899, with a Dictionary Cata-
logue and Indexes." Ph. D. dissertation, Univ. of
Chicago, 1932.

_____. "Of the Chief Novels and Short Stories by Ameri-
can Authors Dealing with the Civil War and Its Effects,"
Bulletin of Bibliography 16 (Sept.-Dec. 1939), 193-94;
17 (Jan.-Apr. 1940), 10-12; 17 (May-Aug. 1940), 33-
35; 17 (Sept.-Dec. 1940), 53-55; 17 (Jan.-Apr. 1941),
72-75.

Thiessen, N. J. An Annotated Bibliography of American
Historical Fiction. Kansas State Teachers College.
Bulletin of Information. vol. 18, no. 5. Emporia,
Kansas, 1938. 65p.

Wegelin, Oscar. Early American Fiction 1774-1830. 3d ed.
N. Y.: Peter Smith, 1929. 37p. plus index.

Wolfe, Dorothey E. "An Annotated Bibliography of the Short

Story." M.S. thesis, Kansas State Teachers College, 1932. 204p.

Wright, Lyle H. American Fiction 1774-1850; A Contribution Toward a Bibliography. San Marino, Calif., 1939. 246p.

NATIONAL POETRY BIBLIOGRAPHY

The Biographical Dictionary of Contemporary Poets; The Who's Who of American Poets. N.Y.: Avon House, 1938. 536p.

Wegelin, Oscar. Early American Poetry. 2d ed. rev. and enl. N.Y.: Peter Smith, 1930. 2 vols. in 1.

Winslow, Ola E. American Broadside Verse from Imprints of the 17th and 18th Centuries. New Haven, Conn.: Yale Univ. Press, 1930. 224p.

POETRY COLLECTIONS

Braithwaite, William S. Anthology of Magazine Verse. N.Y.: Gomme, 1913-29. 17 vols.

Davis's Anthology of Newspaper Verse. Ed. by Athie S. Davis. N.Y.: Henry Harrison, 1918-? (annual).

Del Vecchio, Thomas, ed. Contemporary Men Poets; An Anthology of Verse by 459 Living Poets. N.Y.: Henry Harrison, 1937. 176p.

Gordi, Tooni, ed. Contemporary American Women Poets. N.Y.: Henry Harrison, 1936. 320p.

Nelson, Margaret, ed. American Voices; An Anthology of Poetry Selected from Entries Submitted by More than 6000 Poets, with Biographical Notes of the Authors. N.Y.: Avon House, 1936. 462p.

_____. Yearbook of Contemporary Poetry 1936-37. N.Y.: Avon House, 1936-37. 2 vols.

New Yorker. New Yorker Book of Verse; An Anthology of
Poems First Published in the New Yorker 1925-1935.
N. Y.: Harcourt, Brace, 1935. 311p.

Stevenson, Burton E., ed. Poems of American History.
Rev. ed. Boston: Houghton Mifflin, 1936. 720p.

Warren, Edith, ed. Important American Poets. N. Y.:
Valiant House, 1938. 756p.

NATIONAL DRAMA BIBLIOGRAPHY

Best One-Act Plays 1937-1960. Ed. by Margaret G. Mayorga. N. Y.: Dodd, Mead, 1938-91. 24 vols.

The Best Plays Series. N. Y.: Dodd, Mead, 1919- (annual).
First edited by Burns Mantle, then by John Chapman,
Louis Kronenberger, and Otis L. Guernsey.

The Best Plays of 1909-1919 and the Yearbook of the Drama
of America. Ed. by Burns Mantle and Garrison P.
Sherwood. N. Y.: Dodd, Mead, 1933. 702p.

Halline, Allan G., ed. American Plays. N. Y.: American
Book Co., 1935. 787p.

Hill, Frank P. American Plays Printed 1714-1830; A Bibliographical Record. Palo Alto, Calif.: Stanford Univ.
Press, 1934. 152p.

Mayorga, Margaret G. A Short History of the American
Drama; Commentaries on Plays Prior to 1920. N. Y.:
Dodd, Mead, 1932. 493p.

One-Act Plays for Stage and Study. First to ninth series.
N. Y.: Samuel French, 1925-38.

Quinn, Arthur H. A History of the American Drama from
the Beginning to the Civil War. N. Y.: Harper, 1923.
486p.

_____. A History of the American Drama from the Civil
War to the Present Day. N. Y.: Harper, 1927. 2
vols.

_____. A History of the American Drama from the Civil
War to the Present Day. Rev. ed. N.Y.: F. S.
Crofts, 1936. 432p.

Yearbook of Short Plays. Ed. by Claude M. Wise and Lee
O. Snook. First to sixth series. Evanston, Ill.: Row,
Peterson, 1931-40.

REGIONAL BIBLIOGRAPHY

Elliott, William Y. "Local Color in Southern Literature:
A Bibliography." M.A. thesis, Univ. of Alabama,
1929. 59p.

Major, Mabel, et al. Southwest Heritage; A Literary History
with Bibliography. Albuquerque: Univ. of New Mexico
Press, 1938. 165p.

Rusk, Ralph L. The Literature of the Middle Western Frontier. N.Y.: Columbia Univ. Press, 1925. 2 vols.

REGIONAL FICTION BIBLIOGRAPHY

Agnew, Janet. A Southern Bibliography: Fiction 1929-1938.
Louisiana State Univ. Univ. Bulletin, n.s. 30, no. 7.
Library School Bibliography Series, no. 1. Baton
Rouge: Louisiana State Univ. Press, 1939. 63p.

Davidson, Levette J. "Early Fiction of the Rocky Mountain
Region," Colorado Magazine 10 (1933), 161-72.

Greer, Hilton R., ed. Best Short Stories from the Southwest. Dallas, Texas: Southwest Press, 1928. 386p.;
2d series, 1931. 380p.

Hibbard, Clarence A., ed. Stories of the South, Old and
New. Chapel Hill: Univ. of North Carolina Press,
1928. 520p.

Longmire, Rowena. "Dictionary Catalog of the Short Stories
of Arkansas, Missouri, and Iowa from 1869 to 1900."
Ph.D. dissertation, Univ. of Chicago, 1932.

McLeod, John A. "Southern Highlands in Prose Fiction."
M.A. thesis, Univ. of North Carolina, 1930.

Spotts, Carl B. "The Development of Fiction on the Missouri Frontier (1830-1860)." Ph.D. dissertation, Penn
State Univ., 1934.

_____. "The Development of Fiction on the Missouri
Frontier (1830-1860)," Missouri Historical Review 28
(1934), 195-205, 275-86; 29 (Oct. 1934-July 1935),
17-26, 100-08, 186-94, 279-94.

REGIONAL POETRY BIBLIOGRAPHY

Botkin, Benjamin A., ed. The Southwest Scene: An Anthology of Regional Verse. Oklahoma City: The Economy Co., 1931. 115p.

Ivey, B. S., ed. Pirate Gold; An Anthology of Southwestern
Verse 1898-1928. Austin, Texas; Morgan Printing Co.,
1928. 99p.

Parks, Edd W., ed. Southern Poets; Representative Selections, with Introduction and Notes by Edd W. Parks.
N.Y.: American Book Co., 1936. 419p.

Westward. Poets of the Western Scene; Poems from West-
ward, a National Magazine of Verse. Ed. and with a
Foreword by Hans A. Hoffmann. San Leandro, Calif.:
Greater West Pub. Co., 1937. 111p.

STATE BIBLIOGRAPHY

DeMenil, Alexander N. "A Century of Missouri Literature,"
Missouri Historical Review 15 (Oct. 1920), 74-125.

Gaer, Joseph, ed. Bibliography of California Literature;
Fiction of the Gold-Rush Period; Drama of the Gold-
Rush Period; Poetry of the Gold-Rush Period. 1935.
123 leaves (mimeo.).

Goodrich, Madge K. A Bibliography of Michigan Authors. Richmond, Va.: Richmond Press, 1928. 222p.

Hart, Bertha S. Introduction to Georgia Writers. Macon, Ga.: J. W. Burke, 1929. 322p.

Hazeltine, Mary E. One Hundred Years of Wisconsin Authorship, 1836-1937; A Contribution to a Bibliography of Books by Wisconsin Authors. Madison: Wisconsin Library Association, 1937. 140 leaves (mimeo.)

Hinkel, Edgar J., ed. Bibliography of California Fiction, Poetry, Drama. Produced on a WPA Project. Sponsored by the Alameda County Library, Oakland, Calif. Oakland, 1938. 3 vols. (mimeo.).

Janeway, William R. A Selected List of Ohio Authors and Their Books. Columbus, Ohio: H. L. Hedrick, 1933. 248p.

McClanahan, Mary E. "A Descriptive Bibliography of Tennessee Authors with Biographical Notes." M.A. thesis, Vanderbilt Univ., 1932. 106p.

Marable, Mary H., and Boylan, Elaine. A Handbook of Oklahoma Writers. Norman: Univ. of Oklahoma Press, 1939. 300p.

"North Carolina Bibliography," North Carolina Historical Review, the April issue of each year, beginning in 1935.

Pearson, Alice L. "The Upper Peninsula of Michigan in Literature." M.A. thesis, Univ. of Colorado, 1939.

Ray, Frank J. "Tennessee Writers; A Bibliographical Index." M.A. thesis, Univ. of Tennessee, 1929.

Wheeler, Eva F. "A Bibliography of Wyoming Writers," Univ. of Wyoming Publications 6 (Feb. 15, 1939), 11-37.

STATE LITERARY HISTORY

Dillard, Irene. "A History of Literature in South Carolina."

Ph. D. dissertation, Univ. of North Carolina, 1924.
308p.

Givens, Bessie. "A Literary History of Mississippi." M. A.
thesis, Vanderbilt Univ., 1932.

Healey, Margaret M. "The Short Story in Louisiana During
the Local-Color Period, 1869-1899." M. A. thesis,
Univ. of Chicago, 1935.

Payne, Leonidas W. A Survey of Texas Literature. N. Y.:
Rand, McNally, 1928. 76p.

Pollard, Lancaster. "Washington Literature; A Historical
Sketch." Pacific Northwest Quarterly 29 (1938), 227-54.

Powers, Alfred. History of Oregon Literature, Illustrated
with Manuscripts, Title Pages, Photographs of Sculpture,
and Crayon Drawings by Bernard Hinshaw. Portland,
Oregon: Metropolitan Press, 1935. 809p.

Schumpert, Mary F. "A Survey of Mississippi Fiction and
Verse since 1900." M. A. thesis, Univ. of Mississippi,
1931.

Wauchope, George A. Literary South Carolina; A Short Account of the Progress of Literature and the Principal
Writers and Books from 1700 to 1923. Univ. of South
Carolina Bulletin, no. 133. Columbia, S. C., 1923.
160p.

STATE LITERARY COLLECTIONS

Boyer, Mary G. Arizona in Literature. Glendale, Calif.:
Arthur H. Clarke, 1935. 574p.

Hungerpiller, John C., ed. South Carolina Literature with
Biographical Notes and Critical Comments. Columbia,
S. C.: Press of R. L. Bryan Co., 1931. 249p.

Wood, Warren. Representative Authors of West Virginia.
Ravenswood, W. Va.: Worth-while Book Co., 1926.
322p.

STATE FICTION BIBLIOGRAPHY

Foster, Bernice M. Michigan Novelists. Ann Arbor, Mich.:
George Wahr, 1928. 30p.

Fox, Maynard. "Book-Length Fiction by Kansas Writers,
1915-1938." Master's thesis, Fort Hays Kansas State
College, 1939. 99p.

McVoy, Lizzie C., and Campbell, Ruth B. A Bibliography
of Fiction by Louisianians and on Louisiana Subjects.
Louisiana State Univ. Studies, no. 18. Baton Rouge:
Louisiana State Univ. Press, 1935. 87p.

STATE POETRY BIBLIOGRAPHY

Brashear, Minnie M. "Bibliography of Missouri Verse,"
Missouri Historical Review 19 (Oct. 1924), 87-93.

_____. "Missouri Verse and Verse Writers," Missouri
Historical Review 18 (April 1924), 315-44; 19 (Oct.
1924), 36-93.

Ford, Worthington C. Broadsides, Ballads, Etc., Printed
in Massachusetts 1639-1800. Boston: Massachusetts
Historical Society, 1922. 483p.

Jacobi, Gertrude F. "Minor Poets of South Carolina."
M.A. thesis, Univ. of Florida, 1937. 408p.

Kleppel, Placid. A Bibliography of North Carolina Poetry.
Belmont, N.C.: Abbey Press, 1934. 15p.

Wallenberg, Venice. "A Bibliography of Texas Poetry."
M.A. thesis, Texas Christian Univ., 1927. Unpaged
(about 200p.).

STATE POETRY COLLECTIONS

Allsopp, Frederick, ed. Poets and Poetry of Arkansas.

Little Rock, Ark.: Central Printing Co., 1933.
232p.

Braithwaite, William S., ed. Anthology of Massachusetts
Poets. Boston: Small, Maynard, 1922. 145p.

Brown, Mary L., ed. Rhode Island in Verse. Providence,
R.I.: Roger Williams Press, 1936. 244p.

Coates, Walter J. Favorite Vermont Poets. Series 1-4.
North Montpelier, Vt.: 1928-31.

Conner, Aletha C. Anthology of Poetry by Oklahoma Writers.
Guthrie, Okla.: Cooperative Pub. Co., 1935. 153p.

Deavours, Ernestine C., ed. Mississippi Poets. Memphis:
Clarke Bros., 1922. 204p.

Derleth, August W., and Larsson, Raymond E., eds. Poetry
Out of Wisconsin. N.Y.: Henry Harrison, 1937. 334p.

Graham, Philip, ed. Early Texas Verse (1835-1850) Collected from the Original Newspapers. Austin, Texas:
Steck Co., 1936. 131p.

Harrison, Henry, ed. California Poets; An Anthology of 244
Contemporaries. N.Y.: Henry Harrison, 1932. 768p.

_____. Florida Poets: An Anthology of Contemporary
Verse. N.Y.: Henry Harrison, 1931. 144p.

_____. Georgia Poets: An Anthology of 33 Contemporaries.
N.Y.: Henry Harrison, 1932. 111p.

_____. Michigan Poets: An Anthology of 36 Contempora-
ries. N.Y.: Henry Harrison, 1936. 128p.

_____. Pennsylvania Poets. N.Y.: Henry Harrison, 1936.
223p.

James, Alice, ed. Mississippi Verse. Chapel Hill: Univ.
of North Carolina Press, 1934. 94p.

Gordon, Armistead C. Virginia Writers of Fugitive Verse.
N.Y.: James T. White, 1923. 404p.

Merrill, Harrison R., and Brandley, Elsie T., eds. Utah

Sings: An Anthology of Contemporary Verse. Provo: Utah Academy of Sciences, Arts and Letters, 1934-42. 3 vols.

Musgrove, Eugene R. Poems of New Jersey: An Anthology. N.Y.: Gregg Pub. Co., 1923. 472p.

Poetry Society of Alabama. Alabama Poetry. Dallas, Texas: Kaleidograph Press, 1945. 73p.

Poetry Society of Georgia. Prize Poems, Poetry Society of Georgia. Savannah: 1925. 35p.

_____. 25th Anniversary 1923-1948. Athens: University of Georgia, 1949. 60p.

Poetry Society of Oklahoma. State Anthology. Oklahoma City: Times-Journal Pub. Co., 1936. 186p.

Poetry Society of South Carolina. Yearbook for 1921. Ed. by DuBose Heyward and Hervey Allen. Charleston, S.C., 1923. 48p.

Poetry Society of Texas. Book of the Year. Dallas, Texas: 1925. 60p.

Raley, Loker, ed. 300 Years; the Poets and Poetry of Maryland. N.Y.: Henry Harrison, 1937. 171p.

Sterling, George, et al., eds. Continent's End; An Anthology of Contemporary California Poets. San Francisco: Printed for Book Club of California by J. H. Nash, 1925. 237p.

Stevens, Pearle M., ed. Greater Texas; An Anthology of Verse with Poets of the Southwest. San Antonio, Texas: Naylor, 1939. 182p.

LOCAL BIBLIOGRAPHY AND COLLECTIONS

Battle Creek Scribblers' Club. Battle Creek Writers, Poems and Prose. Battle Creek, Mich., 1927. 80p.

DeMenil, Alexander N. The St. Louis Book Authors. St.

Louis: William Harvey Miner, 1925. 69p.

Elam, Charles M., ed. Cincinnati Poetry of the 19th Century. Cincinnati: Open Sesame Press, 1928. 28p.

Elliott, Mary Q. Biographical Sketches of Knox County [Ohio] Writers. Mt. Vernon, Ohio, 1937. 84p.

Hanford, C. H., ed. Seattle and Environs 1852-1924. Chicago: Pioneer Historical Pub. Co., 1924. 3 vols.

Harwood, Pliny L., and Harwood, Rowena M., eds. The Poets of New London: An Anthology. New London, Conn., 1933. 163p.

Johnson, Rossiter. "Rochester in Literature," Rochester Historical Society Publications 1 (1922), 163-87.

National League of American Pen Women. N.Y.C. Branch. Anthology of Modern Poetry by Members of the League. N.Y.: Hogan-Paulus Corp., 1926. 144p.

_____. San Diego Branch. Wind in the Palms; Anthology of San Diego Verse, 1932. San Diego, Calif.: City Print Co., 1932. 129p.

Peoria Book of Verse. Peoria, Ill.: Published for the Peoria Allied English Interests by the Manual Arts Press, 1922. 106p.

Poets Assembly of Philadelphia. Mined on Parnassus; An Anthology by Members of the Poets Assembly of Phila. and the Phila. Unit of the Catholic Poetry Society of America. Phila., 1939. 24p.

Weston, Latrobe. Baltimore in Verse and Prose. Baltimore: H. G. Roebuck, 1936. 84p.

STATE HISTORY SOURCES

Cappon, Lester J. Bibliography of Virginia History since 1865. Charlottesville: Institute for Research in the Social Sciences, University of Virginia, 1930. 900p.

Godcharles, Frederic A. Pennsylvania, Political, Govern-
mental, Military and Civil. N. Y.: American Historical Society, 1933. 4 vols.

Kull, Irving S., ed. New Jersey; A History. N. Y.: American Historical Society, 1930. 4 vols.

McMechen, Edgar. "Literature and the Arts," in History
of Colorado, by James H. Baker. Denver: Linder-
man Co., 1927. Vol. 3, p. 1231-85.

Owen, Thomas M. History of Alabama and Dictionary of
Biography. Chicago: S. J. Clarke, 1921. 4 vols.

Swem, Earl G. Virginia Historical Index. Roanoke, Va.:
Stone Printing and Manufacturing Co., 1934-36. 2 vols.

Torrey, Edwin C. "Early Poets of South Dakota," in Early
Days in Dakota. Minneapolis: Farnham Printing and
Stationery Co., 1925. p. 65-74.

Williams, Stanley T. "The Literature of Connecticut," in
History of Connecticut in Monographic Form, ed. by
Norris G. Osborn. N. Y.: States History Co., 1925.
Vol. 2, p. 483-537.

HUMOR

Blair, Walter. Native American Humor (1800-1900). N. Y.:
American Book Co., 1937. 573p.

A Book of American Humor in Prose and Verse. N. Y.:
Duffield, 1925. 2 parts in 1 vol., 249p. and 251p.

Hudson, Arthur P., ed. Humor of the Old Deep South.
N. Y.: Macmillan, 1936. 548p.

Meine, Franklin J. Tall Tales of the Southwest; An Anthology
of Southern and Southwestern Humor, 1830-1860. N. Y.:
Knopf, 1930. 456p.

Mott, Howard S., Jr. Three Hundred Years of American
Humor (1637-1936). N. Y.: the Author, 1937. 32p.
(Book dealer's catalog.)

AUTHOR BIBLIOGRAPHIES

Alberts, Sydney S. A Bibliography of the Works of Robinson
    Jeffers. N. Y.: Random House, 1933. 262p.

Brussel, Isidore R. A Bibliography of the Writings of
    James Branch Cabell: A Revised Bibliography. Phila.:
    Centaur Book Shop, 1932. 126p.

Clarkson, Paul S. A Bibliography of William Sydney Porter.
    Caldwell, Idaho: Caxton Printers, 1938. 161p.

Cohn, Louis H. A Bibliography of the Works of Ernest
    Hemingway. N. Y.: Random House, 1931. 116p.

Cunningham, Scott. A Bibliography of the Writings of Carl
    Van Vechten. Phila: Centaur Book Shop, 1924. 52p.

Currie, Barton. Booth Tarkington: A Bibliography. Garden
    City, N. Y.: Doubleday, Doran, 1932. 154p.

Currier, Thomas F. Bibliography of John Greenleaf Whittier.
    Cambridge, Mass.: Harvard Univ. Press, 1937. 692p.

Gallup, Donald C. A Catalogue of English and American
    First Editions of Writings of T. S. Eliot Exhibited in
    the Yale University Library. New Haven, Conn.:
    Yale Univ. Library, 1937. 42p.

Hampson, Alfred L. Emily Dickinson: A Bibliography.
    Northampton, Mass.: Hampshire Bookshop, 1930. 36p.

Hogan, Charles B. A Bibliography of Edwin Arlington Robin-
    son. New Haven, Conn.: Yale Univ. Press, 1936.
    221p.

Holt, Guy. A Bibliography of the Writings of James Branch
    Cabell. Phila.: Centaur Book Shop, 1924. 73p.

Johnson, Cecil. A Bibliography of the Writings of George
    Sterling. San Francisco: Windsor Press, 1931. 63p.

Johnson, Merle D. A Bibliography of the Works of Mark
    Twain, Samuel Langhorne Clemens. Rev. ed. N. Y.:
    Harper, 1910. 203p.

Langfeld, William R., and Blackburn, Philip C. Washington Irving: A Bibliography. N. Y.: New York Public Library, 1933. 90p.

Lee, Alfred P. A Bibliography of Christopher Morley. Garden City, N. Y.: Doubleday, Doran, 1935. 277p.

Lippincott, Lillian. A Bibliography of the Writings and Criticisms of Edwin Arlington Robinson. Boston: Faxon Co., 1937. 86p.

MacDonald, Edward D. A Bibliography of the Writings of Theodore Dreiser. Phila.: Centaur Book Shop, 1928. 130p.

Melish, Lawson M. A Bibliography of the Collected Writings of Edith Wharton. N. Y.: Brick Row Book Shop, 1927. 87p.

Robertson, John W. Bibliography of the Writings of Edgar Allan Poe. San Francisco: Edwin and Robert Grabhorn, 1934. 2 vols.

Sanborn, Ralph, and Clark, Barrett H. A Bibliography of the Works of Eugene O'Neill. N. Y.: Random House, 1931. 171p.

Spiller, Robert E., and Blackburn, Philip C. A Descriptive Bibliography of the Works of James Fenimore Cooper. N. Y.: Bowker, 1934. 259p.

Starrett, Vincent. Ambrose Bierce: A Bibliography. Phila.: Centaur Book Shop, 1929. 117p.

_____. Stephen Crane: A Bibliography. Phila.: Centaur Book Shop, 1923. 46p.

Swire, Herbert L. A Bibliography of the Works of Joseph Hergesheimer. Phila.: Centaur Book Shop, 1922. 39p.

Wegelin, Oscar. A Bibliography of the Separate Writings of John Esten Cooke. Heartmen's Historical Series, no. 43. Metuchen, N.J.: C. F. Heartman, 1925. 20p.

Williams, Stanley T., and Edge, Mary A. A Bibliography of

the Writings of Washington Irving: A Checklist. N. Y.: Oxford Univ. Press, 1936. 200p.

Yost, Karl. A Bibliography of the Works of Edna St. Vincent Millay. N. Y.: Harper, 1937. 248p.

BIOGRAPHIES CONTAINING BIBLIOGRAPHIES

Adkins, Nelson F. Fitz-Greene Halleck: An Early Knickerbocker Wit and Poet. New Haven, Conn.: Yale Univ. Press, 1930. Bib., p. 376-87.

Barnes, Homer F. Charles Fenno Hoffman. N. Y.: Columbia Univ. Press, 1930. Bib., p. 317-33.

Bradley, Edward S. George Henry Boker: Poet and Patriot. Phila.: Univ. of Pennsylvania Press, 1927. Bib., p. 343-49.

Herold, Amos L. James Kirke Paulding: Versatile American. N. Y.: Columbia Univ. Press, 1926. Bib., p. 148-60.

Van Doren, Carl. Sinclair Lewis; A Biographical Sketch with a Bibliography by Harvey Taylor. N. Y.: Doubleday, Doran, 1933. Bib., p. 77-187.

APPENDIX B 1940-1959

COMPREHENSIVE NATIONAL BIBLIOGRAPHY

Americana Annual. N. Y.: Americana Corp., 1923- .

Blanck, Jacob. Bibliography of American Literature,
    comp. ... for the Bibliographical Society of America.
    New Haven, Conn.: Yale Univ. Press, 1955- (in
    progress).

Burke, William J., and Howe, Will D. American Authors
    and Books, 1640-1940. N. Y.: Gramercy Pub. Co.,
    1943. 858p.

Hart, James D. Oxford Companion to American Literature.
    N. Y.: Oxford Univ. Press, 1941. 888p. 2d ed.,
    1948; 3d ed., 1956.

Literary History of the United States. Edited by Robert E.
    Spiller et al. Bibliography. Compiled and edited by
    Thomas H. Johnson. N. Y.: Macmillan, 1948. 817p.
    Supplement, 1959.

Millett, Fred B. Contemporary American Authors; A
    Critical Survey and 219 Biobibliographies. N. Y.:
    Harcourt, Brace, 1940. 716p.

Wilson, Carroll A. Thirteen Author Collections of the 19th
    Century and Five Centuries of Familiar Quotations.
    Ed. by Jean C. S. Wilson and David A. Randall.
    N. Y.: Privately printed for Charles Scribner's Sons,
    1950. 2 vols.

NATIONAL FICTION BIBLIOGRAPHY

Brown, Herbert R. The Sentimental Novel in America 1789-
1860. Durham, N.C.: Duke Univ. Press, 1940. 407p.

Coan, Otis W., and Lillard, Richard G. America in Fiction.
Palo Alto, Calif.: Stanford Univ. Press, 1941. 180p.

Dickens, William B. "A Guide to the American Political
Novel 1865-1910." Ph.D. dissertation, Univ. of Michigan, 1954. 402p.

Dickinson, Arthur T. American Historical Fiction. N.Y.:
Scarecrow Press, 1958. 314p.

Fenton, Charles A., ed. The Best Short Stories of World
War II; An American Anthology. N.Y.: Viking Press,
1957. 428p.

Leisy, Ernest E. The American Historical Novel. Norman:
Univ. of Oklahoma Press, 1950. 280p.

Lively, Robert A. Fiction Fights the Civil War; An Unfinished Chapter in the Literary History of the American People. Chapel Hill: Univ. of North Carolina
Press, 1957. 230p.

Mason, F. Van Wyck, ed. The Fighting American; A War
Chest of Stories of American Soldiers from the French
and Indian Wars Through the First World War. N.Y.:
Reynal and Hitchcock, 1943. 747p.

New Yorker. Short Stories From the New Yorker. N.Y.:
Simon & Schuster, 1940. 440p.

_____. 55 Short Stories From the New Yorker. N.Y.:
Simon & Schuster, 1949. 480p.

Newberry Library, Chicago. American Novels with an
American Setting Printed Before 1880; A Checklist of
Books in the Library, August 1941. Chicago, 1941.
36 leaves (mimeo.).

Prestridge, Virginia, comp. Worker in American Fiction;
An Annotated Bibliography. Champaign: Institute of
Labor and Industrial Relations, Univ. of Illinois, 1954.
27p.

Rose, Lisle A. "A Bibliographic Survey of Economic and Political Writings 1865-1900." American Literature 15 (1944), 381-410.

Taylor, Walter F. The Economic Novel in America. Chapel Hill: Univ. of North Carolina Press, 1942. 378p.

Waldmeir, Joseph J. "Ideological Aspects of the American Novels of World War II." Ph.D. dissertation, Michigan State Univ., 1959. 191p.

Warfel, Harry R. American Novelists of Today. N.Y.: American Book Co., 1951. 478p.

Wright, Lyle H. American Fiction 1851-1875. San Marino, Calif.: Huntington Library, 1957. 413p.

_____. American Fiction 1774-1850; A Contribution Toward a Bibliography. Rev. ed. San Marino, Calif.: 1948. 355p.

_____. "Eighteenth-Century American Fiction: Bibliography," in Essays Honoring Lawrence C. Wroth. Portland, Me.: Anthoensen Press, 1951. p.460-73.

NATIONAL POETRY BIBLIOGRAPHY

Browne, Ray B. "American Poets in the 19th Century 'Popular' Song-Books," American Literature 30 (1959), 503-22.

Gregory, Horace, and Zaturenska, Marya. A History of American Poetry 1900-1940. N.Y.: Harcourt, Brace, 1942. 524p.

Irish, Wynot R. The Modern American Muse; A Complete Bibliography of American Verse 1900-1925. Syracuse, N.Y.: Syracuse Univ. Press, 1950. 259p.

Sugarman, Milton H. "A Bibliography of a Collection of Anonymous Poetical Pamphlets of the 18th Century in the Library of the University of Cincinnati." Ph.D. dissertation, Univ. of Cincinnati, 1953. 184p.

U.S. Library of Congress. General Reference and Bibliography

Division. Sixty American Poets, 1896-1944. Selected with Preface and Critical Notes by Allen Tate. A Preliminary Checklist by Frances Cheney. Washington, D.C., 1945. 188p. Revised by Kenton Kilmer in 1954.

University of Pennsylvania Library. Checklist of Poetry by American Authors Published in the English Colonies of North America and the United States Through 1865, in the Possession of the Rare Book Room, University of Pennsylvania. Compiled by Albert von Chorba, Jr. Phila., 1951. 68 leaves (mimeo.).

NATIONAL DRAMA BIBLIOGRAPHY

America's Lost Plays. Princeton, N.J.: Princeton Univ. Press, 1940-42. 20 vols.

Andrews, Mary L. "Modern Poetic Drama in America, 1900-1942." Ph.D. dissertation, New York Univ., 1943. 92p.

Best American Plays. N.Y.: Crown, 1939- .

Elfenbein, Josef A. "American Drama 1782-1812 as an Index to 'Socio-Political Thought." Ph.D. dissertation, New York Univ., 1951. 375p.

Ferguson, Phyllis M. "Women dramatists in the American Theatre 1901-1940." Ph.D. dissertation, Univ. of Pittsburgh, 1957. 362p.

Nannes, Caspar H. "Politics in the American Drama as Revealed by Plays Produced on the New York Stage 1890-1945." Ph.D. dissertation, Univ. of Pennsylvania, 1949. 307p.

Quinn, Arthur H. A History of the American Drama from the Beginning to the Civil War. 2d ed. N.Y.: Appleton-Century-Crofts, 1951. 530p.

Reardon, John D. "Verse Drama in America from 1765 to the Civil War." Ph.D. dissertation, Univ. of Kansas, 1958.

Sper, Felix. From Native Roots; A Panorama of Our Regional Drama. Caldwell, Idaho: Caxton Printers, 1948. 341p.

University of Pennsylvania Library. Checklist of American Drama Published in the English Colonies of North America and the United States Through 1865 in the Possession of the Library, University of Pennsylvania. Comp. by Herbert von Chorba, Jr. With an Introduction by Arthur H. Quinn. Phila., 1951. 92p.

Walbridge, Earle F. "Drames à clef: A List of Plays with Characters Based on Real People: American Drama," Bulletin of the New York Public Library 60 (May 1956), 235-47.

Weingarten, Joseph A. Modern American Playwrights: A Bibliography. N. Y.: 1946. 2 parts.

William L. Clements Library. Early American Drama; A Guide to an Exhibition in the William L. Clements Library. Arranged by Ada P. Booth. Ann Arbor, Mich.: 1945. 18p.

REGIONAL BIBLIOGRAPHY

Frederick, John T., ed. Out of the Midwest; A Collection of Present-Day Writing. N. Y.: Whittlesey House, 1944. 405p.

Harkness, David J. The Southwest and West Coast in Literature. Univ. of Tennessee Newsletter 33, no. 10, October 1954. 55p.

Harwell, Richard B. Confederate Belles-Lettres; A Bibliography and a Finding List of Fiction, Poetry, Drama, Songsters, and Miscellaneous Literature Published in the Confederate States. Hattiesburg, Miss.: Book Farm, 1941. 79p.

Hubbell, Jay B., Jr. The South in American Literature 1607-1900. Durham, N.C.: Duke Univ. Press, 1954. 987p.

Kurtz, Kenneth. Literature of the American Southwest: A
    Selective Bibliography. Los Angeles: Occidental Col-
    lege, 1956. 63p.

Rader, Jesse L. South of Forty from the Mississippi to the
    Rio Grande: A Bibliography. Norman: Oklahoma
    Press, 1947. 336p.

West, Ray B. Writing in the Rocky Mountains with a Bibliog-
    raphy by Nellie Cliff. Lincoln: Univ. of Nebraska
    Press, 1947. 96p.

REGIONAL FICTION BIBLIOGRAPHY

Agnew, Janet. A Southern Bibliography: Historical Fiction
    1929-1938. Louisiana State Univ. Bulletin, n. s. 32,
    no. 8. Library School Bibliography Series, no. 2.
    Baton Rouge: Louisiana State Univ. Press, 1940. 80p.

Dooley, Nelly. "Sectionalism and Local Color in the Short
    Stories of the Plains States, 1870-1938." Master's
    thesis, Fort Hays Kansas State College, 1940. 137p.

Flanagan, John T. "A Bibliography of Middle Western Farm
    Novels," Minnesota History 23 (June 1942), 156-58.

_____. "The Middle Western Historical Novel," Journal
    of the Illinois State Historical Society 37 (Mar. 1944),
    7-47.

Hartin, John S. "The Southeastern United States in the Novel
    Through 1950; A Bibliographic Review." Ph. D. disser-
    tation, Univ. of Michigan, 1957. 646p.

Hitt, Helen. "History in Pacific Northwest Novels Written
    Since 1920," Oregon Historical Quarterly 51 (Sept. 1950),
    180-206.

Jones, Harry H. "Fiction of the Rocky Mountain Area," Univ.
    of Wyoming Publications 20, no. 1 (1956), 124-29.

Jones, Katherine M. , ed. New Confederate Short Stories.
    Columbia: Univ. of South Carolina Press, 1954.
    202p.

Powell, Lawrence C. Heart of the Southwest: A Selective Bibliography of Novels, Stories, and Tales Laid in Arizona and New Mexico and Adjacent Lands. Los Angeles: Printed for Dawson's Book Shop at the Plantin Press, 1955. 42p.

Shaul, Lawana J. "Treatment of the West in Selected Magazine Fiction, 1870-1900; An Annotated Bibliography." M.A. thesis, Univ. of Wyoming, 1954. 123p.

Van Auken, Sheldon. "The Southern Historical Novel in the Early Twentieth Century," Journal of Southern History 14 (1948), 157-91.

REGIONAL POETRY BIBLIOGRAPHY

Agnew, Janet M. A Southern Bibliography: Poetry 1929-1938. Louisiana State Univ. Bulletin, n.s. 32, no. 11. Library School Bibliography Series, no. 3. Baton Rouge: Louisiana State Univ. Press, 1940. 47p.

Jantz, Harold S. "Bibliography of Early New England Verse," Proceedings of the American Antiquarian Society, n.s. 53 (1943), 391-508.

_____. "Unrecorded Verse Broadsides of Seventeenth Century New England," Papers of the Bibliographical Society of America 39 (1945), 1-19.

Major, Mabel, and Pearce, Thomas M., eds. Signature of the Sun; Southwest Verse 1900-1950. Albuquerque: Univ. of New Mexico Press, 1950. 302p.

Rudolph, Earl L. Confederate Broadside Verse; A Bibliography and Finding List of Confederate Broadside Ballads and Songs. New Braunfels, Texas: Book Farm, 1950. 118p.

Southwestern Anthology of Verse; Poets of the Southwest. San Antonio, Texas: Naylor Co., 1941. 241p.

STATE BIBLIOGRAPHY

Alden, John E., ed. Rhode Island Imprints 1727-1900.
N. Y.: Published for Bibliographical Society of America
by R. R. Bowker, 1949. 665p.

Banta, Richard E. Indiana Authors and Their Books 1816-
1916; Biographical Sketches of Authors Who Published
During the First Century of Indiana Statehood with
Lists of Their Books. Crawfordsville, Ind.: Wabash
College, 1949. 352p.

Bonner, John W. "Bibliography of Georgia Authors," Georgia
Review, Winter issue beginning in 1950.

Brenni, Vito J. West Virginia Authors: A Biobibliography.
Morgantown: West Virginia Library Assoc., 1957. 73p.

Cappon, Lester J., and Duff, Stella F. Virginia Gazette
Index 1763-1780. Williamsburg, Va.: Institute of
Early American History and Culture, 1950. 1323p.

Greene, Barbara W. "Resources in Louisiana Literature;
Affective Writers." M.A. thesis, Southwestern Louisiana
Institute, 1959. 282p.

Historical Records Survey, Ohio. A Checklist of Ohio Imprints 1796-1820. Columbus, 1941. 202p.

Kirk, Rudolf, and Kirk, Clara. Authors of New Jersey: A
Checklist. Trenton: Division of the State Library,
Archives and History, 1955. 59p.

"Maryland Bibliography." Maryland Historical Magazine.
March issue of each year, beginning 1952.

Pollard, Lancaster. "A Checklist of Washington Authors,"
Pacific Northwest Quarterly 31 (1940), 3-96; 35 (1944),
233-66.

Spearman, Walter. North Carolina Writers. Univ. of North
Carolina Library Extension Publication 15, no. 1.
Chapel Hill: Univ. of North Carolina Press, 1949.
50p.

Thornton, Mary L. A Bibliography of North Carolina 1589-

1956. Chapel Hill: Univ. of North Carolina Press,
1958. 597p.

Turnbull, Robert J. Bibliography of South Carolina 1563-
1950. Charlottesville: Univ. of Virginia Press, 1956.
5 vols., plus Index published in 1960.

STATE LITERARY HISTORY

Jacobs, Elijah L. "A History of Missouri Literature 1780-
1930." Ph.D. dissertation, Univ. of Southern California, 1949. 150p.

_____, and Wolverton, Forrest E. Missouri Writers; A
Literary History of Missouri, 1780-1955. St. Louis:
State Publishing Co., 1955. 366p.

STATE FICTION BIBLIOGRAPHY

Able, Augustus H. "Fiction as a Mirror of Delaware Life,"
Delaware History 3 (1948), 37-53.

Bailey, Eutopia O. "Small Town in Missouri Twentieth Century Fiction," Missouri Historical Review 49 (April,
July 1955), 230-48, 328-41.

Emch, Lucille B. "Ohio in Short Stories 1824-1839," Ohio
Archeological and Historical Quarterly 53 (1944), 209-53.

Flanagan, John T. "Thirty Years of Minnesota Fiction,"
Minnesota History 31 (1950), 129-47.

Frederick, John T. "Early Iowa in Fiction," Palimpsest 36
(1955), 389-420.

_____. "The Farm in Iowa Fiction," Palimpsest 32 (1951),
121-52.

_____. "Town and City in Iowa Literature," Palimpsest
35 (1954), 49-96.

Jacobson, Harvey K. "A Study of Novels About North Dakota." Master's thesis, Univ. of North Dakota, 1956.

Kraus, Joe W. "Missouri in Fiction; A Review and a Bibliography." Missouri Historical Review 42 (April, July 1948), 209-55, 310-34.

McRory, Mary O. Florida in Fiction; A Bibliography. Tallahassee: Florida State Library, 1958. 67p.

McVoy, Lizzie C., ed. Louisiana in the Short Story. Louisiana State Univ. Studies, no. 41. University: Louisiana State Univ. Press, 1940. 291p.

Odum, Gertrude G. "Georgia Fiction 1926-1950." Georgia Review 5 (1951), 244-57.

Pearson, Alice L. "The Upper Peninsula in Fictional Literature," Michigan History 24 (1940), 329-38.

Powell, William S., ed. North Carolina Fiction 1734-1957. Chapel Hill: Univ. of North Carolina Library, 1958. 189p.

Richards, Horace G. One Hundred South Jersey Novels; A Bibliography of Fiction with a Southern New Jersey Setting. Trenton: New Jersey Folklore Society, 1947. 21p.

Thompson, Lawrence S., and Thompson, Algernon D. The Kentucky Novel. Lexington: Univ. of Kentucky Press, 1953. 172p.

Woodbridge, Hensley C. "The Kentucky Novel 1951-5," Kentucky Historical Society Review 54 (April 1956), 134-36.

_____. "The Kentucky Novel 1956-57," Kentucky Historical Society Review 56 (April 1958), 156-64.

STATE FICTION COLLECTIONS

Jones, Katharine M., and Schlaefer, Mary V., eds. South

Carolina in the Short Story. Columbia: Univ. of South Carolina Press, 1952. 176p.

Peery, William W., ed. 21 Texas Short Stories. Austin: Univ. of Texas Press, 1954. 264p.

Strode, Hudson. Spring Harvest; A Collection of Stories from Alabama. N.Y.: Knopf, 1944. 199p.

Summers, Hollis S., ed. Kentucky Story; A Collection of Short Stories. Lexington: Univ. of Kentucky Press, 1954. 247p.

Walser, Richard G., ed. North Carolina in the Short Story. Chapel Hill: Univ. of North Carolina Press, 1948. 309p.

_____. Short Stories from the Old North State. Chapel Hill: Univ. of North Carolina Press, 1959. 288p.

STATE POETRY BIBLIOGRAPHY

Chicago Public Library Omnibus Project. Bibliography of Illinois Poets since 1900. Chicago, 1942. 216 leaves.

Coates, Walter J. A Bibliography of Vermont Poetry and Gazetteer of Vermont Poets. Montpelier: Vermont Historical Society, 1942- .

STATE POETRY COLLECTIONS

Abbe, George, ed. Contemporary Ohio Poetry; An Anthology of Midcentury Ohio Poetry Sponsored by the Ohio Poetry Society. N.Y.: Poets of America Pub. Co., 1959. 193p.

Burklund, Carl E., ed. New Michigan Verse. Ann Arbor: Univ. of Michigan, 1940. 113p.

Christian, Sheldon, ed. Poems About Maine. N.Y.: Henry Harrison, 1940. 144p.

Iowa Poetry Association. <u>Lyrical Iowa</u>, 1946- . New London, Iowa, 1947- .

Jenney, Adeline M., ed. <u>Prairie Poets; An Anthology of Verse of the South Dakota Poetry Society 1927-1949</u>. Minneapolis: Lund Press, 1949. 209p.

Mississippi Poetry Society. <u>Lyric Mississippi; An Anthology of Selected Poems Written by Members of the Mississippi Poetry Society</u>. Birmingham, Ala.: Vulcan Press, 1955. 54p.

Poetry Society of Colorado. <u>Silver Souvenir 1921-1946</u>. Denver: Sage Books, 1946. 122p.

Richards, Carmen N., ed. <u>Minnesota Skyline; Anthology of Poems About Minnesota</u>. Minneapolis: League of Minnesota Poets, 1944. 141p.

Walser, Richard G., ed. <u>North Carolina Poetry</u>. Richmond, Va.: Garrett and Massie, 1941. 196p.

_____. <u>North Carolina Poetry</u>. Rev. ed. Richmond, Va.: Garrett and Massie, 1951. 222p.

LOCAL BIBLIOGRAPHY AND COLLECTIONS

<u>A Century of Benton County Poetry; A Collection of Original Poetry</u>. Roseburg, Oregon: Poetry Clinic, 1957. 68p.

Cone, Gertrude. <u>A Selective Bibliography of Publications on the Champlain Valley</u>. Plattsburgh?, N.Y., 1959. 144p.

Jillson, Willard. <u>Literary Haunts and Personalities of Old Frankfort 1791-1941</u>. Frankfort: Kentucky State Historical Society, 1941. 130p.

Lewis, Victor E., ed. <u>Poets and Poetry of Wyoming Valley: A Collection of Selected Contemporary Verse, Rhymes, and Poems</u>. Wilkes Barre, Pa.: Llewellyn Bros., 1940. 127p.

<u>A Little Book of Somerset County Verse</u>. Somerset County (Pa.) Historical Society. Sesquicentennial Publications, no. 3. Somerset, Pa., 1945. 37p.

Ross, Grace, and Kuykendall, Mabel, eds. Poetry Out Where the West Begins; A Collection of Poems by Fort Worth Authors. Dallas: Kaleidograph Press, 1949. 184p.

Wingfield, Marshall. Literary Memphis; A Survey of Its Writers and Writings. Memphis: West Tennessee Historical Society, 1942. 223p.

STATE HISTORY SOURCES

Able, Augustus H. "Delaware Literature," in Delaware: A History of the First State, ed. by Henry C. Reed. N.Y.: Lewis Historical Pub. Co., 1947. Vol. 2, p. 935-66.

Bining, Arthur C., et al. Writings on Pennsylvania History: A Bibliography; A List of Secondary Materials Compiled Under the Auspices of the Pennsylvania Historical Association. Harrisburg, Pa.: Historical and Museum Commission, 1946. 565p.

Coleman, J. Winston, Jr. A Bibliography of Kentucky History. Lexington: Univ. of Kentucky Press, 1949. 516p.

Hatcher, Harlan. "Ohio in the Literature of the 20th Century," in The History of the State of Ohio, ed. by Carl F. Wittke. Columbus: Ohio State Archeological and Historical Society, 1942. Vol. 6, p. 267-93.

Merriam, Harold G. "Montana Writing," in A History of Montana, by Merrill G. Burlingame and Ross K. Toole. N.Y.: Lewis Pub. Co., 1957. Vol. 2, p. 265-90.

Schlinkert, Leroy. Subject Bibliography of Wisconsin History. Madison: State Historical Society of Wisconsin, 1947. 213p.

STATE GUIDEBOOKS

Federal Writers' Program. Atlanta; A City of the Modern

South. N. Y.: Smith and Durrell, 1942. 266p. (American Guide Series.)

_____. Michigan; A Guide to the Wolverine State. N. Y.: Oxford Univ. Press, 1941. 696p. (American Guide Series.)

_____. Oklahoma; A Guide to the Sooner State. Norman: Univ. of Oklahoma Press, 1941. 445p. rev. ed., 1957. (American Guide Series.)

_____. Tennessee; A Guide to the State. N. Y.: Viking Press, 1939. 558p. (American Guide Series.)

_____. Wisconsin; A Guide to the Badger State. N. Y.: Duell, Sloan and Pearce, 1941. 651p. (American Guide Series.)

HUMOR

Cerf, Bennett, ed. An Encyclopedia of Modern American Humor. Garden City, N. Y.: Hanover House, 1954. 688p.

Chittick, Victor L., ed. Ring-tailed Roarers; Tall Tales of the American Frontier 1830-1860. Caldwell, Idaho: Caxton Printers, 1941. 316p.

Conroy, Jack, ed. Midland Humor. N. Y.: Current Books, 1947. 446p.

Linscott, Robert N., ed. The Best American Humorous Short Stories. N. Y.: Random House, 1945. 436p.

Seaver, Edwin, ed. Pageant of American Humor. Cleveland: World, 1948. 607p.

White, Elwyn B., and White, Katharine S., eds. A Subtreasury of American Humor. N. Y.: Coward-McCann, 1941. 814p.

AUTHOR BIBLIOGRAPHIES

Bradley, J. J. "An Annotated Bibliography of Material by and about Thornton N. Wilder." Master's thesis, Carnegie Institute of Technology, 1953. 44p.

Branch, Edgar M. A Bibliography of James T. Farrell's Writings, 1921-1957. Phila.: Univ. of Pennsylvania Press, 1959. 142p.

Brewer, Frances J., and Bruccoli, Matthew J. James Branch Cabell. Charlottesville: Univ. of Virginia Press, 1957. 2 vols.

Cox, Martha. Maxwell Anderson Bibliography. Charlottesville: Bibliographical Society, Univ. of Virginia, 1958. 117p.

Currier, Thomas F. A Bibliography of Oliver Wendell Holmes. Ed. by Eleanor M. Tilton. N.Y.: New York Univ. Press, 1953. 707p.

Daniel, Robert W. A Catalog of the Writings of William Faulkner. New Haven, Conn.: Yale Univ. Library, 1942. 32p.

Duke University Library. Catalog of the Whitman Collection in the Duke University Library Being a Part of the Trent Collection Given by Dr. and Mrs. Josiah C. Trent. Compiled by Ellen F. Frey. Durham, N.C.: Duke Univ. Library, 1945. 148p.

Edel, Leon, and Laurence, Dan H. A Bibliography of Henry James. London: Hart-Davis, 1957. 411p. (Soho Bibliography.)

Edelstein, Jerome M. A Bibliographical Checklist of the Writings of Thornton Wilder. New Haven, Conn.: Yale Univ. Library, 1959. 62p.

Edwards, John. A Preliminary Checklist of Ezra Pound, Especially His Contributions to Periodicals. New Haven, Conn.: Kirgo-Books, 1953. 73p.

Feinberg, Charles E. Walt Whitman: A Selection of the

Manuscripts, Books, and Association Items Gathered by Charles E. Feinberg. Catalogue of an Exhibition Held at the Detroit Public Library, Detroit, Michigan, 1955. Detroit: 1955. 128p.

Gallup, Donald C. A Bibliographical Checklist of the Writings of T. S. Eliot. New Haven, Conn.: Yale Univ. Library, 1947. 128p.

_____. T. S. Eliot: A Bibliography, Including Contributions to Periodicals and Foreign Translations. N. Y.: Harcourt, Brace, 1953. 177p.

Haas, Robert B., and Gallup, Donald C. A Catalog of the Published and Unpublished Writings of Gertrude Stein Exhibited in the Yale University Library. New Haven, Conn.: Yale Univ. Library, 1941. 64p.

Hagle, A. D. "Hamlin Garland: A Bio-Bibliography." Master's thesis, Catholic Univ. of America, 1958. 100p.

Heartman, Charles F. Bibliographical Checklist of the Writings of the Poet, Charles West Thomson. Heartman's Historical Series, no. 60. Hattiesburg, Miss.: Book Farm, 1941. 15p.

_____, and Canny, James R. A Bibliography of the Writings of Edgar Allen Poe Together with a Record of First and Contemporary Later Prints of His Contributions to Annuals, Anthologies, Periodicals and Newspapers Issued During His Lifetime. Rev. ed. Hattiesburg, Miss.: Book Farm, 1943. 294p.

Holmes, Thomas J. Cotton Mather: A Bibliography of His Works. Cambridge, Mass.: Harvard Univ. Press, 1940. 3 vols.

Johnson, Elmer D. Of Time and Thomas Wolfe: A Bibliography with a Character Index of His Works. N. Y.: Scarecrow Press, 1959. 226p.

Jonas, Klaus W. Carl Van Vechten: A Bibliography. N. Y.: Knopf, 1955. 82p.

Lauter, Paul. E. E. Cummings: Index to First Lines and

Bibliography of Works by and about the Poet. Denver: A. Swallow, 1955. 44 leaves (mimeo.).

Lewis, Mary D. "Stephen Vincent Benét: His Major Work, His Preparation for It, and a Bibliography of His Writings." Ph.D. dissertation, Univ. of Illinois, 1953. 279p.

Lohf, Kenneth A., and Sheehy, Eugene P. Frank Norris: A Bibliography. Los Gatos, Calif.: Talisman Press, 1959. 107p.

Lyle, Guy R., and Brown, H. Tatnall. A Bibliography of Christopher Morley. Washington, D.C.: Scarecrow Press, 1952. 198p.

McDonald, J. P. "A Bibliography of Works by and about Willa Cather." Master's thesis, Drexel Institute of Technology, 1951. 57p.

Matheson, J. W. "Theodore Roethke: A Bibliography." Master's thesis, Univ. of Washington, 1958. 68p.

Morse, Samuel F. Wallace Stevens: A Preliminary Checklist of His Published Writings, 1898-1954. Published in Connection with an Exhibition Held in Honor of the Poet's 75th Birthday, 2 Oct. 1954. New Haven, Conn.: Yale Univ. Library, 1954. 66p.

New York Public Library. Berg Collection. Nathaniel Hawthorne: The Years of Fulfillment 1804-1853. An Exhibition from the Berg Collection: First Editions, Manuscripts, Autograph Letters. Compiled by John D. Gordon. N.Y.: New York Public Library, 1954. 50p.

Payne, M. H. "Dorothy Canfield Fisher: Biobibliography." Master's thesis, Florida State Univ., 1959. 84p.

Potter, Jack. A Bibliography of John Dos Passos. Chicago: Normandie House, 1950. 95p.

Rogers, T. T. "Marjorie Kinnan Rawlings, Regional Writer: An Annotated Bibliography." Master's thesis, Florida State Univ., 1954. 43p.

Rowe, Hershel D. Hart Crane: A Bibliography. Denver: A. Swallow, 1955. 30p.

Russo, Anthony, and Russo, Dorothy R. A Bibliography of James Whitcomb Riley. Indianapolis: Indiana Historical Society, 1944. 351p.

Russo, Dorothy R. A Bibliography of George Ade, 1866-1944. Indianapolis: Indiana Historical Society, 1947. 314p.

_____, and Sullivan, Thelma L. Bibliographical Studies of Seven Authors of Crawfordsville, Indiana: Lew and Susan Wallace, Maurice and Will Thompson, Mary Hannah and Caroline Virginia Krout, and Meredith Wilson. Indianapolis: Indiana Historical Society, 1952. 486p.

_____, and _____. A Bibliography of Booth Tarkington, 1869-1946. Indianapolis: Indiana Historical Society, 1949. 303p.

Samuels, Lee. A Hemingway Checklist. N.Y.: Scribner's, 1951. 63p.

Sawyer, Julien. Gertrude Stein: A Bibliography. N.Y.: Arrow Editions, 1941. 162p.

U.S. Library of Congress. Reference Dept. Walt Whitman: A Catalog Based upon the Collections of the Library of Congress, with Notes on Whitman Collections and Collectors by Charles E. Feinberg. Washington, D.C.: 1955. 147p.

University of Virginia Library. The Barrett Library: Bret Harte: A Checklist of Printed and Manuscript Works. Charlottesville: Univ. of Virginia Press, 1957. 64p.

_____. The Barrett Library: William Dean Howells: A Checklist of Printed and Manuscript Works of William Dean Howells in the Library of the University of Virginia. Compiled by Fannie Mae Elliott and Lucy Clark. Charlottesville: Univ. of Virginia Press, 1959. 68p.

Weber, Clara C., and Weber, Carl J. A Bibliography of the Published Writings of Sarah Orne Jewett. Colby College Monograph, no. 18. Waterville, Me: Colby College Press, 1949. 105p.

Wegelin, Oscar. A Bibliography of the Separate Writings of

John Esten Cooke. Rev. ed. Heartman's Historical
Series, no. 43. Hattiesburg, Miss.: Book Farm, 1941.
13p.

_____ . A Bibliography of the Separate Writings of William
Gilmore Simms of South Carolina, 1806-1870. 3d ed.
Heartman's Historical Series, no. 58. Hattiesburg,
Miss.: Book Farm, 1941. 24p.

Williams, Ames W., and Starrett, Vincent. Stephen Crane:
A Bibliography. Glendale, Calif.: John Valentine, 1948.
161p.

AUTHOR BIBLIOGRAPHIES IN PERIODICALS
(Arranged alphabetically by name of periodical)

Branch, Edgar M. "A Chronological Bibliography of the
Writings of Samuel Clemens to June 8, 1867," American Literature 18 (1946), 109-59.

Brenni, Vito J. "Edna Ferber: A Selected Bibliography,"
Bulletin of Bibliography 22 (1958), 152-55.

_____ . "Pearl Buck: A Selected Bibliography," Bulletin
of Bibliography 22 (1957), 65-68, 94-95.

Egly, William H. "Bibliography of Ellen Anderson Gholson
Glasgow," Bulletin of Bibliography 17 (1940), 47-50.

Goldsmith, Robert H. "Ring W. Lardner: A Checklist of
His Published Writings," Bulletin of Bibliography 21
(1954), 104-06.

Kallich, Martin. "A Bibliography of John Dos Passos,"
Bulletin of Bibliography 19 (1949), 231-35.

Maddocks, Gladys L. "Stephen Vincent Benét: A Bibliography," Bulletin of Bibliography 20 (1951), 142-46; 20
(1952), 158-60.

Pizer, Donald. "Hamlin Garland: A Bibliography of Newspaper and Periodical Publications (1885-1895)," Bulletin of Bibliography 22 (1957), 41-44.

Quesenbery, W. D., Jr. "Ellen Glasgow: A Critical Bibliography," Bulletin of Bibliography 22 (1959), 201-06, 230-36.

Smythe, Katherine H. "Eudora Welty: A Checklist," Bulletin of Bibliography 21 (1956), 207-08.

Sprague, M. D. "Richard Wright: A Bibliography," Bulletin of Bibliography 21 (1953), 39.

Sylvester, William A. "Selected and Critical Bibliography of the Uncollected Works of Katherine Anne Porter," Bulletin of Bibliography 19 (1947), 36.

White, William. "John P. Marquand: A Preliminary Checklist," Bulletin of Bibliography 19 (1949), 268-71.

Cahoon, Herbert. "Herman Melville: A Checklist of Books and Manuscripts in the Collections of the New York Public Library," Bulletin of the New York Public Library 55 (1951), 263-75, 325-38.

Gibson, William M., and Arms, George. "A Bibliography of William Dean Howells," Bulletin of the New York Public Library 50 (1946), 675-98, 857-68, 909-28; 51 (1947), 91-105, 213-48, 341-45, 384-88, 431-57, 486-512. Published in 1948 with slight revisions as a book by the Library.

Gordon, John D. "Ralph Waldo Emerson, 1803-1862; Catalog of an Exhibition from the Berg Collection," Bulletin of the New York Public Library 57 (1953), 392-408, 433-60.

Schwartz, Edward. "Katherine Anne Porter: A Critical Bibliography," Bulletin of the New York Public Library 57 (1953), 211-47.

Sheehy, Eugene P., and Lohf, Kenneth A. "The Achievement of Marianne Moore: A Bibliography," Bulletin of the New York Public Library 62 (1958), 131-49, 183-90, 249-59.

Griscom, Joan. "Bibliography of Caroline Gordon," Critique 1 (1956), 74-78.

Meriwether, James B. "A James Gould Cozzens Checklist,"

Critique 1, no. 3 (1958), 57-63.

Hogan, Charles B. "Edwin Arlington Robinson: New Bibliographic Notes," Papers of the Bibliographic Society of America 35 (1941), 115-44.

Baker, Carlos. "R. P. Blackmur: A Checklist," Princeton University Library Chronicle 31 (1942), 99-106.

Carlson, Eric W. "Benedict Thielen: An Introduction and a Checklist," Princeton University Library Chronicle 13 (Spring 1952), 143-55.

Meriwether, James B. "William Faulkner: A Checklist," Princeton University Library Chronicle 18 (Spring 1957), 136-58.

Mizener, Arthur. "Edmund Wilson: A Checklist," Princeton University Library Chronicle 5 (1944), 62-78.

Patrick, J. Max, and Stallman, Robert W. "John Peale Bishop: A Checklist," Princeton University Library Chronicle 7 (Feb. 1946), 62-79.

Piper, Henry D. "F. Scott Fitzgerald: A Checklist," Princeton University Library Chronicle 12 (1951), 196-208.

Thorp, Willard. "Allen Tate: A Checklist," Princeton University Library Chronicle 3 (1942), 85-98.

Young, Malcolm, and McLaury, Helen. "James Boyd: A Checklist," Princeton University Library Chronicle 6 (1944-45), 77-81.

Hagemann, E. R. "A Checklist of the Writings of John William De Forest (1826-1906)," Studies in Bibliography 8 (1956), 185-94.

Robbins, J. Albert. "Some Unrecorded Poems of James Kirke Paulding: An Annotated Checklist," Studies in Bibliography 3 (1950), 229-40.

Callan, Edward. "An Annotated Checklist of the Works of W. H. Auden," Twentieth Century Literature 4 (April 1958), 30-50.

Porter, Bernard H. "The First Publications of F. Scott Fitzgerald," Twentieth Century Literature 5 (1959), 176-82.

Rowe, Hershel D. "Hart Crane: A Bibliography," Twentieth Century Literature 1 (July 1955), 94-113.

AUTHOR BIBLIOGRAPHIES
IN BIOGRAPHIES AND COLLECTED WORKS

Bartlett, William I. Jones Very: Emerson's "Brave Saint." Durham, N.C.: Duke Univ. Press, 1942. Bib., p. 209-27.

Graham, Philip, and Thies, Frieda C. "Bibliography," in Centennial Edition of the Works of Sidney Lanier. Baltimore: Johns Hopkins Press, 1945. Vol. 6, p. 379-412.

Leary, Lewis. That Rascal Freneau; A Study in Literary Failure. New Brunswick, N.J.: Rutgers Univ. Press, 1941. Bib., p. 418-80.

Mizener, Arthur. The Far Side of Paradise; A Biography. Boston: Houghton Mifflin, 1951. Bib., p. 350-56.

Randel, William P. Edward Eggleston: Author of The Hoosier School-Master. N.Y.: King's Crown Press, 1946. Bib., p. 263-313.

APPENDIX C 1960-1975

COMPREHENSIVE NATIONAL BIBLIOGRAPHY

Burke, William J., and Howe, Will D. American Authors
and Books, 1640 to the Present. 3d rev. ed. Revised
by Irving and Anne Weiss. N.Y.: Crown, 1972. 719p.

Hart, James D. Oxford Companion to American Literature.
4th ed. N.Y.: Oxford Univ. Press, 1965. 991p.

Harvard University Library. Widener Library. Widener
Library Shelflist, 26: American Literature. Cambridge, Mass.: Harvard University Library, 1970.
2 vols.

Index to Early American Periodicals to 1850. Readex Microprint Edition. N.Y.: Readex Microprint Corp.,
1964- .

Kirkham, Edward and Fink, John W. Indices to American
Literary Annuals and Gift Books 1825-1865. New
Haven, Conn.: Research Publications, 1975. 628p.

Literary History of the United States. Edited by Robert E.
Spiller and others. Bibliography Supplement II. N.Y.:
Macmillan, 1972. 366p.

Literature and Language Bibliographies from the American
Year Book 1910-1919. Introduction and Indexes by
Arnold N. Rzepecki. Ann Arbor, Mich.: Pierian Press,
1970. 259p.

Seven Gables Bookshop, N.Y.C. First Books by American
Authors 1765-1964. N.Y.: 1965. 106p.

NATIONAL FICTION BIBLIOGRAPHY

Blotner, Joseph. The Modern American Political Novel 1900-1960. Austin: Univ. of Texas Press, 1966. 424p.

Butler, Michael D. "The Literary Landscape of the Trans-Mississippi West 1826-1902." Ph.D. dissertation, Univ. of Illinois, 1970. 340p.

Coan, Otis W., and Lillard, Richard G. America in Fiction: An Annotated List of Novels that Interpret Aspects of Life in the U.S., Canada, and Mexico. 5th ed. Palo Alto, Calif.: Pacific Books, 1967. 232p.

Dickinson, Arthur T. American Historical Fiction. 3d ed. Metuchen, N.J.: Scarecrow Press, 1971. 380p.

Grieder, Theodore. American Fiction in the Fales Library 1774-1900; A Checklist. New York Univ. Libraries. Bibliographic Series, no. 7. N.Y., 1971. 43p.

Karolides, Nicholas J. The Pioneer in the American Novel. Norman: Univ. of Oklahoma Press, 1967. 324p.

Mack, Garnett L. "Domestic Short Fiction in America 1820-1860." Ph.D. dissertation, George Washington Univ., 1972. 254p.

McCloskey, John C. "American Satires, 1637-1957; A Selective Checklist, Part II: Fiction." Augmented and Updated by Carol and Donald Kay. Satire Newsletter 10, no. 2 (1973), 97-122.

McGarry, Daniel D., and White, Sarah H. Historical Fiction Guide; Annotated, Chronological, Geographical and Topical List of 5000 Selected Historical Novels. Metuchen, N.J.: Scarecrow Press, 1963. 628p. 2d ed., 1973.

Ohio State University Libraries. The William Charvat American Fiction Collection: An Exhibition of Selected Works. Columbus: 1967-68. 3 parts.

Sumner, David N. "American Industrial Labor Novels, 1870-1945; A Preliminary Socio-Cultural Study." Ph.D. dissertation, Brown Univ., 1972. 287p.

VanDerhoof, Jack. A Bibliography of Novels Related to American Frontier and Colonial History. Troy, N. Y.: Whitston Pub. Co., 1971. 501p.

Waldmeir, Joseph. American Novels of the Second World War. The Hague: Mouton, 1968. 180p.

Wright, Lyle H. American Fiction 1774-1850. 2d rev. ed. San Marino, Calif.: Huntington Library, 1969. 411p.

_____. American Fiction 1851-1875. San Marino, Calif.: 1965. 438p.

_____. American Fiction 1876-1900. San Marino, Calif.: Huntington Library, 1966. 683p.

Wright, R. Glenn, ed. Author Bibliography of English Language Fiction in the Library of Congress Through 1950. Boston: G. K. Hall, 1973. 8 vols.

_____. Chronological Bibliography of English Language Fiction in the Library of Congress through 1950. Boston: G. K. Hall, 1974. 8 vols.

NATIONAL FICTION COLLECTIONS

The Best Little Magazine Fiction. N. Y.: New York Univ. Press, 1970- (annual).

Free, William J. "American Fiction in the Columbian Magazine 1786-1792; An Annotated Checklist," Bulletin of Bibliography 25 (1968), 150-51.

Hudson Review. Anthology. Ed. by Frederick Morgan. N. Y.: Vintage, 1961. 461p.

Kenyon Review. Gallery of Modern Fiction: Stories from the Kenyon Review. Ed. by Robie Macauley. N. Y.: Salem Press, 1966. 396p.

New Yorker. Stories from the New Yorker, 1950-1960. N. Y.: Simon and Schuster, 1960. 780p.

NATIONAL POETRY BIBLIOGRAPHY

Andrews, Charles R. "A Thematic Guide to Selected American Poetry About the Second World War." Ph.D. dissertation, Case Western Reserve Univ., 1967. 428p.

Brown University Library. Dictionary Catalog of the Harris Collection of American Poetry and Plays. Boston: G. K. Hall, 1972. 13 vols.

Davis, Lloyd, and Irwin, Robert. Contemporary American Poetry; A Checklist. Metuchen, N.J.: Scarecrow Press, 1975. 179p.

Hart, James A. "American Poetry of the First World War, 1914 to 1920; A Survey and Checklist." Ph.D. dissertation, Duke Univ., 1965. 526p.

Huddleston, Eugene L. "Feminist Verse Satire in America; A Checklist 1700-1800," Bulletin of Bibliography 32 (1975), 115-21.

_____. "Topographical Poetry in America 1783-1812." Ph.D. dissertation, Michigan State Univ., 1965. 299p.

_____. "Topographical Poetry in America; A Checklist 1783-1812," Bulletin of Bibliography 25 (Sept.-Dec. 1966), 8-13; 25 (Jan.-Apr. 1967), 35-36, 39.

Lemay, J. A. Leo. A Calendar of American Poetry in the Colonial Newspapers and Magazines and in Major English Magazines Through 1765. Worcester, Mass.: American Antiquarian Society, 1972. 353p.

Murphy, Rosalie. Contemporary Poets. London: St. James Press, 1970. 1243p. 2d ed., 1975.

Stoddard, Roger E. "A Catalog of Books and Pamphlets Unrecorded in Oscar Wegelin's Early American Poetry 1650-1820," Books of Brown 23 (1969), 1-84.

_____. "Further Addenda to Wegelin's Early American Poetry," Papers of the Bibliographical Society of America 65 (April 1971), 169-72.

University of Virginia Library. The Barrett Library: Wegelin

Collection of Later Nineteenth-Century Minor American Poetry. Compiled by Lucy Clark. Charlottesville: Univ. of Virginia Press, 1962. 107p.

Williams, Galen. A Partial Directory of American Poets. N.Y.: Poets and Writers, 1971. 155p.

Zulauf, Sander W., and Weiser, Irwin H. Index of American Periodical Verse: [year]. Metuchen, N.J.: Scarecrow Press, 1973- (annual).

POETRY COLLECTIONS

Allen, Donald M., ed. New American Poetry 1945-1960. N.Y.: Grove Press, 1960. 454p.

Berg, Stephen, and Mezey, Robert, eds. Naked Poetry; Recent American Poetry in Open Forms. Indianapolis: Bobbs-Merrill, 1969. 387p.

Lowenfels, Walter, and Braymer, Nan, eds. Where Is Vietnam? American Poets Respond; An Anthology of Contemporary Poems. N.Y.: Doubleday, 1967. 160p.

New Yorker. The New Yorker Book of Poems; Poems Selected by the Editors of the New Yorker. N.Y.: Viking Press, 1969. 835p.

Owen, Guy, and Williams, Mary C., eds. New Southern Poets; Selected Poems from Southern Poetry Review. Chapel Hill: Univ. of North Carolina Press, 1974. 113p.

Poetry Society of America. The Diamond Anthology. Edited by Charles Angoff and others. South Brunswick, N.J.: A. S. Barnes, 1971. 323p.

Steinmetz, Lee, ed. The Poetry of the American Civil War. East Lansing: Michigan State Univ. Press, 1960. 264p.

Virginia Quarterly Review. Poems from the Virginia Quarterly Review 1925-1967. Charlottesville: Univ. Press of Virginia, 1969. 259p.

NATIONAL DRAMA BIBLIOGRAPHY

Bergquist, G. William, ed. Three Centuries of English and American Plays: A Checklist: England 1500-1800; United States 1714-1830. N.Y.: Hafner Pub. Co., 1963. 281p.

Bonin, Jane F. Major Themes in Prize-Winning American Drama. Metuchen, N.J.: Scarecrow Press, 1975. 188p.

Brown University Library. Dictionary Catalog of the Harris Collection of American Poetry and Plays. Boston: G. K. Hall, 1972. 13 vols.

Collins, John D. "American Drama in Anti-Slavery Agitation 1792-1861." Ph.D. dissertation, Univ. of Iowa, 1963. 449p.

Douglas, James S. "The Small Town in American Drama, 1900-1940." Ph.D. dissertation, Washington State Univ., 1970. 302p.

Guernsey, Otis L., ed. Directory of the American Theater 1894-1971. N.Y.: Dodd, Mead, 1971. 343p.

Herron, Ima H. The Small Town in American Drama. Dallas, Texas: Southern Methodist Univ. Press, 1969. 564p.

McCloskey, John C. "American Satires, 1637-1957; A Selective Checklist. Part I: Drama," Satire Newsletter 2, no. 2 (1965), 101-09.

Moe, Albert F., and Moe, Margaret G. American Drama Through 1830; A Checklist. Oakland, Calif.: 1968. 80p.

Nannes, Caspar H. Politics in the American Drama. Washington, D.C.: Catholic Univ. of America Press, 1960. 256p.

Peavy, Linda. "A Bibliography of Provincetown Players' Dramas, 1915-1922." Papers of the Bibliographical Society of America 69 (1975), 569-74.

Stoddard, Roger E. "A Guide to 'Spencer's Boston Theatre,'
1855-1862." Procs. of the American Antiquarian Society 79 (1969), 45-98.

_____. "Some Corrigenda and Addenda to Hill's American
Plays Printed 1714-1830." Papers of the Bibliographical Society of America 65 (1971), 278-95.

_____. Two Hundred Years of American Plays 1765-1964;
An Exhibition from the Harris Collection. Providence:
Brown Univ. Library, 1965. 51p.

Wegner, William H. "The Representation of the American
Civil War on the New York Stage 1860-1900." Ph.D.
dissertation, New York Univ., 1966. 336p.

Whitney, Blair. "American Poetic Drama 1900-1966."
Ph.D. dissertation, Univ. of Illinois, 1967. 224p.

REGIONAL BIBLIOGRAPHY

Bradbury, John M. Renaissance in the South; A Critical
History of the Literature 1920-1960. Chapel Hill: Univ.
of North Carolina Press, 1963. 222p.

"Current Bibliography," Great Lakes Review, Summer 1974-
(biennial).

Major, Mabel, and Pearce, Thomas M. Southwest Heritage;
A Literary History with Bibliographies. 3d ed. Albuquerque: Univ. of New Mexico Press, 1972. 378p.

REGIONAL LITERARY COLLECTIONS

Corrington, John W., and Williams, Miller, eds. Southern
Writing in the Sixties. Baton Rouge: Louisiana State
Univ., 1966-67. 2 vols.

Havighurst, Walter, ed. The Great Lakes Reader. N.Y.:
Macmillan, 1966. 421p.

Shockley, Martin, ed. Southwest Writers Anthology. Austin, Texas: Steck-Vaughn, 1967. 328p.

Sonnichsen, Charles N. The Southwest in Life and Literature. N. Y.: Devin-Adair, 1962. 554p.

Taylor, J. Golden, ed. The Literature of the American West. N. Y.: Houghton Mifflin, 1971. 592p.

REGIONAL FICTION BIBLIOGRAPHY

Bray, Robert. "In Pursuit of Distinctive Utterance: Realistic Novels in the Midwest, 1871-1914." Ph.D. dissertation, Univ. of Chicago, 1971. 326p.

Gaston, Edwin W., Jr. The Early Novel of the Southwest. Albuquerque: Univ. of New Mexico, 1961. 318p.

Kennedy, Patricia. "The Pioneer Woman in Middle Western Fiction." Ph.D. dissertation, Univ. of Illinois, 1968. 244p.

Meyer, Roy W. The Middle Western Farm Novel in the Twentieth Century. Lincoln: Univ. of Nebraska, 1965. 265p.

REGIONAL FICTION COLLECTIONS

Western Writers of America. Bad Men and Good; A Roundup of Western Stories by Members of the WWA. N. Y.: Dodd, Mead, 1953. 240p.

_____. Holsters and Heroes; Stories from the WWA. N. Y.: Macmillan, 1954. 207p.

_____. Legends and Tales of the Old West by Members of the WWA. Garden City, N. Y.: Doubleday, 1962. 408p.

_____. Spurs West, By Members of the WWA. Ed. by

S. Omar Barker. Garden City, N. Y.: Doubleday, 1960. 332p.

_____. Wild Streets; Tales of the Frontier Towns. Garden City, N. Y.: Doubleday, 1958. 285p.

REGIONAL POETRY BIBLIOGRAPHY

Hill, Gertrude. "The Southwest in Verse: A Selective Bibliography of Arizona and New Mexico Poetry," Arizona Quarterly 23 (1967), 306-12.

Hummel, Ray O., Jr., ed. Southeastern Broadsides Before 1877: A Bibliography. Richmond: Virginia State Library, 1971. 501p.

Le Master, J. R., ed. Poets of the Midwest. Appalachia, Va.: Young Publications, 1966. 404p.

Larson, Clinton F., and Stafford, William. Modern Poetry of Western America. Provo, Utah: Brigham Young Univ., 1975. 234p.

Stryk, Lucien, ed. Heartland: Poems of the Midwest. De Kalb: Northern Illinois Univ. Press, 1967. 261p.

_____. Heartland II: Poets of the Midwest. De Kalb: Northern Illinois Univ. Press, 1975. 255p.

STATE BIBLIOGRAPHY

Coward, Robert Y., and Coward, Hester H., eds. Catalog of the David Demaree Banta Indiana Collection. 2d ed. Menasha, Wis.: George Banta Co., 1965. 212p.

Coyle, William, ed. Ohio Authors and Their Books; Biographical Data and Selective Bibliographies for Ohio Authors, Native and Resident, 1796-1950. Preliminary Research by Mr. and Mrs. Wessen. Sponsored by the Martha Kinney Cooper Ohioana Library Association. Cleveland: World, 1962. 741p.

Harvey, Alice G. Nebraska Writers. Rev. ed. Omaha,
Neb.: the Author, 1964. 182p.

Hilbert, Rachel M., ed. Michigan Authors. Ann Arbor:
Michigan Association of School Librarians, 1960. 68p.

Paluka, Frank. Iowa Authors; A Biobibliography of Sixty
Native Writers. Iowa City: Friends of the Univ. of
Iowa Libraries, 1967. 244p.

Richey, Ish. Kentucky Literature 1784-1963. Tompkinsville, Ky.: Monroe County Press, 1963. 236p.

Thompson, Donald E. Indiana Authors and Their Books 1917-
1966. Crawfordsville, Ind.: Wabash College, 1974.
688p.

Tourville, Elsie A. Alaska: A Bibliography 1570-1970.
Boston: G. K. Hall, 1974. 738p.

STATE LITERARY HISTORY

Andrews, Clarence A. A Literary History of Iowa. Iowa
City: Univ. of Iowa Press, 1972. 287p.

Browning, Mary C. Kentucky Authors; A History of Kentucky Literature. Owensboro, Ky.: Brescia College
Bookstore, 1968. 357p.

Jody, Marilyn. "Alaska in the American Literary Imagination: A Literary History of Frontier Alaska with a
Bibliographical Guide to the Study of Alaskan Literature." Ph.D. dissertation, Indiana Univ., 1969. 272p.

Lemay, Joseph A. "A Literary History of Colonial Maryland." Ph.D. dissertation, Univ. of Pennsylvania,
1964. 413p.

_____. Men of Letters in Colonial Maryland. Knoxville:
Univ. of Tennessee Press, 1972. 407p.

Shumaker, Arthur W. A History of Indiana Literature.
Indianapolis: Indiana Historical Bureau, 1962. 611p.

Walser, Richard G. Literary North Carolina: A Brief Historical Survey. Raleigh, N. C.: North Carolina State Dept. of Archives and History, 1970. 137p.

Williams, Benjamin B. "A Literary History of Alabama to 1900." Ph. D. dissertation, Vanderbilt Univ., 1971. 551p.

STATE LITERARY COLLECTIONS

Calhoun, Richard J., and Guilds, John C., eds. A Tricentennial Anthology of South Carolina Literature 1670-1970. Columbia: Univ. of South Carolina Press, 1971. 580p.

Lee, W. Storrs, ed. California: A Literary Chronicle. N. Y.: Funk & Wagnalls, 1968. 537p.

_____. Maine: A Literary Chronicle. N. Y.: Funk & Wagnalls, 1968. 487p.

Powell, Lawrence C. California Classics; The Creative Literature of the Golden State. Los Angeles: Ward Ritchie Press, 1971. 393p.

STATE FICTION BIBLIOGRAPHY

Coad, Oral S. New Jersey in the Revolution: A Bibliography of Historical Fiction 1784-1963. New Brunswick, N. J.: New Brunswick Historical Club, 1964. 39p.

Black, Albert G. Michigan Novels; An Annotated Bibliography. Ann Arbor: Michigan Council of Teachers of English, 1963. 64p.

"Michigan in Novels," Michigan in Books 12 (Summer-Autumn 1971), 4-14.

Peyroutet, Jean A. "The North Dakota Farmer in Fiction," North Dakota Quarterly 39 (Winter 1971), 59-71.

Wolfe, Hilton J. "Alaskan Literature; the Fiction of America's Last Wilderness." Ph.D. dissertation, Michigan State Univ., 1973. 355p.

STATE POETRY BIBLIOGRAPHY

Elliott, William. "Minnesota North Country Poetry; A Bibliography," Society for the Study of Midwestern Literature, Newsletter 4, no. 1 (1974), 8-10.

Hilbert, Rachel M., ed. Michigan Poets with Supplement to Michigan Authors. Ann Arbor: Michigan Association of School Librarians, 1964. 77p.

Johnson, Elmer D. "A Preliminary Checklist of Louisiana Poetry in English," Southwestern Louisiana Journal 4 (Jan. 1960), 43-60.

Williams, Benjamin B. "Alabama Civil War Poets," Alabama Review 15 (1962), 243-52.

STATE POETRY COLLECTIONS

Gilbert, Margaret, and Finlan, William J., eds. An Anthology of Verse about Michigan's Upper Peninsula. Escanaba, Mich.: Photo Offset Print. Co., 1965. 234p.

Gildner, Gary, and Gildner, Judith, eds. Out of This World; Poems from the Hawkeye State. Ames: Iowa State Univ. Press, 1975. 134p.

Lyon, Mabelle A., et al. Sing Naked Spirit; A Compilation of Verse from Members of the Arizona State Poetry Society. Mesa, Ariz.: Printed by P. Gillespie, 1970. 178p.

Marvin, Francis M., ed. Book of Poems; Poetic Gleams of Light in a Troubled World. Bartonville, Pa.: the Compiler, 1960. 260p.

Meyer, Vivian M., et al., eds. Cosmic Cadence; An Anthology of Poems. Pitman: New Jersey Poetry Society, 1971. 64p.

Owen, Guy, and Williams, Mary C., eds. North Carolina Poetry; The Seventies. Raleigh, N.C.: Southern Poetry Review Press, 1975. 80p. (A special issue of the Southern Poetry Review in 1975.)

Pennsylvania Poetry Society. Prize Poems 1969; 20th Anniversary Year. Harrisburg, Pa.: Keystone Press, 1969. 48p.

Poetry Society of Alaska. One Hundred Years of Alaska Poetry. Denver: Big Mountain Press, 1966. 165p.

Poetry Society of Michigan. Forty Salutes to Michigan Poets; Fortieth Anniversary Anthology. The Society, 1975. 128p.

Stibitz, Edward Earle, ed. Illinois Poets; A Selection. Carbondale: Southern Illinois Univ. Press, 1968. 227p.

Walser, Richard G., ed. Poets of North Carolina. Richmond, Va.: Garrett and Massie, 1963. 142p.

Wright, Mary M., ed. Avalon Anthology of Texas Poets. Compiled by Lilith Lorraine (pseud.). Corpus Christi, Texas: Different Press, 1963. 62p.

STATE DRAMA BIBLIOGRAPHY

Heyl, Edgar. "Plays by Marylanders 1870-1916," Maryland Historical Magazine 62 (1967), 438-47; 63 (1968), 70-77, 179-87, 420-26; 64 (1969), 74-77, 412-19.

Nolan, Paul T. "Alabama Drama, 1870-1916; A Checklist," Alabama Review 18 (1965), 65-72.

_____, and Simpson, Amos E. "Checklist of Arkansas Playwrights," Arkansas Historical Quarterly 22 (Spring 1963), 67-75.

LOCAL BIBLIOGRAPHY AND COLLECTIONS

Adams, John R. Books and Authors of San Diego. San
     Diego, Calif.: San Diego State College Press, 1966.
     64p.

Bukowski, Charles, et al., eds. Anthology of L.A. Poets.
     Los Angeles: Laugh Literary, 1972. 64p.

Fisher, Perry G. Materials for the Study of Washington:
     A Selected Annotated Bibliography. Washington, D.C.:
     George Washington University, 1974. 63p.

Hinshaw, John V., ed. East of America; An Anthology of
     Cape Cod Poets. Chatham, Mass.: Chatham Press,
     1969. 80p.

Ireland, Joe, and Gallmeyer, Ann, eds. New Orleans
     Poets; Anthology. New Orleans: New Orleans Public
     Library, 1972. 62p.

Padgett, Ron, and Shapiro, David, eds. An Anthology of
     New York Poets. N.Y.: Random House, 1970. 588p.

Reid, Alfred S., ed. "Literature," The Arts in Greenville,
     1800-1860. Greenville, S.C.: Furman Univ. Book-
     store, 1960. p. 97-102, 106-08.

_____. "Poets of Greenville," Furman Studies, n.s. 11
     (Nov. 1963), 1-44.

Rosenblum, Martin J., ed. Brewing: 20 Milwaukee Poets.
     Lyme Center, N.H.: Giligia Press, 1972. 143p.

Tremble, Stella C., ed. A Book of Chicago Poets. Chicago:
     Columbus Press, 1964. 68p.

True, Michael. Worcester Poets, with Notes Toward a
     Literary History. Worcester, Mass.: Worcester
     Poetry Association, 1972. 44p.

Whisnant, Charleen, and Grey, Robert W., eds. Eleven
     Charlotte Poets. Charlotte, N.C.: Red Clay Pub-
     lishers, 1971. 98p.

STATE HISTORY SOURCES

Ellis, Helen H. Michigan in the Civil War; A Guide to the
    Material in Detroit Newspapers 1861-1866. Lansing:
    Michigan Civil War Centennial Observance Commission,
    1965. 404p.

Rouse, Sarah A. "Literature 1890-1970," in A History of
    Mississippi, ed. by Richard A. McLemore. Hatties-
    burg: Univ. and College Press of Mississippi, 1973.
    Vol. 2, p.446-76.

Sinclair, Donald A. The Civil War and New Jersey; A Bib-
    liography. New Brunswick: Published by Friends of
    Rutgers Univ. Library for New Jersey Civil War Cen-
    tennial Commission, 1968. 186p.

Smith, Sam B., and Banker, Luke H., eds. Tennessee
    History; A Bibliography. Knoxville: Univ. of Tennes-
    see Press, 1974. 498p.

HUMOR

Anderson, John Q., ed. With the Bark On; Popular Humor
    of the Old South. Compiled and Edited with Introduc-
    tion and Notes by John Q. Anderson. Nashville, Tenn.:
    Vanderbilt Univ. Press, 1967. 337p.

Ault, Philip H., ed. The Home Book of Western Humor.
    N.Y.: Dodd, Mead, 1967. 364p.

Cohen, Hennig, and Dillingham, William B., eds. Humor
    of the Old Southwest. 2d ed. Athens: Univ. of
    Georgia Press, 1975. 427p.

Green, Roger L., ed. A Century of Humorous Verse 1850-
    1950. N.Y.: Dutton, 1961. 289p.

Hall, Wade H. The Smiling Phoenix; Southern Humor from
    1865 to 1914. Gainesville: Univ. of Florida Press,
    1965. 375p.

Miles, Elton. Southwest Humorists. Southwest Writers

Series, no. 26. Austin, Texas: Steck-Vaughn, 1969. 44p.

Walser, Richard, ed. Tar Heel Laughter. Chapel Hill: Univ. of North Carolina Press, 1974. 309p.

Weber, Brom, ed. An Anthology of American Humor. N.Y.: Crowell, 1962. 584p.

AUTHOR BIBLIOGRAPHIES

Ashley, Franklin. James Dickey: A Checklist. Detroit: Gale Research Co., 1972. 98p.

Atkinson, Jennifer M. Eugene O'Neill: A Descriptive Bibliography. Pittsburgh: Univ. of Pittsburgh Press, 1974. 410p.

Avery, Laurence G. A Catalog of the Maxwell Anderson Collection at the University of Texas. Tower Bibliographical Series no. 6. Austin: Humanities Research Center, Univ. of Texas, 1968. 175p.

Billings, Harold W. A Bibliography of Edward Dahlberg. Tower Bibliographical Series no. 8. Austin: Humanities Research Center, Univ. of Texas, 1971. 122p.

Brenni, Vito J. Edith Wharton: A Bibliography. Morgantown: West Virginia Univ. Library, 1966. 99p.

_____. William Dean Howells: A Bibliography. Metuchen, N.J.: Scarecrow Press, 1973. 212p.

Bruccoli, Matthew J. F. Scott Fitzgerald: A Descriptive Bibliography. Pittsburgh: Univ. of Pittsburgh Press, 1972. 369p. (Pittsburgh Series in Bibliography.)

_____. John O'Hara: A Checklist. N.Y.: Random House, 1972. 136p.

_____. Kenneth Millar/Ross MacDonald: A Checklist. Detroit: Gale Research Co., 1971. 86p.

_____. Raymond Chandler: A Checklist. Kent, Ohio: Kent State Univ. Press, 1968. 35p.

_____. Ring W. Lardner: A Descriptive Bibliography. Pittsburgh: Univ. of Pittsburgh Press, 1975. 424p. (Pittsburgh Series in Bibliography.)

Buckingham, Willis J. Emily Dickinson: An Annotated Bibliography; Writings, Scholarship, Criticism, and Ana, 1850-1968. Bloomington: Indiana Univ. Press, 1970. 322p.

Butterick, George F., and Glover, Albert. Bibliography of Works by Charles Olson. N.Y.: Phoenix Book Shop, 1967. 90p.

Edelstein, Jerome M. Wallace Stevens: A Descriptive Bibliography. Pittsburgh: Univ. of Pittsburgh Press, 1973. 429p. (Pittsburgh Series in Bibliography.)

Fallwell, Marshall, Jr., et al. Allen Tate: A Bibliography. N.Y.: David Lewis, 1969. 112p.

Field, John P. Richard Wilbur: A Bibliographical Checklist. Serif Series: Bibliographies and Checklists, no. 16. Kent, Ohio: Kent State Univ., 1971. 85p.

Gallup, Donald C. A Bibliography of Ezra Pound. London: R. Hart-Davis, 1963. 454p. (Soho Bibliographies.)

_____. T. S. Eliot: A Bibliography. New ed. London: Faber, 1969. 414p.

Gefvert, Constance J. Edward Taylor: An Annotated Bibliography 1668-1970. Serif Series: Bibliographies and Checklists, no. 19. Kent, Ohio: Kent State Univ. Press, 1971. 83p.

Gottesman, Ronald. Upton Sinclair: An Annotated Checklist. Serif Series: Bibliographies and Checklists, no. 24. Kent, Ohio: Kent State Univ. Press, 1973. 544p.

Hanneman, Audre. Ernest Hemingway: A Comprehensive Bibliography. Princeton, N.J.: Princeton Univ. Press, 1967. 568p. Supplement, 1975. 393p.

Hayashi, Tetsumaro. John Steinbeck: A Concise Bibliography, 1930-1965. Metuchen, N.J.: Scarecrow Press, 1967. 164p.

_____. A New Steinbeck Bibliography 1929-1971. Me-
tuchen, N.J.: Scarecrow Press, 1973. 225p.

Hopkins, John R. James Jones: A Checklist. Detroit:
Gale Research Co., 1974. 67p.

Hudgens, Betty L. Kurt Vonnegut, Jr. Detroit: Gale Research Co., 1972. 67p.

Huff, Mary N. Robert Penn Warren: A Bibliography. N.Y.:
David Lewis, 1968. 171p. (Fugitive Bibliographies.)

Johnson, Elmer D. Tom Wolfe: A Checklist. Serif Series:
Bibliographies and Checklists, no. 12. Kent, Ohio:
Kent State Univ. Press, 1970. 278p.

Kelly, William W. Ellen Glasgow: A Bibliography. Charlottesville: Printed for Bibliographical Society of Virginia by Univ. Press of Virginia, 1964. 330p.

Kherdian, David. A Bibliography of William Saroyan, 1934-
1964. San Francisco: Roger Beacham, 1965. 204p.

_____. Six Poets of the San Francisco Renaissance:
Portraits and Checklists. Fresno, Calif.: Giligia
Press, 1967. 183p.

Kosofsky, Rita N. Bernard Malamud: An Annotated Checklist. Serif Series: Bibliographies and Checklists, no.
7. Kent, Ohio: Kent State Univ. Press, 1969. 63p.

Lindsay, Robert O. Witter Bynner: A Bibliography. Univ.
of New Mexico Publications. Library Series no. 2.
Albuquerque: Univ. of New Mexico Press, 1967. 112p.

McCollum, Kenneth C. Nelson Algren: A Checklist. Detroit: Gale Research Co., 1973. 107p.

McLeod, James R. Theodore Roethke: A Bibliography.
Serif Series: Bibliographies and Checklists, no. 27.
Kent, Ohio: Kent State Univ. Press, 1973. 241p.

Massey, Linton R. William Faulkner, "Man Working," 1919-
1962; A Catalog of the William Faulkner Collections at
the University of Virginia. Charlottesville: Bibliographical Society of the University of Virginia, 1968.
250p.

Mazzaro, Joseph. The Achievement of Robert Lowell, 1939-1959. Detroit: Univ. of Detroit Press, 1960. 41p.

Meriwether, James B. James Gould Cozzens: A Checklist. Detroit: Gale Research Co., 1973. 85p.

Michel, Pierre. James Gould Cozzens: An Annotated Checklist. Serif Series: Bibliographies and Checklists, no. 22. Kent, Ohio: Kent State Univ. Press, 1971. 123p.

Mullaly, Edward J. Archibald MacLeish: A Checklist. Serif Series: Bibliographies and Checklists, no. 26. Kent, Ohio: Kent State Univ. Press, 1973. 95p.

Novik, Mary. Robert Creeley: An Inventory 1945-1970. Serif Series: Bibliographies and Checklists, no. 28. Kent, Ohio: Kent State Univ. Press, 1975. 210p.

O'Donnell, Thomas F., et al. A Bibliography of Writings by and About Harold Frederic. Research Bibliographies in American Literature, no. 4. Boston: G. K. Hall, 1975. 342p.

Pizer, Donald, et al. Theodore Dreiser: A Primary and Secondary Bibliography. Research Bibliographies in American Literature, no. 3. Boston: G. K. Hall, 1975. 515p.

Ramsey, Richard and Ramsey, David. Edmund Wilson: A Bibliography. N.Y.: David Lewis, 1971. 345p.

Ricks, Beatrice, and Adams, Joseph D. Herman Melville: A Reference Bibliography 1900-1972, with Selected 19th Century Materials. Boston: G. K. Hall, 1973. 532p.

Sackton, Alexander. The T. S. Eliot Collection at the University of Texas at Austin. Tower Bibliographical Series, no. 9. Austin: Humanities Research Center, Univ. of Texas, 1975. 402p.

Schwartz, Joseph, and Schweik, Robert C. Hart Crane: A Descriptive Bibliography. Pittsburgh: Univ. of Pittsburgh Press, 1972. 168p.

Sheehy, Eugene P. and Lohf, Kenneth A. Sherwood Anderson: A Bibliography. Los Gatos, Calif.: Talisman Press, 1960. 125p.

Stallman, Robert W. Stephen Crane: A Critical Bibliography. Ames: Iowa Univ. Press, 1972. 642p.

Stefanik, Ernest C. John Berryman: A Descriptive Bibliography. Pittsburgh: University of Pittsburgh Press, 1974. 285p. (Pittsburgh Series in Bibliography.)

Taylor, C. Clarke. John Updike. Serif Series: Bibliographies and Checklists, no. 4. Kent, Ohio: Kent State Univ. Press, 1968. 82p.

Triesch, Manfred. The Lillian Hellman Collection at the University of Texas. Austin: Humanities Research Center, Univ. of Texas, 1967. 167p.

University of Virginia Library. The Barrett Library: Edwin Lassetter Bynner: A Checklist of Printed and Manuscript Works. Comp. by Lucy T. Clark. Charlottesville: Univ. of Virginia Press, 1961. 9p.

_____. The Barrett Library: Oliver Wendell Holmes: A Checklist of Printed and Manuscript Works in the Library of the University of Virginia. Comp. by Anita Rutman, Lucy Clark, and Marjorie Carver. Charlottesville: Univ. Press of Virginia, 1969. 109p.

_____. The Barrett Library: Richard Harding Davis: A Checklist of Printed and Manuscript Works. Charlottesville: Univ. of Virginia Press, 1963. 31p.

_____. The Barrett Library: Robinson Jeffers: A Checklist of Printed and Manuscript Works. Compiled by Anita Rutman and Lucy Clark, the Manuscripts by Marjorie Carver. Charlottesville: Univ. of Virginia Press, 1960. 41p.

Van Doren, Mark. Carl Sandburg. With a Bibliography of Sandburg Materials in the Collections of the Library of Congress. Washington, D.C.: Library of Congress, 1969. 83p.

Waldrip, Louise, and Bauer, Shirley A. A Bibliography of the Works of Katherine Anne Porter. Metuchen, N.J.: Scarecrow Press, 1969. 219p.

White, William. Edwin Arlington Robinson: A Supplementary Bibliography. Serif Series: Bibliographies and checklists, no. 17. Kent, Ohio: Kent State Univ. Press, 1971. 168p.

_____ . John Ciardi: A Bibliography. Detroit: Wayne State Univ. Press, 1959. 65p.

_____ . W. D. Snodgrass: A Bibliography. Detroit: Wayne State Univ. Press, 1960. 32p.

Wilson, Robert A. A Bibliography of Works by Gregory Corso, 1954-1965. N. Y.: Phoenix Bookshop, 1966. 40p.

_____ . Gertrude Stein: A Bibliography. N. Y.: Phoenix Bookshop, 1974. 227p.

Woodbridge, Hensley C., et al. Jack London: A Bibliography. Georgetown, Calif.: Talisman Press, 1966. 422p.

_____ . Jack London: A Bibliography. Enl. ed. Millwood, N. Y.: Kraus Reprint Co., 1973. 554p.

AUTHOR BIBLIOGRAPHIES IN PERIODICALS
(Arranged alphabetically by name of periodical)

Branch, Edgar M. "A Supplement to the Bibliography of James T. Farrell's Writings," American Book Collector 11 (Summer 1961), 42-48.

_____ . "Bibliography of James T. Farrell, a Supplement," American Book Collector 17 (May 1967), 9-19.

_____ . "Bibliography of James T. Farrell, Sept. 1970-Feb. 1975, a Supplement," American Book Collector 26 (Jan.-Feb. 1976), 17-22.

Manley, Francis. "William Inge: A Bibliography," American Book Collector 16 (Oct. 1965), 13-21.

Biglane, Jean N. "Sherwood Bonner: A Bibliography of Primary and Secondary Materials," American Literary Realism 5 (1972), 39-60.

Carleton, Reese M. "Mary Noailles Murfree (1850-1922): An Annotated Bibliography," American Literary Realism 7 (1974), 293-378.

Eichelberger, Clayton L., and Lyon, Zoë. "A Partial Listing of the Published Writing of Harris M. Lyon," American Literary Realism 3 (1970), 41-52.

Marovitz, Stanford E., and Fried, Lewis. "Abraham Cahan (1860-1951): An Annotated Bibliography," American Literary Realism 3 (1970), 197-243.

Swanson, Jeffrey. "A Checklist of the Writings of Henry Blake Fuller," American Literary Realism 7 (1974), 211-43.

Woodward, Robert H. "Frederic's Short Fiction: A Checklist," American Literary Realism 1 (1968), 73-76.

Brittain, Joan T. "Flannery O'Connor: A Bibliography," Bulletin of Bibliography 25 (1967-68), 98-100, 123-24, 142.

Buchan, Vivian. "Sara Teasdale, 1884-1933," Bulletin of Bibliography 25 (1967), 94-97, 120-23.

Bush, George E. "James Purdy," Bulletin of Bibliography 28 (1971), 5-6.

Fabre, Michel, and Margolies, Edward. "Richard Wright (1908-1960): A Bibliography," Bulletin of Bibliography 24 (1965), 131-33, 137.

Gilliam, Loretta. "Gore Vidal: A Checklist," Bulletin of Bibliography 30 (1973), 1-9, 44.

Grissom, Margaret S. "Shirley Ann Grau," Bulletin of Bibliography 28 (1971), 76-78.

McDaniel, John N. "Philip Roth: A Checklist 1954-1973," Bulletin of Bibliography 31 (1974), 51-53.

Napier, James J. "Joseph Hergesheimer: A Selected Bibliography 1913-1945," Bulletin of Bibliography 24 (1963-64), 46-48, 52, 69-70.

Schatt, Stanley. "LeRoi Jones," Bulletin of Bibliography 28 (1971), 55-57.

Sherman, Dean. "Owen Wister: An Annotated Bibliography," Bulletin of Bibliography 28 (1971), 7-16.

Shivers, Alfred S. "Jessamyn West," Bulletin of Bibliography 28 (1971), 1-3.

Stefanik, Ernest C. "A John Berryman Checklist," Bulletin of Bibliography 31 (1974), 1-4, 28.

Bryer, Jackson R. "John Barth," Critique 6, no. 2 (1963), 86-89.

_____. "John Hawkes," Critique 6, no. 2 (1963), 89-94.

Evarts, Prescott, Jr. "John Fowles: A Checklist," Critique 13, no. 3 (1972), 105-07.

Hanna, Allan. "An Allan Seager Bibliography," Critique 5, no. 3 (1963), 75-90.

Schneider, Harold W. "Two Bibliographies: Saul Bellow and William Styron," Critique 3 (Summer 1960), 71-91.

Smith, James P. "A Peter Taylor Checklist," Critique 9, no. 3 (1967), 31-36.

Weixlmann, Joseph N. "John Barth: A Bibliography," Critique 13, no. 3 (1972), 45-56.

Stanford, Ann. "Anne Bradstreet: An Annotated Checklist," Early American Literature 3 (Winter 1968/69), 217-28.

Witherington, Paul. "Charles Brockden Brown: A Bibliographic Essay," Early American Literature 9 (Fall 1974), 164-87.

Princeton University Library Chronicle 25 (Autumn 1963). The whole issue, consisting of 115 pages, is on seven Princeton poets. An essay followed by a checklist is given for each poet.

Katz, Joseph. "The Shorter Publications of Frank Norris," Proof 3 (1973), 155-220.

Meriwether, James B. "The Shorter Fiction of William Faulkner: A Bibliography," Proof 1 (1971), 293-329.

Pizer, Donald. "The Publications of Theodore Dreiser: A Checklist," Proof 1 (1971), 247-92.

Blanck, Jacob. "BAL Addenda," Papers of the Bibliographical Society of America 55 (1961), 46-47.

Doyle, Paul A. "Mary Lavin: A Checklist," Papers of the Bibliographical Society of America 63 (1969), 317-21.

Jonas, Klaus W. "Additions to the Bibliography of Carl Van Vechten," Papers of the Bibliographical Society of America 55 (1961), 42-45.

Lawton, James N. "The Authorship of Item 165 in Lyle Wright's American Fiction 1851-1875," Papers of the Bibliographical Society of America 64 (1970), 83.

Phillips, Robert S. "Shirley Jackson: A Checklist," Papers of the Bibliographical Society of America 56 (1962), 110-13.

_____. "Shirley Jackson: A Chronology and a Supplementary Checklist," Papers of the Bibliographical Society of America 60 (1966), 203-13.

Smith, Nolan E. "Author Identification for Six Wright I Titles: Cleveland and Doughty," Papers of the Bibliographical Society of America 65 (1966), 173-74.

Kolin, Philip C. "A Classified Edward Albee Checklist," Serif 6 (Sept. 1969), 16-32.

Krause, Sydney J., and Nieset, Jane. "A Census of the Works of Charles Brockden Brown," Serif 3 (Dec. 1966), 14-16.

White, William. "Robinson Jeffers: A Checklist 1959-1965," Serif 3 (June 1966), 36-39.

_____. "Walt Whitman's Poetry in Periodicals," Serif 11 (Summer 1974), 31-38.

Aderman, Ralph M. "James Kirke Paulding's Contributions to American Magazines," Studies in Bibliography 17 (1964), 141-51.

Woodward, Robert H. "Harold Frederic: A Bibliography," Studies in Bibliography 13 (1960), 247-57.

Robinson, Frank K. "Edgar Lee Masters; An Exhibition in Commemoration of the Centenary of His Birth; Catalogue and Checklist," Texas Quarterly 12 (Spring 1969), 4-68.

Hollenberg, Susan W. "Theodore Roethke: Bibliography," Twentieth Century Literature 12 (1967), 216-22.

Kellogg, George. "Frederick Manfred: A Bibliography," Twentieth Century Literature 11 (1965), 30-35.

McNally, Nancy L. "Checklist of Elizabeth Bishop's Published Writings," Twentieth Century Literature 11 (1966), 201.

Reinhart, Virginia S. "John Dos Passos 1950-1966: Bibliography," Twentieth Century Literature 13 (1966), 167-78.

Rule, Margaret W. "An Edward Albee Bibliography," Twentieth Century Literature 14 (1968), 35-44.

AUTHOR BIBLIOGRAPHIES
IN BIOGRAPHIES

Holloway, Jean. Hamlin Garland: A Biography. Austin: Univ. of Texas Press, 1960. Bib., p. 314-32.

Schorer, Mark. Sinclair Lewis: An American Life. N. Y.: McGraw-Hill, 1961. Bib., p. 815-26.

BIBLIOGRAPHY

(Sources for most of the titles discussed in the
text and included in the appendices)

Andrews, Clarence A. "The Literature of the Midwest: A
Beginning Bibliography," Great Lakes Review 1 (Summer 1974), 35-68.

Bibliographic Index; A Cumulative Index to Bibliographies,
1937- . N.Y.: H. W. Wilson, 1938- .

Cantrell, Clyde H., and Patrick, Walton R. Southern Literary Culture; A Bibliography of Masters' and Doctors'
Theses. Tuscaloosa: Univ. of Alabama Press, 1955.
124p.

Cohen, Hennig. Articles in Periodicals and Serials on South
Carolina Literature 1900-1950. Columbia: South Carolina Archives Dept., 1956. 87p.

Comprehensive Dissertation Index 1861-1972. Ann Arbor,
Mich.: Xerox Univ. Microfilms, 1973. 37 vols. plus
annual vols.

Cumulative Book Index; A World List of Books in the English
Language. N.Y.: H. W. Wilson, 1898- .

Dissertation Abstracts. Ann Arbor, Mich.: University
Microfilms, 1952-68.

Dissertation Abstracts International: A: The Humanities
and the Social Sciences. Ann Arbor, Mich.: Univ.
Microfilms International, 1969- .

Etulain, Richard W. Western American Literature; A Bibliography of Interpretive Books and Articles. Vermilion, S.D.: Dakota Press, 1972. 137p.

Gohdes, Clarence L. Bibliographic Guide to the Study of the Literature of the U.S.A. 3d ed. Durham, N.C.: Duke Univ. Press, 1970. 134p.

_____. Literature and Theater of the States and Regions of the U.S.A.; An Historical Bibliography. Durham, N.C.: Duke Univ. Press, 1967. 276p.

Havlice, Patricia P. Index to American Author Bibliographies. Metuchen, N.J.: Scarecrow Press, 1971. 204p.

Kirby, David K. American Fiction to 1900; A Guide to Information Sources. Detroit: Gale Research, 1975. 296p.

Leary, Lewis. Articles on American Literature 1900-1950. Durham, N.C.: Duke Univ. Press, 1954. 437p.

_____, et al. Articles on American Literature 1950-1967. Durham, N.C.: Duke Univ. Press, 1970. 751p.

Literary History of the United States, ed. by Robert E. Spiller and others. Bibliography, ed. by Thomas H. Johnson. N.Y.: Macmillan, 1948; Supplement, 1959; Supplement II, 1972.

McNamee, Lawrence F. Dissertations in English and American Literature; Theses Accepted by American, British, and German Universities, 1865-1964. N.Y.: Bowker, 1968. 1124p. Supplements, 1969 and 1974.

Nilon, Charles H. Bibliography of Bibliographies in American Literature. N.Y.: Bowker, 1970. 483p.

Rubin, Louis D., ed. A Bibliographic Guide to the Study of Southern Literature. With an Appendix Containing Sixty-Eight Additional Writers of the Colonial South by J. A. Leo Lemay. Baton Rouge: Louisiana State Univ., 1969. 351p.

Ryan, Pat M. American Drama Bibliography. Fort Wayne, Ind.: Fort Wayne Public Library, 1969. 240p.

Sheehy, Eugene P., et al. Guide to Reference Books. 9th ed. Chicago: American Library Assoc., 1976. 1015p.

Tanselle, G. Thomas. Guide to the Study of U.S. Imprints. Cambridge, Mass.: Belknap Press of Harvard Univ. Press, 1971. 2 vols.

United States Catalog; Books in Print. N.Y.: H. W. Wilson, 1899; 2d ed, 1902; 3d ed., 1912; 4th ed., 1928.

Winther, Oscar O. A Classified Bibliography of the Periodical Literature of the Trans-Mississippi West (1811-1957). Indiana Univ. Social Science Series, no. 19. Bloomington: Indiana Univ. Press, 1961. 626p. Supplement (1957-67). Indiana Univ. Social Science Series, no. 26. Bloomington: Indiana Univ. Press, 1970. 340p.

Woodress, James L. American Fiction, 1900-1950; A Guide to Information Sources. Detroit: Gale Research, 1974. 260p.

SECONDARY REFERENCES

"Charles F. Heartman," New York Times, March 10, 1953, p. 88, column 4.

"Clifton Waller Barrett," Current Biography, 1965, p.15-18.

Ferguson, Phyllis M. "Women Dramatists in the American Theatre 1901-1940," Dissertation Abstracts 18 (1958), 231 (Univ. of Pittsburgh).

Stoddard, Roger E. "C. Fiske Harris, Collector of American Poetry and Plays," Papers of the Bibliographical Society of America 57 (1963), 14-32.

_____. "Oscar Wegelin, Pioneer Bibliographer of American Literature," Papers of the Bibliographical Society of America 56 (1962), 237-47.

Thompson, Ralph. American Literary Annuals and Gift Books 1825-1865. N.Y.: H. W. Wilson, 1936.

Who's Who in America, 1974-75.

GENERAL REFERENCES

Flanagan, John T. "American Literature Bibliography in the Twentieth Century," in Bibliography: Current State and Future Trends, ed. by Robert B. Downs and Frances B. Jenkins. Urbana: Univ. of Illinois, 1967, p.214-36.

Tanselle, G. Thomas. "The Descriptive Bibliography of American Authors," Studies in Bibliography 21 (1968), 1-24.

_____. "The Historiography of American Literary Publishing," Studies in Bibliography 18 (1965), 3-39.

_____. "The State of Reference Bibliography in American Literature," Resources for American Literary Study 1 (Spring 1971), 3-16.

INDEX

Able, Augustus H. 41
Adams, John R. 70, 84
Adams, Joseph D. 73
Ade, George 47
Agnes Surriage (1886) 74
Agnew, Janet 13, 36, 40
Alabama: drama bibliography
  69; fiction anthology 44
Alaska: bibliography 66; fic-
  tion bibliography 68;
  poetry anthology 69
Albee, Edward 80
Albert, Sydney S. 23
Aldrich, Bess Streeter 67
Algren, Nelson 76
Alice of Old Vincennes (1900)
  36
All the King's Men (1946) 64
Allen, Francis H. 2
America in Fiction (1941) 31;
  1967 ed. 56
American Authors and Books
  (1640-1940): 1943 ed.
  30, 51; 1972 ed. 54, 81
American Broadside Verse
  from Imprints of the 17th
  and 18th Centuries (1930)
  7-8
"American Drama in Anti-
  Slavery Agitation 1792-1861"
  (1963) 60
American Fiction 1774-1850
  (1948) 31
American Fiction 1774-1850
  (1969) 55
American Fiction 1851-1875
  (1965) 55
American First Editions (1929)
  3; 1936 and 1942 eds. 29
American Guide Series 46

American Historical Fiction
  (1958) 31, 51
American Historical Novel
  (1950) 32, 51
American Literary Annuals
  and Gift Books (1936) 54;
  index (pub. 1975) 54
American Literary Realism
  80
American Novels of the Second
  World War (1968) 56
American Plays (1935) 10
American Plays Printed 1714-
  1830 (1934) 10, 59, 83
"American Poetry of the First
  World War, " (1965) 57
American Writers Series 13
American Yearbook (1910-
  1950) 4, 54
Americana Annual 30
Anderson, John Q. 71, 85
Anderson, Maxwell 78
Andrews, Clarence A. 67,
  84
Andrews, Mary L. 35
Annotated Bibliography of
  American Historical Fic-
  tion (1938) 5
Anthology of American Humor
  (1962) 71, 85
Anthology of New York Poets
  (1970) 70, 84
Anthony, Henry B. 56
Archer Pilgrim (1942) 43
Arizona: anthology 15; poetry
  anthology 69
Arizona in Literature (1935) 15
Arkansas: drama bibliography
  69
Arms, George 29, 49

Arnow, Harriette 65
Arrington, Alfred W. 20
Artemus Ward's Travels
    (1865) 19
Atkinson, Jennifer M. 78
Author bibliographies 20-25,
    47-51, 72-81, 82, 85-86,
    88; first author bibliog-
    raphy 1; compiled for
    book collectors 1; im-
    portance of 26
Author biographies 24-25,
    50-51, 81, 86
Avery, Laurence G. 78

BAL see Bibliography of
    American Literature
Baltimore: anthology 17, 85
Baltimore in Verse and
    Prose (1936) 85
Banker, Luke 70
Banta, David D. 64
Banta, Richard E. 40-41,
    52, 84
Barnes, Homer F. 24
Barrett, C. Waller 7, 74
Barrett Collection of the Uni-
    versity of Virginia 48
Barrett Library Collection of
    American Authors (Uni-
    versity of Virginia) 73-
    74, 77
Barth, John 81
Bartlett, William 51
Battle Creek, Michigan:
    anthology 17
Battleground (1902) 37
Bayou Folk (1894) 15
Bechdolt, Frederick 38
Bellamy, Edward 33
Benét, William R. 4
Bergquist, G. William 59
Berryman, John 77, 79
Best American Plays Series
    35
Best Plays of the [year] and
    Yearbook of the American
    Drama (1919 to date) 11
Best Plays of 1909-1919 and
    the Yearbook of the Drama
    of America (1933) 11
Best Short Stories of [year]

and the Yearbook of the
    American Short Story 6
Best Short Stories of World
    War II (1957) 34
Bibliographical Society of
    America 28
Bibliography of American
    Literature (1955 to date)
    27-29, 54, 79, 83
"Bibliography of Early New
    England Verse" (1943)
    39, 84
Bibliography of Edwin Arling-
    ton Robinson (1936) 76;
    supplement 76
Bibliography of Henry David
    Thoreau (1908) 2
Bibliography of Illinois Poets
    Since 1900 (1942) 44
Bibliography of John Green-
    leaf Whittier (1937) 21,
    28
Bibliography of Kentucky
    History (1949) 46
Bibliography of North Carolina
    (1958) 40, 52, 84
Bibliography of Novels Related
    to American Frontier and
    Colonial History (1971)
    56, 81
Bibliography of Oliver Wendell
    Holmes (1963) 47
Bibliography of Robinson
    Jeffers (1933) 23
Bibliography of South Carolina
    (1956) 40
Bibliography of Virginia History
    Since 1865 (1930) 18
Bibliography of William Saroyan
    1934-1964 (1965) 79
Bibliotheca Americana (1855
    volume) 29
Bingham, Millicent T. 28
Biographical Dictionary of
    Contemporary Poets (1938)
    8, 9
"Biographical Dictionary of
    Poets in the United States"
    (1926) 8
Bishop, Elizabeth 80
Bishop, John Peale 50
Bivouac of the Dead and Its
    Author (1875) 13

Black, Albert G. 84
Blackburn, Philip C. 22
Blair, Walter 18-19, 20, 85
Blanck, Jacob 28-29
Blotner, Joseph 56
Boker, George H. 24
Bolts of Melody (1945) 28
Bonin, Jane F. 60
Bonner, Sherwood 80
Bonney Family (1928) 44
Book Farm 49
Books and Authors of San
    Diego (1966) 70, 84
Botkin, Benjamin A. 13
Bowers, Fredson 74
Boyer, Mary G. 15
Boylan, Elaine 84
"A Boy's Adventure" (1880)
    22
Bradbury, John M. 60
Bradley, Edward S. 24
Bradstreet, Anne 80
Braithwaite, William S. 8
Branch, Edgar M. 80
Brashear, Minnie 16
Braymer, Nan 59
Brenni, Vito J. 74
Brewer, Frances J. 48
Bromfield, Louis 37
Brown, Charles Brockden
    80
Brown, Herbert R. 33
Brown University Library
    56, 57, 59
Browning, Mary C. 65, 82
Bruccoli, Matthew J. 48, 74,
    75, 78, 87
Brussel, Isidore R. 24
Buckingham, Willis J. 73
Bulletin of Bibliography 49,
    79
Bulletin of the New York
    Public Library 49, 52
Burke, William J. 51, 54
Burns Mantle Series 11;
    volume for 1899-1909 35;
    index for 1894-1971 (1971)
    60, 81
Butterick, George F. 78
Bynner, Edwin L. 73-74
Bynner, Witter 77
Byrne, Don 29

CHAL see Cambridge History
    of American Literature
Cabell, James B. 24, 26, 48
Cable, George W. 15, 36
Cagle, William R. 74
Cahan, Abraham 80
California: bibliography of
    literature 14; literature
    anthology 68; poetry
    anthology 17; bibliography
    of short stories 39
California Classics (1971) 68
California Poets (1932) 17
Cambridge History of Ameri-
    can Literature 2, 83
Campbell, Ruth B. 16
Canny, James R. 49
Cape Cod: poetry anthology
    70
Cappon, Lester J. 18
Catalog of American Poetry in
    the Colonial Newspapers and
    Magazines (1972) 81
Catalog of the David Demaree
    Banta Indiana Collection
    (1965) 64
Catalog of the Maxwell Ander-
    son Collection at the Uni-
    versity of Texas (1968)
    78
Cawein, Madison 65
Century of Benton County
    [Oregon] Poetry (1957)
    45, 84
Cerf, Bennett 46, 85
Champlain Valley, New York
    State: fiction 45
Chandler, Raymond 76
Charles Fenno Hoffman (1930)
    24
Charlotte, North Carolina:
    poetry anthology 70
Cheney, Frances 34
Chew, Beverly 1
Chicago Public Library 44
Chittick, Victor L. 46
Chopin, Kate 15
Ciardi, John 78
Cincinnati, Ohio: poetry
    anthology 17
City anthologies 17, 45, 70,
    84-85

Civil War: drama 60; fiction
5, 32-33; literature in
New Jersey 71; poetry
anthology 59; poetry
bibliography 40, 59;
poetry in Michigan 70
Clair, Colin 29
Clark, Lucy T. 48
Clark, Walter Van Tilburg 30
Clemens, Samuel L. 19, 22,
33
Cliff, Nellie 35
Coan, Otis W. 31, 56
Coates, Walter J. 17
Cohen, Hennig 72, 85
Cohn, Louis H. 85
Coleman, J. Winston 46
Collins, John D. 60
Colorado: poetry anthology
45
Cone, Gertrude 45
Confederate States: poetry
bibliography 40
Connecticut: literature 18
Conroy, Jack 47, 85
Contemporary American
Authors (1940) 30
Contemporary American
Literature (1922) 3;
rev. ed. (1929) 3
Contemporary American Men
Poets (1937) 9
Contemporary Poets (1970)
57; 2d ed. (1975) 58
Cooke, John Esten 20, 49
Cooper, James F. 22
Copperhead (1893) 33
Corey, Paul 30
Corso, Gregory 78
Cozzens, James G. 76
Coyle, William 64, 82
Crane, Stephen 24, 33, 73
Crawfordsville, Indiana:
writers of 48
Creeley, Robert 77
Critique 81
Currie, Barton 23
Currier, Thomas F. 21, 47,
52, 87

Dahlberg, Edward 76
Davidson, Levette J. 13

Davis's Anthology of News-
paper Verse (1918-?) 9
Day of Doom (1701) 7
De Forest, John W. 33, 50
Delaware: fiction 41; litera-
ture 45
DeMenil, Alexander N. 15
Democracy (1880) 71
"Development of Fiction on the
Missouri Frontier" (1934)
13
Diamond Anthology (1971) 58
Dickens, William B. 33
Dickey, James 78
Dickinson, Arthur T. 31, 51
Dickinson, Emily 23, 28,
72-73
Dictionary Catalog of the Har-
ris Collection of American
Poetry and Plays (1972)
56, 59, 81, 83, 87
"Dictionary Catalog of the
Short Stories of Arkansas,
Missouri, and Iowa from
1869 to 1900" (1932)
12-13
Dictionary of Books Relating
to America (1868-92) 24
Dillingham, William B. 72,
85
Directory of the American
Theatre 1894-1971 (1971)
81
Dollmaker (1954) 66
Donahue, Edward 46
Dooley, Nelle 38
Dos Passos, John 80
Doubleday, Doran Co. 22-23
Douglas, James S. 60
Drama: American drama in
anti-slavery agitation 60;
anthologies 10, 11, 35;
bibliography 59, 83;
early American 2, 10,
34, 59; 19th and 20th
centuries 10, 11, 34-35,
59, 60; history 10; one-
act plays 11-12; political
60; regional 35; small
town in 60; socio-political
thought in early drama 35
Drama in Pokerville (1847) 19
Dreiser, Theodore 23, 74, 80

Early American Literature 80
Early American Poetry (2d ed.,
    1930) 7, 57
Early Days in Dakota (1925)
    18
Early Novel of the Southwest
    (1961) 62, 83
Ebenezer Pemberton's Sermon
    on the Death of Whitefield
    (1771) 7
Economic Novel in America
    (1942) 33, 51
Edelstein, Jerome 77
Edwards, Jonathan 27
Eggleston, Edward 51
Elegy on the Death of Mr.
    Buckingham St. John
    (1771) 7
Elfenbein, Josef 35
Eliot, T. S. 48, 85, 87
Elliott, Fannie M. 48
Elliott, William Y. 13
Ellis, Helen H. 70
Emch, Lucille B. 42
Emerson, Ralph Waldo 2
Encyclopedia of Modern Ameri-
    can Humor (1954) 46, 85
Erichsen, Howard 62
"Expedition of Timothy Taurus"
    7

Far Side of Paradise (1951)
    50
Farm (1933) 37
Farmer's Almanac 19
Farrell, James T. 80
Faulkner, William 48, 50,
    75, 80
Favorite Vermont Poets (1928-
    31) 17
Feinberg, Charles E. 48, 78
Ferber, Edna 62
Ferguson, Phyllis M. 35
Fiction: bibliography 5, 6,
    31, 55-56, 83; economic
    5, 33; historical 4-5,
    31-33, 34, 36, 56; po-
    litical 5, 33, 56; satiri-
    cal 56; short stories:
    bibliography 5, 6; an-
    thologies 5-6

Fiction Fights the Civil War
    (1957) 32
Field, Joseph M. 19
Fields (1946) 32
Fink, John 54
First Books by American
    Authors 1765-1964 (1965)
    55
Fisher, Perry G. 70, 84
Fitzgerald, F. Scott 74
Flanagan, John T. 37, 51
Florida: fiction about: bib-
    liography 42; poetry
    anthology 17
Flory, Claude R. 5
"Flowering Judas" 61
Flying Cloud (1854) 29
Folks (1934) 44
Ford, Worthington C. 16
Fort Worth Poems (1949) 45,
    84
Fort Worth, Texas: poetry
    anthology 45
Foster, Bernice M. 16
"Four Generations" 44
Fowles, John 81
Frederic, Harold 33, 73, 80
Frederick, John T. 42, 84
Freneau, Philip 7
From Native Roots (1948) 35
Fugitive Bibliographies (pub.
    by David Lewis) 75, 76
Fuller, Henry B. 80
Fullerton, Bradford 3
Fulton, Maurice G. 13

Gale Research Co. 76, 77,
    78
Gallup, Donald C. 29, 48,
    76, 85, 87
Garland, Hamlin 33, 68, 81
Gaston, Edwin 62, 83
Gefvert, Constance J. 73
Genius: 1923 reissue of Theo-
    dore Dreiser's novel 23
George Henry Boker (1927)
    24
Georgia: bibliography of
    writers 14, 40; fiction
    about 42; literature 14;
    poetry anthology 17

Georgia Review 40
Giant (1952) 62
Gibson, William M. 29, 49
Gift, A Xmas and New Year's
 Present (1843) 54
Gift books 54; index 54
Glasgow, Ellen 37, 49, 74
Glaspell, Susan 68
Glover, Albert 78
Goodrich, Madge K. 14
Gordi, Tooni 9
Gordon, Armistead C. 16
Goren, Paul 29
Gottesman, Ronald 75
Grandissimes (1880) 36
Grapes of Wrath (1939) 68
Grau, Shirley 79
Great Gatsby (1925) 71, 74
Great Lakes Review 62
Greene, Barbara W. 40
Greensboro, North Carolina:
 poetry anthology 70
Greensboro Reader (1968) 70
Greenville, South Carolina:
 poetry anthology 70
Greer, Hilton R. 13
Gregory, Horace 34
Greyslaer (1842 ed.) 24
Griswold, Francis 30
Griswold, Rufus W. 1
Guernsey, Otis L. 60, 81
Guide to the Best Historical
 Novels and Tales (1929)
 4

Hagemann, E. R. 50
Hall, Wade H. 71, 85
Halline, Allen G. 10
Hamlin Garland (1960) 81
Handbook of Oklahoma Writers
 (1939) 14, 84
Hanneman, Audre 75, 85
Harbinger, A Maygift (1833)
 54
Harkness, David J. 36
Harris, C. Fiske 56
Harris, Gerrard 62
Harris, Joel C. 13
Harris Collection of American
 Poetry and Plays (Brown
 University) 56, 59
Harrison, Henry 9, 17, 84

Hart, Bertha S. 14
Hart, James A. 57
Hartin, John S. 36
Harvey, Alice G. 64
Harwell, Richard B. 35
Hatcher, Harlan 45
Hawthorne, Nathaniel 2, 54
Hayashi, Tetsumaro 75
Heartland (1967) 63; Heart-
 land II (1975) 63
Heartman, Charles F. 49
Heartman's Historical Series
 48-49
Helliwell, Louise 12
Hellman, Lillian 78
Hemingway, Ernest 75
Hergesheimer, Joseph 24,
 79
Hermann, John 38
Herold, Amos L. 24
Herron, Ima H. 60
Heyl, Edgar 69
Hilbert, Rachel M. 64, 69
Hill, Frank P. 10, 59, 83
Hinkel, Edgar J. 14
Historical Fiction Guide (1963
 and 1973 eds.) 56
History of American Drama
 from the Beginning to the
 Civil War (1923) 10;
 2nd ed. (1943) 34
History of American Drama
 from the Civil War to the
 Present (1927; rev. ed.,
 1936) 10
History of American Poetry
 (1900-1940) (1942) 34
History of Connecticut in
 Monographic Form (volume
 2, 1925) 18
History of Indiana Literature
 (1962) 67
History of Mississippi (vol. 2,
 1973) 70
History of the State of Ohio
 (vol. 6, 1942) 45
Hitt, Helen 38
Hoffman, Charles F. 24
Holloway, Jean 81
Holman, C. Hugh 68
Holmes, Oliver Wendell 2,
 54
Holmes, Thomas J. 47

Holt, Guy 24
Home Ballads and Poems
(1860) 21
Home Book of Western Humor
(1967) 72
Hosmer, William H. C. 28
Houghton Mifflin Co. 2
House of the Seven Gables
(1851) 71
Howe, Will D. 51, 54
Howells, William Dean 49,
73
Hubbell, Jay B. 35, 68, 83
Huddleston, Eugene L. 57
Hudson, Arthur P. 20, 85
Huff, Mary N. 75
Humanities Research Center
at the University of
Texas 76, 78
Hummel, Ray O. 63, 84
Humor 88; anthologies
19-20, 46, 71-72, 85;
bibliography 19
Humor of the Old Deep South
(1936) 20, 85
Humor of the Old Southwest
(1975) 72, 85
Hunter's Horn (1958) 65

Illinois: poetry bibliography
44
Important American Poets
(1938) 9
Index of American Periodical
Verse (1973 to date) 58,
81, 83
Indiana: biobibliography 41,
63-64; literary history
67; literature bibliog-
raphy 64
Indiana Authors and Their
Books 1816-1916 (1949)
41, 52, 84; supplement
(1974) 63
Indiana Authors and Books
1917-1966 (1974) 82
Indiana Historical Society 47
Ingraham, Joseph H. 29
Introduction to Georgia
Writers (1929) 14
Iowa: fiction 42-44; literary
history 67

Iowa Interiors (1926) 44
Irish, Wynot R. 83
Ivey, B. S. 13

Jackson, Don 43
Jacobi, Gertrude 16
Jacobs, Elijah L. 41
Jacobson, Harvey K. 44
James, Henry 2
James Kirke Paulding (1926)
24
Jantz, Harold S. 39, 84
Jeffers, Robinson 23
Jody, Marilyn 68, 81
Johnson, Elmer D. 69
Johnson, Merle 3, 22, 29
Johnson, Thomas H. 27, 28
Jones, Harry H. 39
Jones, James 76
Jones, LeRoi 79

Karolides, Nicholas J. 56
Keese, John 1
Kelly, William W. 74
Kennedy, Patricia 63
Kentucky: biobibliography 64-
66; fiction bibliography
46; fiction anthology 44;
fiction about 42
Kentucky Authors (1967) 65
"Kentucky Is My Land" 64
Kentucky Novel (1953) 42, 51
Kettell, Samuel 1
Kheridan, David 79
Kirk, Clara 41
Kirk, Rudolf 41
Kirkham, Edward 54
Kirkland, Joseph 37
Krout, Caroline V. 67
Kurtz, Kenneth 36
Kuykendall, Mabel 45, 84

LHUS see Literary History
of the United States
Landis, Frederick 67
Lanier, Sydney 14
Lantern in Her Hand (1928)
67
Lardner, Ring 74
Lawton, James 79

Leary, Lewis 50
Lee, Alfred P. 22
Leisy, Ernest 32, 51
Lemay, J. A. 57
Leon, Francis G. 1
Lewis, David 75, 76
Lewis, Sinclair 24, 81
Lewis, Victor E. 84
Library of Congress 34, 48
"Light Competition" 12
Lillard, Richard G. 31, 56
Lindsay, Robert O. 77
Literary History of Iowa
    (1972) 67, 84
Literary History of the United
    States: Bibliography vol.
    (1948) 27, 53; Bibliog-
    raphy Supplement (1959)
    28, 51, 53; Bibliography
    Supplement II (1972) 54,
    81
Literary Memphis (1942) 45,
    84
Literature of the American
    West (1971) 62
Literature of the Middle
    Western Frontier (1925)
    12
Literature of the Southwest
    (1956) 36
Lively, Robert A. 32-33
London, Jack 68, 73
Longfellow, Henry Wadsworth
    1
Longmire, Rowena 12
Louisiana: fiction anthology
    44; literature bibliogra-
    phy 40; novelists: bib-
    liography 16; poetry
    bibliography 69
Lowell, James Russell 2
Lowenfels, Walter 59
Lyon, Harris M. 80

MacDonald, Edward 23
McGarry, Daniel D. 56
MacLeish, Archibald 78
McLemore, Richard A. 70
McLeod, James R. 77
McTeague (1899) 68
McVoy, Lizzie C. 16
Madness in the Heart 46

Major, Mabel 12, 40, 62
Malamud, Bernard 76
Manfred, Frederick 80
Manly, John 3
Mann, Charles W. 74
Mantle, Burns 10
Marable, Mary H. 84
Maryland: bibliography of
    authors; drama bibliog-
    raphy 70
Maryland Historical Magazine
    41, 70
Mason, F. Van Wyck 34
Massachusetts: poetry bib-
    liography 16
Massey, Linton R. 75
Materials for the Study of
    Washington (1974) 70, 84
Mather, Cotton 47
Mayorga, Margaret G. 10
Meine, Franklin J. 20
Melish, Lawson M. 23
Melville, Herman 73
Memphis, Tennessee: literary
    history 45
Meriwether, James B. 68,
    76, 80
Meyer, Roy W. 62, 83
Michel, Pierre 76
Michigan: bibliography of
    authors 14; Civil War
    poetry 70-71; fiction
    bibliography 16, 42;
    poetry anthology 17, 69;
    poetry bibliography 69
Michigan in the Civil War
    (1965) 70-71
Michigan Novels (1963) 69,
    84
Michigan Poets with Supple-
    ment to Michigan Authors
    (1964) 69
Middle West: farm novels;
    bibliography 62; fiction
    12, 62, 63; historical
    novel 37; humor anthology
    47; literature 12
Middle Western Farm Novel
    in the Twentieth Century
    (1965) 62, 83
Midland Humor (1947) 47, 85
Mike Fink, King of Mississippi
    Keelboatmen (1933) 20

Millar, Kenneth 78
Miller, Joaquin 68
Millett, Fred B. 3, 30
Milwaukee, Wisconsin: poetry
    anthology 70
Mince Pie (1919) 22
Minnesota: poetry bibliog-
    raphy 69
Miss Ravenel's Conversion
    from Secession to Loyalty
    (1867) 33
Mississippi: literature 70
Missouri: fiction 13; literary
    history 41; literature 15;
    poetry 16
Mizener, Arthur 50
Moby Dick (1851) 71
Modern American Muse (1950)
    83
Modern American Political
    Novel 1900-1960 (1966)
    56
Montana: literature 45
Moore, Marianne 50
Morley, Christopher 22
Mott, Howard S. 19
Muir, John 68
Murfree, Mary N. 80
Murphy, Rosalie 57

Naked Poetry (1960) 58
Nannes, Caspar H. 35, 60
Native American Humor (1800-
    1900) (1937) 18-19, 85
New England: poetry bibliog-
    raphy 39
New Hope (1942) 44
New Jersey: bibliography of
    authors 41; Civil War
    literature 71; fiction 41;
    poetry anthology 69
New Jersey: A History (vol.
    4, 1930) 18
New London, Connecticut:
    poetry anthology 17
New Naked Poetry (1976) 58
New Orleans, Louisiana:
    poetry anthology 70
New Southern Poets (1974)
    59
New York City: poetry
    anthology 70

New Yorker 8, 34
New Yorker Book of Poems
    (1969) 58
Newberry Library 31
Newsboy 28
Nield, Jonathan 4
Nolan, Paul T. 69
Norris, Frank 33, 68, 80
North Carolina: fiction about:
    bibliography 42; fiction
    anthology 44; humor an-
    thology 72; poetry an-
    thologies 45, 69; state
    bibliography 15, 40
North Carolina English Teachers
    Association 42
North Carolina Fiction 1734-
    1957 (1958) 42, 51
North Carolina Library Asso-
    ciation 42
North Dakota: novels 44
Novels see Fiction
Novik, Mary 77
Nowell-Smith, Simon 29

O'Brien, Edward J. 6
O'Connor, Flannery 79
Odum, Gertrude G. 42
O'Hara, John 75
O'Hara, Theodore 13
O. Henry Memorial Award
    Prize Stories (1920 to
    date) 5
Ohio: short stories about 42;
    20th century literature 45
Ohio Authors and Their Books
    (1962) 64, 82
Oklahoma: bibliography of
    writers 14; guide book
    46; literature 14, 46;
    poetry anthology 17
Olson, Charles 78
O'Malley of Shanganagh (1925)
    29
One-Act Plays for Stage and
    Study (1925-1938) 11
O'Neill, Eugene 23, 78;
    anthology of early poems
    23
O'Neill, Perry 29
Oxford Anthology of American
    Literature (1938) 4

Oxford Companion to American Literature (1941) 30, 51; 4th ed. (1965) 81

Pacific Northwest: fiction 39
Pacific Northwest Quarterly 41
Padgett, Ron 84
Pageant of American Humor (1948) 46, 85
Paluka, Frank 64
Parks, Edd W. 13
Paulding, James K. 24, 50
Pearce, Thomas M. 12, 40, 62
Pearson, Alice L. 42
Pearson, Norman H. 4, 29
Peavy, Linda 60
Pennsylvania: literature bibliography 46; poetry anthology 69
Peoria, Illinois: poetry anthology 17
Phoenix Book Shop (New York City) 75, 77, 78
Pioneer in the American Novel (1967) 56
"Pit and the Pendulum" 54
Pizer, Donald 80
Plains States: short stories 38
Plays see Drama
Poe, Edgar Allan 20, 49, 54
Poems by Alfred W. Arrington (1869) 20
Poems by Irwin Russell (1888) 13
Poems by Philip Freneau (1909) 7
Poems; Medley and Palestrina (1902) 50
Poems of American History (1936) 9-10
Poetical Works of William H. C. Hosmer (1854) 28
Poetry: anthologies 7-10, 58-59; bibliographies 6-7, 34, 56, 57, 58, 83; topographical 57
Poetry of the American Civil War (1960) 59

Poetry societies 17, 45, 58, 68
Poetry Society of America 58
Poetry Society of Colorado 45
Poetry Society of Georgia 17
Poetry Society of Oklahoma 17
Poets: biographical dictionaries 8, 57; contemporary American men 9; contemporary American women 9
Poets and Poetry of Wyoming Valley [Pennsylvania] Poetry (1940) 45, 84
Poets of America (1840-42) 1
Pollard, Lancaster 41
Porter, Katherine Anne 49, 61, 75
Pound, Ezra 76, 87
Powell, Lawrence C. 68
Powell, William S. 42, 51, 84
Prince and the Pauper (1882) 22
Princeton University Library Chronicle 50
Proof 79-80
Pulsifer, Pauline F. 21
Purdy, James 79

Quinn, Arthur H. 10, 34

Rader, Jesse L. 35
Ranck, George W. 13
Randel, William P. 51
Random House 22-23
Readers' Guide to Periodical Literature 14
Readex Microprint Corporation 55
Reardon, John D. 35
Red Badge of Courage (1895) 33
Regional literature 12-13, 35-40, 60-63, 83-84
Reid, Alfred S. 70
Renaissance in the South (1963) 60
"The Representation of the

American Civil War on the
New York Stage 1860-1900"
(1966) 60
Research Bibliographies in
American Literature (G.
K. Hall) 73, 74
"Retired" 44
Richey, Ish 64, 82
Richter, Conrad 32, 62
Rickert, Edith 3
Ricks, Beatrice 73
Riddle, A. G. 38
Riley, James Whitcomb 41,
47
Robbins, J. Albert 50
Robert Creeley: An Inventory
1945-1970 (1975) 77
Robertson, John W. 20
Robinson, Edwin A. 26, 76
Rocky Mountains: fiction
13, 36, 39
Roethke, Theodore 77, 80
Roorbach, Orville A. 29
Rose, Lisle A. 5, 33
Ross, Grace 45, 84
Roth, Philip 79
Roundup 63
Rouse, Sarah A. 70
Rubin, Louis D. 68
"Rural Community" 44
Rusk, Ralph L. 12
Russell, Irwin 13
Russo, Anthony 47
Russo, Dorothy 47, 48
Rzepecki, Arnold 54

Sabin, Joseph 24
Samuels, Lee 85
San Diego, California: fiction
70; poetry anthology 17
Sanctuary (1931) 71
Saroyan, William 79
Savage, George 11
Scarecrow Press 58
Schlinkert, Leroy 46
Schorer, Mark 81
Schwarz, Edward 49
Sea Island Today (1939) 30
Sea of Grass (1937) 62
Sea Wolf (1904) 68
Seager, Allan 81

Seattle, Washington: poetry
17
Seattle and Its Environs
(1924) 17
Seaver, Edwin 85
Selective Bibliography of
American Literature
(1775-1900) (1932) 3
Sentimental Novel in America
(1940) 33
Serif 80
Serif Series (Kent State Uni-
versity) 73, 75, 76, 77
Seven Gables Bookshop (New
York City) 55
Shapiro, David 84
Shaul, Lawana J. 38
Sherman, Dean 79
Sherwood, Garrison P. 11
Short History of the American
Drama (1932) 10
Short stories see Fiction
Shumaker, Arthur W. 67
Shurter, Robert L. 5
Signature of the Sun: South-
west Verse 1900-1950
(1950) 40
Simms, William G. 49
Simpson, Amos E. 69
Sinclair, Donald A. 71
Sinclair, Upton 75
Sinclair Lewis (1961) 81
Sinclair Lewis (1933) 24
Sister Carrie (1900) 24
Sixty American Poets 1896-1944
(1945) 34; rev. ed.
(1954) 34
Smiling Phoenix (1965) 71-72,
85
Smith, Elizabeth O. 28
Smith, Rebecca W. 5, 12
Smith, Sam 70
Snodgrass, William 78
Soho Bibliography Series (R.
Hart-Davis, London) 76
Somerset County (Pennsylvania):
poetry anthology 45
Son of Earth 62
Song of the Vermonters 21
Sonnichsen, Charles L. 62
South: fiction bibliography 13,
36; historical novels, 36-

37; history of humor
71; humor anthology 71-
72; literature bibliography
35; literary history 60-
61; local color bibliography 13; poetry antholo-
gies 13; poetry bibliog-
raphy 40, 63
South Carolina: fiction anthology 44; literature
anthology 68; poetry 16;
state bibliography 40
South Dakota: poetry 18;
poetry anthology 45
South Dakota Poetry Society
45
South in American Literature
1607-1900 (1954) 83
South of Forty from the Mississippi to the Rio Grande
(1947) 35
Southeastern Broadsides Before
1877 (1971) 63, 83
Southern Bibliography: Fiction
1929-1938 (1939) 13
Southern Poetry Review 59
Southern Poets (1936) 13
Southwest: bibliography 12,
36; fiction anthologies
13, 72; literature 12,
13; poetry anthologies
13, 40; tall tales 20
Southwest Heritage (1938)
12, 83
Southwest in Life and Litera-
ture (1962) 62
Specimens of American Poetry
(1829) 1
Spencer, Elizabeth 60
Spencer, William V. 59
Sper, Felix 35
Spiller, Robert E. 22
Spotts, Carl B. 13
Stallman, Robert W. 73
Stanford, Ann 80
Starrett, Vincent 73
State Anthology [Oklahoma]
(1936) 17
State literature 14-17, 40-
45, 63-71
Stein, Gertrude 48, 75
Steinbeck, John 68, 75
Steinmetz, Lee 59

Stevens, Wallace 48, 77
Stevenson, Burton 9
Stoddard, Roger E. 57, 59,
81, 83
Storrs, Lee W. 68
Stryk, Lucien 63
Stuart, Jesse 64
Studies in Bibliography 50
Subject Bibliography of Wis-
consin History (1947) 46
Subtreasury of American
Humor (1941) 46
Suckow, Ruth 43-44
Sugarman, Milton H. 34

Tall tales 20, 46
Tall Tales of the Southwest
(1930) 20
Tar Heel Laughter (1974) 72
Tarkington, Booth 23, 41,
48, 67, 85
"Tascosa" 38
Tate, Allen 34, 50, 76
Taylor, Edward 73
Taylor, Harvey 24
Taylor, J. Golden 62
Taylor, Peter 81
Taylor, Walter F. 33, 51
Teasdale, Sara 79
Tennessee: fiction bibliog-
raphy 70
Tennessee History: A Bibliog-
raphy (1974) 70
Texas: fiction anthology 44;
poetry bibliography 16
That Rascal Freneau (1941)
50
Theses for master's and
doctoral degrees: con-
tribution to subject analy-
sis of American literature
26
Thielen, Benedict 50
Thiessen, N. J. 5
Thompson, Algernon 42, 51
Thompson, Donald E. 63,
82
Thompson, Lawrence R. 29
Thompson, Lawrence S. 42,
51
Thompson, Maurice 36
Thompson, Ralph 54

Thomson, Charles W. 49
Thoreau, Henry D. 2
Thornton, Mary L. 15, 40,
    52, 84
Thorp, Willard 50
Three Centuries of English
    and American Plays
    (1963) 59
Three Hundred Years of
    American Humor (1637-
    1936) (1937) 19
Three Miles Square (1939)
    30
Tilton, Eleanor M. 47
Todd, Mabel L. 28
Token 54
"Topographical Poetry in
    America 1783-1812"
    (1965) 57
Torrey, Edwin C. 18
Tory's Daughter (1888) 38
Tourville, Elsie A. 82
Tower Bibliography Series
    (University of Texas)
    76, 78
Track of a Cat (1949) 30
Treasure of the Land (1917)
    63
Trees (1940) 32
Triesch, Manfred 78
True, Michael 70
Trumbull, John 7
Turnbull, Robert J. 40
Twain, Mark see Clemens,
    Samuel L.
Twentieth Century Literature
    80
Twenty Best Plays of the
    Modern American Theatre
    (1939) 35

United States. Library of
    Congress 34, 48
University of Pennsylvania
    Library 34
University of Pittsburgh
    Series in Bibliography
    74, 77, 79, 87
University of Virginia Press
    48
"Untitled Story" 29
Updike, John 76

Utah: poetry anthologies 17
Utah Sings (1934-42) 17
Utopias: in fiction 5

Van Auken, Sheldon 36
VanDerhoof, Jack 56, 81
Van Doren, Carl 24
Van Vechten, Carl 85
Vecchio, Thomas Del 9
Vermont: poetry anthologies
    17
Very, Jones 51
Vidal, Gore 79
Vietnam War: poetry anthology
    59
Vigil of Faith (1842) 24
Virginia: literature bibliog-
    raphy 18; poetry 17;
    poetry anthology 17
Virginia Quarterly Review 58
Voice at the Back Door (1956)
    60
Vonnegut, Kurt 76

WPA see Works Progress
    Administration
Waldmeir, Joseph J. 32, 33,
    51, 56
Wallenberg, Venice 16
Walser, Richard G. 45, 69,
    72, 84
Ward, William 20
Warren, Edith 9
Warren, Greenliffe 29
Warren, Robert Penn 49,
    64-65, 75
Washington: bibliography of
    authors 41
Washington, D.C.: bibliog-
    raphy 70; fiction bibliog-
    raphy 70
Weber, Brom 71, 85
Wegelin, Oscar 1, 6-7, 20,
    48-49, 57, 83
Wegner, William H. 60
Weingarten, Joseph H. 34
Weiss, Anne 54
Weiss, Irving 54
West: fiction 39; humor
    anthology 72; literature
    36

West, Jessamyn 79
West, Ray B. 35
West Virginia: biobibliography 40
West Virginia Authors (1957) 40
Western Captive (1842) 28
Weston, Latrobe 85
Western Writers of America 63
Wharton, Edith 23, 74
Wheatley, Phillis 7
Where Is Vietnam? 59
White, Sarah H. 56
White, William 76, 78, 80, 87
White Mule (1937) 31
Whitman, Walt 4, 48
Whittier, John Greenleaf 21
Who's Who in America 16
Widener Library, Harvard University 55
Wigglesworth, Michael 7
Wilbur, Richard 78
Wilder, Thornton 48
Williams, Ben Ames 73
Williams, Blanche C. 5
Williams, Galen 58
Williams, Stanley T. 18
Williams, William Carlos 31
Wilson, Edmund 50
Wilson, Robert A. 75, 78
Wingfield, Marshall 45, 84
Winslow, Ola E. 7
Wisconsin: bibliography of authors 14; fiction bibliography 46
Wister, Owen 79
With the Bark On: Popular Humor of the Old South (1967) 71, 85

Witherington, Paul 80
Wittke, Carl F. 45
Wolfe, Dorothy E. 5
Wolfe, Hilton J. 68, 82
Wolfe, Thomas 76
Wolverton, Forrest E. 41
Woodbridge, Hensley C. 42, 73
Worcester, Massachusetts: poets 70
Works Progress Administration 55
World Historical Fiction Guide (1973) 56
World War I: fiction 34; poetry bibliography 57
World War II: fiction bibliography 33, 56; ideology of American novels 33; short stories: anthology 34
Wright, Lyle H. 31, 51, 55, 83
Wright, R. Glenn 55-56, 83
Wright, Richard 79
Writing in the Rocky Mountains (1947) 36
Writings of James Russell Lowell (1890) 28
Writings on Pennsylvania History (1946) 46
Wyoming Valley, Pennsylvania: poetry anthology 45

Yale University Library 48
Yearbook of Short Plays (1931-1940) 11
Zaturenska, Marya 34
Zury: The Meanest Man in Spring County (1887) 37